*William Carlos Williams
and the Painters,
1909–1923*

William Carlos Williams and the Painters, 1909–1923

William Marling

Ohio University Press
Athens, Ohio

Library of Congress Cataloging in Publication Data

Marling, William, 1951-
   William Carlos Williams and the painters, 1909-1923.

   Bibliography: p.
   Includes index.
   1. Williams, William Carlos, 1883-1963.   2. Williams, William
Carlos, 1883-1963—Knowledge—Art.   3. Art and literature.
4. Painting, Modern—20th century—History.   I. Title.
PS3545.I544Z629   811'.52   82-6312
ISBN 0-8214-0655-8   AACR2

To Cindy

Table of Contents

Acknowledgments

William Carlos Williams, PICTURES FROM BRUEGHEL, copyright © 1955, 1962, William Carlos Williams. COLLECTED EARLIER POEMS of William Carlos Williams. Copyright © 1938 by New Directions Publishing Corporation. SELECTED LETTERS of William Carlos Williams. Copyright © 1957 by William Carlos Williams. "Yes, Mrs. Williams," by William Carlos Williams. Copyright © 1959 by William Carlos Williams. THE AUTOBIOGRAPHY of William Carlos Williams. Copyright © 1951 by William Carlos Williams. SELECTED ESSAYS of William Carlos Williams. Copyright © 1954 by William Carlos Williams.
Reprinted by permission of New Directions.

Excerpts from the unpublished writings of William Carlos Williams copyright © 1982 by Paul and William Eric Williams.

Excerpts from the unpublished writings of William Carlos Williams cited with the permission of the Poetry/Rare Books Collection, University Libraries, the State University of New York at Buffalo, and the Collection of American Literature, Beinecke Rare Book and Manuscript Library, Yale University.

Excerpts from the unpublished writings of Marsden Hartley cited with the permission of the Estate of Norma Berger, and the permission of the Collection of American Literature, Beinecke Rare Book and Manuscript Library, Yale University.

Excerpts from the writings of Alfred Stieglitz cited with the permission of Georgia O'Keefe, and the Collection of American Literature, Beinecke Rare Book and Manuscript Library, Yale University. Not to be reproduced without permission.

Excerpts from the unpublished writings of Walter Conrad Arensberg cited by permission of the Arensberg Archives of the Francis Bacon Library, Pomona, California.

1. *A Question of Circles*

"The moment sight ceases, art ceases."

Williams

"I almost became a painter," wrote William Carlos Williams in 1954, "and had it not been that it was easier to transport a manuscript than a wet canvas, the balance might have been tilted the other way."[1]

This statement contains some hyperbole and a good deal of truth. In 1907 Williams *was* poised between the two arts, but his momentum had always been toward poetry. He continued his painting until he was in his early thirties, however, and he was serious about it. Raised in the traditions and ambiance of painting, he sought out and made friends with painters all his life.

The importance of painting in Williams' career has been recognized for some time. Unfortunately, cursory surveys and facile judgments about its importance to his poetry were long the rule. Not until 1969, when Bram Dijkstra published *Cubism, Stieglitz, and the Early Poetry of William Carlos Williams*, did a serious scholar see that painting might be central to a study of Williams. Along with Dickran Tashjian's portrait of Williams in the twenties (*Skyscraper Primitives*, 1975) and his catalog for the Whitney Museum exhibit, this effort has given us a new conception of painting and Williams' poetry. More recently, new studies have augmented this work.[2]

But all of this research proceeded in the absence of solid biographical information on Williams. The result is that we have now a picture of Williams as a cosmopolitan *littérateur*, an *avant-gardist* whose putative sources range from Lao-tzu to Larbaud to Toulouse-Lautrec. He would have done nothing but read had he glanced at even the first page of every magazine and journal that scholars have described as his "sources." Fortunately he did not; Williams was a man of limited time. Besides being a husband and father, he kept two medical offices, delivered babies at two

New Jersey hospitals, made house calls, took post-graduate classes at two New York hospitals, and dedicated himself to a number of sweaty home-improvement projects. Even though he was nearly the first man in Rutherford to own an automobile, he was still two hours from the controversies of Manhattan.

The unusual demands on his time and energy make Williams a kind of textbook case in the question of "influences" or, in this study, the question of circles. The time that he took to devote to "literature" was time stolen from other responsibilities, and he used the better part of it to write poetry. Ezra Pound may have been urging him to read Remy de Goncourt and Provençal poets, and it would be a boon to assistant professors of English if he had. But as more biographical studies reveal the facts of Williams' life, it becomes increasingly doubtful that he did. His "influences" seem of the simplest, most explicable sort: his brother and his mother, his college classmates, his close friends.

The current conception of Williams' interest in painting bears little relation to this new data however. This skewing is the inadvertent result of the pioneering study by Dijkstra, who filled a biographical lacuna with the influence of the "Stieglitz circle." At the center of this conception, which turns on Dijkstra's argument that Williams "came to, or perhaps wanted to, forget" who his friends and mentors were, stands a letter from Williams to Alfred Stieglitz in 1922. Dijkstra writes:

> Stieglitz had sent Williams a copy of Marsden Hartley's *Adventures in the Arts*, which had just been published by Boni and Liveright, largely at Stieglitz's instigation. Williams wrote back to thank him, and remarked that he would "stop in to see you at your rooms some evening soon, perhaps tomorrow. Do not alter any of your plans on my account but unless something unforeseen occurs (I am a slave you know) I shall appear at your place this Friday evening at perhaps eight o'clock." Williams closed his letter by remarking "it has been a nice quiet winter, hasn't it, with everybody away"—a statement which presupposes the existence of common acquaintances and shared experiences.[3]

According to Dijkstra, this is "incontrovertible evidence that by this time they knew each other quite intimately." But the fact is that this letter, which has always been available in its entirety, when quoted in full and augmented by biographical data, suggests a different picture.

Dear Stieglitz:

Suddenly Hartley's book appeared without another word being spoken. I didn't know whether you are—I didn't know. I presume though, now that no bill has followed it, that you have sent it to me, most kindly, as a gift. I thank you very much. I want to take advantage of this to stop in to see you at your rooms some evening soon, perhaps tomorrow.

Do not alter any of your plans on my account but unless something unforeseen occurs (I am a slave you know) I shall appear at your place this Friday evening at perhaps eight o'clock. I want to bring with me my friend Wallace Gould, an old friend of Hartley's from his home in Maine, whose work you may remember having seen in *The Little Review*.

It's been a nice quiet winter, hasn't it, with everyone away?

Sincerely yours,

W. C. Williams.[4]

Stieglitz' biographers write that the photographer often sent books to people whom he considered of "sufficient means," and then billed them for the favor. His parsimony on this and other scores, in fact, became legendary. Obviously Williams had heard about this tactic or been victimized previously, as the initial reticence in his letter shows. Nonetheless, he wished "to take advantage of this to stop in" and to introduce Gould to Stieglitz. In light of what biographers Whittemore and Mariani reveal about Williams in this period, this seems to be his primary purpose. Williams and Marsden Hartley had been promoting Gould in the *Little Review* as Le Douanier Rousseau of American letters, a point on which the poet tweaks Stieglitz' memory. Gould could no longer be printed in Williams' *Contact*, which folded in 1921, but Stieglitz' magazine *391* was still publishing. It seems that Gould, who was sleeping in Williams' living-room, needed new literary contacts.

Nor is the supposition of "intimacy" born out by other letters in the Stieglitz Archive at Yale University. In a letter of May 6, 1925, Williams began formally: "Dear Alfred Stieglitz: Georgia O'Keefe suggested that I write to you. . . ." Williams' wife Florence also said that she and her husband had been on better terms with Miss O'Keefe than with her husband, Stieglitz. The "influence" of Stieglitz' magazines is equally doubtful, for a letter that Williams wrote when he was preparing a bibliography of little magazines for the second series of *Contact* in 1931 begins: "Dear Stieglitz: I want to know precisely when you inaugurated C. W. [Camera Work], how many numbers there were, etc. . . ."[5] It sounds unlikely that the poet subscribed to any of Stieglitz' journals (the most famous, *Camera Work*, had a peak paid circulation of only a few hundred subscribers). All these letters end with "Best wishes," a formal closing for Williams.

For his part Stieglitz did not rave about Williams in his letters either. To Hartley he wrote in 1923: "Enjoyed your feelings about Williams and his writings. I have never quite warmed up to most of his writings but have always liked him when I met him."[6] Hartley was one of Williams' few friends who *did* get along with Stieglitz. Charles Demuth, whose early work Stieglitz had shown, was exiled because his watercolors threatened the commercial success of John Marin. The politic Frenchman Marcel Duchamp instinctively kept Stieglitz at arm's length: "Dear Mr. Stieglitz" begin several of his frosty letters.[7] Later Duchamp and other members of the Arensberg Circle came to regard Stieglitz' stream of promotions and questionnaires as an annoyance.

Dear Stieglitz:

Even a few words I don't feel like writing. You know exactly what I think about photography. I would like to see it make people despise painting until something else will make photography unbearable. There we are.

Marcel Duchamp[8]

This tireless self-promotion also annoyed Wiliams: "That and his eternal talking. I got sick of it. . . . Like a spider he built his net to attract those he wished to browbeat or entrap using the pictures as a come-on."[9] When Stieglitz died, Williams wrote an appraisal of him, "What of Alfred Stieglitz?" which posited the photographer's egotism as his most salient characteristic:

One of Stieglitz' favorite stories was of the two doors over one of which was written, "This way to see God!" and over the other "This way to hear a lecture about God!" The crowd was going in at the second door. Stieglitz was behind the other.[10]

Such a tone became the staple of Dijkstra's argument that Williams was fudging on his debt to Stieglitz. But that doesn't seem the case, especially as more of the history of the period is published. Alfred Kazin knew Stieglitz well, and wrote recently:

> He liked to talk of the "spiritual" in art. The withered lady aesthetes who surrounded him actually talked of the adored master in the third person. Stieglitz had made them see everything in a new light. His manner was complaining, impatient. . . . He did not have enough to do and he was surrounded by pictures he usually would refuse to sell. He found most people unworthy of the pictures he loved most . . . in his truculent old man's voice, he complained endlessly. . . . Stieglitz would always remain the biggest item in his own gallery. Picturing himself on the point of death, he remained the proverbially important Jewish son—*he* was the magnet around which even Picasso and Braque collected.[11]

Other biographies bear similar testimony, leading one to assume that Williams, with his usual indiscretion, simply told the truth from the start.

Stepping back from the controversies about painting and Williams' life, one is struck—in biographical data and his letters—by the continuity and depth of his relationships with other people. Unlike the fleeting alliances of Ezra Pound or Robert McAlmon, Williams' friendships endured sometimes twenty or thirty years. He was a family man and seems to have extended familial values into his social world. As his critics and confidants he preferred friends such as Pound, his brother Ed, and Charles Demuth—people he had known a long time. Much of what he saw, read and did, he pursued on the strength of their recommendations. In like manner he shunned the more Bohemian, Dionysian aspects of Village life in the teens and twenties. He was not so prim as Wallace Stevens, but he was more at home above 14th Street than below it. Essentially a "shy" man, he needed an introduction to the art world, and he got it from Demuth and Pound. They introduced him to the *Others* group that met at nearby Grantwood, and after 1915 in Walter Arensberg's salon. There was a cautious gentility there much like that of middle-class Rutherford, an ambiance in which he saw himself "raising a glass of yellow Rhine wine in the narrow space just beyond the light-varnished woodwork" and smiling "the smile of water tumbling from one ledge to another."[12]

The Arensberg Circle itself had a distinct beginning and end. Although Walter Arensberg participated in several artistic ventures with Allan and Louise Norton, including the publication of *Rogue*, it was not until he moved into a sumptuous studio apartment at 33 West 67th Street in 1915 that Arensberg's home became a central gathering point. By late 1918 he and his wife tired of the continual entertaining, and restricted the number of nights that their apartment was "open" to one or two per week. But they still lacked a private life and when financial problems arose in 1921, they moved to Hollywood without telling anyone of the crisis. In the interim, however, the apartment was the most important New York gathering place of painters and poets. Mabel Dodge ruled the social scene, and Stieglitz prevailed in penurious fashion over the infant world of photography, but ambitious painters and poets headed for Arensberg's.

The composition of the Arensberg Circle is best explained by Beatrice Wood: "At the time I didn't even know we were a 'circle,' but I can see now that we were. Although there were new people—different people—every night, there were people who came back, or who were always there." Williams, she adds, was one of those there fairly frequently, although "he spent his time talking to the men."[13] In his research on the circle Patrick L. Stewart lists the following as the main members between 1914 and 1918: dancer Isadora Duncan; European painters Marcel Duchamp, Francis Picabia, Albert Gleizes, and Jean Crotti; American painters Arthur Dove, Marsden Hartley, Charles Sheeler, Man Ray, John Covert, Morton Schamberg, Charles Demuth and Joseph Stella; poets Alfred Kreymborg, William Carlos Williams, Wallace Stevens, Carl Van Vechten and Mina Loy; *littérateurs* Max Eastman, Arthur Craven and the Baroness Elsa von Freitag Loringhoven; and intellectuals Martin Barzun, Ernest Southard, and Henri Roche.[14] Outside of Gertrude Stein's parlor or the tenement called the Bateau-Lavoir in Montmarte, it is doubtful that a more diverse and brilliant group of artists met so regularly. The awe that a threadbare poet registered in their presence was described by Kreymborg, who wrote that "looking from Fania Marinoff to Carl Van Vechten, from Donald Evans to Walter Conrad Arensberg . . . with a side-long glance at the redoubtable Mina Loy," he knew "they were the handsomest set in town."[15]

The Arensbergs' studio was hung to the ceiling with a stunning, ever-changing array of modern art. Art historian Ann d'Harnoncourt has written that at one point the feature pieces were Brancusi's "Prodigal Son," several superb Braque collages, work by Sheeler and Schamberg, Matisse's "Portrait of Mme. Landsberg," and Duchamp's re-touched photo of "Nude Descending a Staircase."[16] The apartment was so large, said Beatrice Wood, and the notion of artistic reflection so sacred, that she often wandered off and stared at work by Matisse without interruption for an hour.[17] According to other reports, there were "long evenings of chess playing, poetry writing and fiery debates."[18] No doubt Williams, when his mercurial genius called, was among the furtive corner scribblers. It was an ambiance of gentility and electricity, the perfect counterpoint to his medical practice among Rutherford's poor.

It is tempting to assume that the Arensberg Circle had no aesthetic, that it was an open opera in which anyone was welcome to sing. But at least as far as painting goes, this was not the case; it explains, in fact, the conspicuous absence of painters from the Ashcan School or academicians. "The influence of the Puteaux Cubists was important to the Arensberg Circle from the beginning," writes Stewart. The "Puteaux Cubists" consisted principally of Duchamp and his brother Villon, Roche, Gleizes, Crotti and Picabia, all of whom had met after 1911 on a weekly basis at Puteaux, a suburb of Paris. They had been brought together by an interest in the Futurist manifestos published in *Le Figaro* in 1909 and 1910, and became "preoccupied with the intellectual, social and aesthetic characteristics of a new art for a new era." Something of a self-improvement society, they read and discussed the latest developments in science and technology; their common library consisted of Bergson, Nietzsche and Whitman. "These stylistic and theoretical preoccupations were to be brought to America during and after the Armory Show," writes Stewart:

> They exerted a pervasive influence on the direction of American art and thought. Two aspects dominate: the presence of a Cubo-Futurist style in American avant garde art from 1913 to 1918, and an increasing emphasis on a modernistic faith in America's artistic progress at the expense of Europe.[19]

This concern continued when the chief members of the Puteaux group found themselves together in the Arensbergs' apartment. Certainly not everyone who visited there became a cubo-futurist; Wallace Stevens alone would defeat such a claim. But as Williams attests, he felt "tremendously stirred" by the people he met there.[20]

There is, in fact, no more obvious source for Williams' shift away

7

from the neo-Keatsian, traditionally-oriented poetry that he wrote before 1914 to the lean, rapid poetry he wrote afterward than the Arensberg Circle. It provided a milieu that Williams found conducive to his development because its concerns built upon his own life-long interests in painting and in poetry—and in the possibility of a nexus between the two. Even in childhood, the *visual* was of great importance to Williams. As he grew older, especially into adolescence and early manhood, he associated the turbulent feelings of his new sexuality with the components of visual—and especially painted—schemes. He conceived of his emotions and his reactions to them in visual terms. "Pictures pressed into my mind with a great power of argument," he wrote of his youth.[21] In his letters, essays and poetry, there is an association of masculinity with form and line, of femininity with color and mass, which gradually reveals itself. From the concerns and membership of the Arensberg Circle, Williams learned to use these associations as a way of working out and balancing his personal inner turbulence. The elements that make up painting, with which Williams had a life-long familiarity, could be translated into words.

Thinking in these visual terms was something Williams called "pre-writing."[22] Using the visual paradigms that he created, he mediated in his poems between his desire and his knowledge, his expectations and his sense of fate. The results of his experiments between 1909 and 1923 present the reader with carefully wrought, finely balanced "pictures." While not all of Williams' work has this preternaturally visual quality, a great deal of it does—and is the work for which he is usually acclaimed. Frequently it gives the appearance that Williams avoided thought—"No ideas but in things"—and leads some scholars to declare that he succeeded in a "primordial union of subject and object."[23] Although Williams was not averse to such a view, it hits his method only a glancing blow. In these famous, very visual poems, Williams' "deliberations" are simply to be found in the pictures that the poems create. "A design in the poem and a design in the picture," he said, "should make them more or less the same thing."[24]

8

2. *Mother, Brother and Charles*

> *It is inevitable that, in the end, individuals, brothers though they may be and closely allied as they have lived . . . they will find themselves strangers.*

> Williams

If Williams were among us today, he would probably seem much as he did to his friend Marsden Hartley:

> Williams you know is a very lovely fellow for himself and he certainly has made a splendid struggle to plasticize all his various selves and he is perhaps more people at once than anyone I've every known—not vague persons but he's a small town of serious citizens in himself. I never saw so many defined human beings in one being.[1]

Such impressions gained Williams an early reputation as a poetic "primitive" and an artist not inclined to thinking. He was thought to imitate the ideas of friends or the programs in vogue. Imitation is absent from his work, but the gentleness that many reported of him seems to have made this portrait credible.

Few have noted that Williams was aware of his self-division, and that he guarded it as an asset. Discussing his "formlessness" in a letter to John Riordan in 1926, Williams wrote:

> . . . my failure to work inside a pattern—a positive sin—is the cause of my virtues . . . I cannot work inside a pattern because I can't find a pattern that will have me. My whole effort—in light of your observations—is to find a pattern large enough, modern enough, flexible enough to include my desires. And if I should find it I'd die.[2]

Patterns that are large, modern and flexible enough to accommodate all of our various selves are difficult for our friends to discern in us, difficult for scholarship to ferret out. The lack of biographical work on Williams, until recently, has also hampered the reconstruction of his world view.

But the work that does exist appears to support Williams' comment to Riordan. To maintain his sense of self, he defined himself by opposition to other artists, ideas and movements. It was not the vehement opposition of the threatened ego, but rather an exploration designed to find out whether or not an idea was "large enough" to "contain" him. It is equally apparent that all these patterns and Williams' investigations of them were ruled by a dominant theme, which he himself recognized in writing the first draft of *The Autobiography*, but deleted from later versions. Recounting his childhood days with his brother, Williams wrote:

> Ed and I grew up together to become as one person. All that I experienced as a growing child and up to the time of my marriage was shared with him. We were constantly together for nearly twenty years.
> . . . I have had several but not many intimate friendships with men during my life, patterned I suppose, on my youthful experience with my brother . . . all artists [here he mentions Pound, Demuth and McAlmon]. . . . On the other hand, there is Flossie, my wife, who is the rock on which I have built.
> Men have given the direction to my life and women have always supplied the energy.[3]

By giving "direction," men became the classic, guiding forces in Williams' life. In "supplying energy," women became avatars of his romantic, formless feelings. In itself this division and assignment of values may not be unusual, but in Williams' life it linked with the *visual* and assumed tremendous importance.

A movement in opposition to "patterns" is ingrained in the lore of the Williams family, as is the love of painting. Williams' paternal grandmother, who figures so prominently in his early poems, took as her second husband "an itinerant photographer up in New York from St. Thomas for the purchase of supplies."[4] Their son William George Williams was also inclined to the arts. Though he sold "Florida water" for a living, he found time to memorize long passages of Shakespeare, to

younger brother Ed. "When my mother had got through with her painting, we had left her half-squeezed-out tubes in our attic, with their memory of d'Archambeau and Ludovic. . . ."

> It was nip and tuck with us when we discovered my mother's discarded
> oils . . . I remember cobalt, smaller than the other tubes because it was
> expensive, and the palette showing heavy use. I might easily have become
> a painter and in some ways I regret that I did not go on with it. . . . I did
> seem to have some ability in colors and Mother had done pretty good work
> there.[11]

When he composed his early poetry, Williams wrote later, "I was conscious of my mother's influence all through this time of writing . . . I've always held her as a mythical figure, remote from me, detached, looking down on an area in which I happened to live . . . after the years in Paris where she had been an art student. Her interest in art became my interest in art. I was personifying her, her detachment from the world of Rutherford."[12] Still later he wrote about her in "The Painting," a poem that sketches Elena's "Portrait of a Niece in Mayaquez."

> Starting from black or
> finishing
> with it
> her defeat stands
> a delicate
> look
> of blond hair dictated
> by the
> Sorbonne
> this was her last
> clear
> act
> a portrait of a
> child
> to which
> she was indifferent
> beautifully
> drawn
> then she married and
> moved to
> another country.[13]

Toward the end of her life, Williams and his brother decided to send Elena to Rome for a year. There she lived in a small pension near the Pincio Gardens: "The place had been chosen by my brother as one notably easy of access . . . and furthermore the tram to the American Academy passed by the corner." She saw many paintings by her favorite painters and the trip rejuvenated her, but it was not an unqualified success. "Never did my mother go out, but she was in fear of being lost,"[14] Williams noted. It was this feeling of being lost, of personal formlessness that Williams came to understand as the chief danger of his mother's romanticism.

A few years later she broke her hip and became permanently bedridden. Williams jotted down her aphorisms, homilies and stories; and the resulting volume shows that she kept her foregone career in the air constantly. "I think I would have been a good portrait painter," she says. "I like so much to study faces." She describes how an itinerant painter had painted a landscape on a mirror in her father's icehouse in Puerto Rico. She remarks on "Le Corbusier and his new-fangled houses on stilts: it makes me think of the house where I was born."[15]

After Elena died, Williams and his brother discovered in the attic "a prize, in each case, which she had won by her painting and drawing in Paris, at the School for Industrial Design in 1877, '78, and '79. And in all these years she had kept those medals secret."[16]

Elena became Williams' first, most important influence. She was remote; she was a romantic and a painter, a fortune-teller who held seances and talked with spirits, and who seemed terribly "lost" to Williams even late in life. She was "almost without speech—her life spent in that place completely out of her choice . . . Only her son, the bridge between herself and a vacancy as of the sky at night, the terrifying emptiness of non-entity." Elena made Williams aware early of this region into which even words could not penetrate, where paint sometimes sufficed, but which was really "an appetite, a feeling and a love."

Elena set a mark on Williams that made him attentive to the painter's concerns. When he spent 1898 at Chateau de Lancy, near Geneva, he said he "stared into the windows of the exhibitors of paintings before which I passed on my way about the street and to and from my fencing lessons."[17] Back home at Horace Mann the same books that introduced Williams to *Il Penseroso, Comus* and *Paradise Lost* contained superb illustrations.

I'll never forget how I studied Gustave Dore's pictures of those beautiful but damned ladies and with what profound disappointment I failed to discover from them the anatomical secrets which so fascinated me at the time.[18]

Art classes per se were not a part of Williams' regimen; under his father's direction, he took mathematics, English, science and Latin.

To know something about Williams' brother is to understand more about Williams' development in this period. Only one year Williams' junior, Edgar, too, was awed by his mother's stories and ability to paint. As the second son he was allowed to indulge in these interests in school. He took art classes, and mastered drawing. It became apparent that he had a vocation in art, possibly in architecture or in design. By temperament and by role within the family, he seems to have been a conservative spirit. His was an orderly personality, and his initial attraction to art was disciplined by a classic education in painting and drawing. For Williams he was an intimate who advised rationality and restraint, and the split in their views on art and life was understood by neither of them until later.

Williams' life changed abruptly when he was taken out of high school before graduation and enrolled at the University of Pennsylvania Medical School in Philadelphia. On his first morning there, he met a neighbor named Van Cleve who played violin. "I told him that I wasn't interested in music, but I was interested in writing and somewhat in painting." Van Cleve saw that Williams met another student interested in writing, Ezra Pound. The extent of Pound's friendship with Williams and the "direction" he gave can be exaggerated, but he clearly succeeded Ed as Williams' conservative male intimate.

Williams appears to have been moved in an equal and opposite way by Charles Demuth, who was studying at Drexel Institute. Demuth was a painter who nursed ambitions of becoming a writer; often his paintings took literary works as their subjects, and later he illustrated work by Zola, James, Proust and Poe. Williams encouraged Demuth to write and was encouraged by him. "I met Charles Demuth over a dish of prunes at Mrs. Chain's boarding house on Locust Street and formed a lifelong friendship on the spot with dear Charlie," Williams wrote. This account is not nearly so sentimental as an earlier version:

Mrs. Chain's prunes were the most wonderful. Watery tidbits. It was

prunes or applesauce. Her daughter was simple I guess. Did her best to
land one of the students, kept it up for twenty years. At that table I met one
of my dearest friends. Will you have some bread? Yes. That look. It was
enough. Youth is so rich. It needs no stage setting. Out went my heart to
that face. There was something there, a reticence, a welcome, a loneliness
that called to me. And he, he must have seen it in me too. We looked. It was
gauged accurately at once and sealed for all time. The other faces are so
many prunes.

Demuth took Williams in hand at a critical moment. "I was undecided,"
Williams wrote, "whether or not I should become a painter. I coldly
re-calculated all the chances."[19] Not only was Demuth more sympathetic
and less egocentric than Pound, but he eased Williams into the social
world. Williams wrote to his mother, "Demuth, that fellow who is studying here, has invited me to a dance at his school on Saturday evening. I
am to take a girl who I have never seen, but who is very nice nevertheless." Their sensibilities meshed in other ways:

> . . . when supper would be over and we felt disinclined to return to our
> rooms, Charles Demuth used to take long walks with me in West Phila-
> delphia. . . . There was a high brick wall along the south side of Locust
> Street, just west of Thirty-sixth, inside of which there must have been an
> old garden, long neglected. The thought of it fascinated me. Charlie
> laughed when I spoke of it. "Not many could enjoy such a thing as that,"
> he said, "by merely looking at the outside of the wall."

Neither Williams nor his friend realized it, but Demuth was a
homosexual. Williams was attracted not only by his sensitivity and winning ways, but by his representation of the "energy" of the female attitude: he was one who, like Elena, knew of unspeakable spaces. Demuth
"had an evasive way of looking aslant at the ground or up at the ceiling
when addressing you, followed by short, intense looks of inquiry," Williams said.[20]
From Demuth Williams inherited a number of artistic tastes, including a fondness for Watteau and Fragonard—Demuth's favorites.
His role was important enough for Williams to mention him in the
almost familial spaces of his letters to Ed: ". . . the Academy of Arts was
close at hand. I turned up Broad St. and soon was conversing with my
friend Demuth. He was in the best of health, is painting exceptionally

well, asked after you. . . ."[21] When Williams dramatically discovered his poetic vocation a year later, the only person other than Ed in whom he confided was Demuth, who wrote back:

> Carlos, Carlos, how good your letter did sound . . . you have no idea how your letter affects me. I have always felt that it would happen to you some day—that you would simply *have* to write. However, hearing that it would happen this winter was grand news. . . .
>
> I will not be able to see you before I go—yes, *it is* too bad. Still, Carlos, when I come back—*when I come back*, well, we may both have a start in a small way then. . . .
>
> And Carlos even though nothing happens after your six months' work up in Boston, don't give up, will you? It's worth all the worry & tears, after all.[22]

In 1905 Demuth introduced Williams to Dot Wilson, a friend of his from Drexel. Thereafter Williams relaxed after classes and on weekends at her home in a shabbier section of Philadelphia. The attraction was her father.

> I used to go on Sunday afternoons to the second-story room of a house on North 34th St. and sit with a dirty little old man in whose company I was transported to a colloquy with the angels. He would have a commission to complete, a pastoral scene in oils, a few cows standing or lying down in a meadow, for which he was known among the lesser dealers.

Wilson seemed a "grubby little figure," but Williams respected his resourcefulness. "He used to paint, right out of his head, landscapes with cows, 24 × 36 inches or so, that sold as 'art' for from ten to twenty dollars." What Williams liked was that he "had not lost the spark that made him love his vocation." He was a figure in opposition to the pattern of life.

> My delight was in going down to the old boy's second floor, north-light studio and sitting there all Sunday afternoon while he'd work, putting in his trees and cows with a low toned sky in the background, over and over the same thing. At first I used to sit and hear him talk until one day he said "How about trying it yourself? Here, I'll set you up a canvas," which he did. "Here are some clean brushes, here are the colors"—at which he jammed a handful of other brushes, hairs in the air, into a small jar and placed it before me—"There, paint that."

And he turned away to get on with his work. That was fun.
. . . He gave me no instruction more than to nod his head in approval
when he thought I had done well.[23]

After graduation Williams held a series of internships, not in Boston, but in New York City. Without an Elena or a Demuth to guide the "energy" in his life, Williams confronted his personal drives nakedly for the first time. Pound had gone to London; Williams wrote to Ed that there was no one to show him how to give "direction" to this force:

To do what I mean to do and to be what I must be in order to satisfy my own self I must discipline my affections, and until a fit opportunity affords, like no one in particular except you, Ed, and my nearest family. From nature, Ed, I have a weakness wherever passion is concerned. No matter how well I may reason and no matter how clearly I can see the terrible results of yielding up to desire, if certain conditions are present I might as well never have arrived at a consecutive conclusion for good in all my life, for I cannot control myself. As a result in order to preserve myself as I must, girls cannot be my friends.[24]

Williams was forced out of his last residence, at a children's hospital in Hell's Kitchen. But he profited by his exposure to New York. "I have been trying to get out and see the city this year and get my share of the good things the city is giving away," he wrote to Ed in 1908. "I have visited the Metropolitan Museum frequently and with a catalogue I'll soon be able to distinguish a few of the characteristics of the principal schools of painting." Evidently he was getting some ideas, too, for nine months later he wrote to Ed: "Art is intrinsic, it is not a plaything, it is an everyday affair and does not need a museum for its expositions; it should breathe in the common places and inspire us at the moments of decision in our work and play."[25]

He was also writing the pieces that became *Poems*, and he still felt a lack of "direction" in his work. To Ed, who had prepared the cover art, he wrote after *Poems* was published:

You are an artist and your work runs parallel with all art therefore if we can establish an analogy between your architecture and my poetry or rather discover the analogy which must exist we can help each other to succeed in a way that mighty few people can do. For if you can influence the best that is in me by your architecture which you can do and if I can influence the best that is in you by expressing what I feel there could not possibly be any more joyful outlet to our love.[26]

Williams' father had promised to send him to Europe for a year if Ed won the Prix de Rome for architecture at the American Academy in Italy—and Ed won it. Much to the disgust of Pound, who was in the literary center of London, Williams spent his year studying pediatrics in Leipzig. It was not a lost year, despite Pound's ire, but it did mark the beginning of rocky relations between the two.

Williams sailed to Europe in 1909 with other young doctors who were headed overseas for a year of German medicine. "We had wonderful weather on the Channel," he wrote, "with the most wonderful J. M. W. Turner skies—you know the kind with little frost-like fingers. . . ." He landed in Belgium and went directly to Leipzig, but he had overestimated his fluency, and disliked German culture. "The German art is quite ponderous," he wrote to Ed, "but it is founded on German thought and independence. It is solid and good but often there comes out a monstrosity."[27]

Pound asked Williams to visit him in London, and after a year Williams did. On the way, he passed through Holland, visiting museums that apparently impressed him: ". . . the Dutch picture galleries. . . ." "I remember Holland as a place through which I passed in 1910. I remember the museums and the coffee (and chocolate) houses. . . ." "We marvel at the masterpieces of Holbein, of Rembrandt . . . it does not occur to us that faces do not exist to that degree of intensity today."[28]

Pound lived in a small room on Church Walk in Kensington. Williams had only a week and chose to spend part of it with Ivy Peabody's parents in Olney, a decision that irritated Pound. But they crowded the remaining days, attending one of Yeats' readings, dropping in on members of the Abbey Theatre, and visiting the literary scenes. They "went together to the National Gallery to see the Elgin marbles and certain of the pictures upstairs, work of Bellini and the early Renaissance." An attractive woman was there and Williams noted that Pound made a farce of the occasion by "leaning back on his cane" and posturing for her.

From London Williams went to Paris, where he stayed with distant relatives and rested before going to Rome. He walked "up the avenue de l'Opera, etc., seeing the famous dancers on the portico, all verdigris, and dirtied by the birds." He saw St. Sulpice "with its severe front" and Notre Dame, of which he wrote "It is the lack of solution hardened into this form, twin-towered, all the paraphernalia of the aisles. We should not be down-hearted if we can't solve it pronto. . . . Of what else are all the great liturgies built?"[29]

In Rome Ed took charge of the poet's amorphous impressions and directed them skillfully. It was a short course in classic architecture, in the judicious use of line and mass.

> In Italy Ed took me under his wing, introducing me to the wonders of medieval and renaissance architecture and painting: Siena, in one sudden burst; Bramonte's [sic] dome of the Duomo; the frescos of Pinturicchio. There was the trip to Fiesole; the golden Greek temples at Paestum; Amalfi, of course; Sorrento, Capri, and the call we made on Elihu Vedder there. Wild Anacapri out on its point of rocks . . . Pompeii, Naples . . .[30]

Rome especially impressed him. Williams and his brother visited the Museo Nazionale delle Terine, where they saw "the great ruined dome of Diocletian's tepidarum." They went to the Vatican, the standard tourist sights, but despite all the classicism Williams felt he was somehow at

> ". . . the place of his birth. . . . the place where the word begins. . . . There must be in Rome a greater thing inclusive of the world of love and of delight; unoppressive—loosing the mind so that men shall again occupy that center from which they have been avulsed by their own sordidness— and failure of imagination.[31]

This impression of Rome stuck with Williams all his life. Fifty years later, he said, "Painting is much more my meat. Maybe, we'll say, the Renaissance, the big murals at the Vatican—they make much more sense to me. . . ." In *The Autobiography* he wrote of "the great baths of Diocletian and the Venus Andromeda before which I would stand until I was ashamed to be seen in its presence."[32]

From Rome they went to Florence, where Ed gave Bill another short course on architecture. Williams noted the buildings: "Buonarot-

ti's cornice overhung the street. . . . he lifted his eyes to Giotto's tower
of colored stone. . . . Boboli Gardens . . . Pitti Palace . . . Santa
Croce . . . passing by chance Donatello's St. Michael . . ." He remembered the art: ". . . the great marble David. . . . The false crudity
of Angelo, the delicate torment. . . ."[33]

After Florence they visited Naples, Pompeii, and Herculaneum.
There may have been a short trip to Venice, to which Williams would
return in 1924. After several months, Williams set sail for America. En
route he disembarked at Gibraltar; since the steamship company had no
outward bound vessels for a month, Williams visited Seville and Gra-
nada and "then Madrid and the Goyas. El Escorial, nothing like it for bare
Spain."[34]

No doubt his European year added much to Williams' comprehension of painting, but it also showed him plainly how he contrasted
with his brother. "Edgar was a master at drawing," Florence Williams
said later, "and Bill used to paint."[35] She provides a useful distinction.
Within art there is a tension between drawing, with its distinct lines,
discrete shapes and illusions of depth, and painting, in which color,
mass and brush stroke are important. Drawing is definite; painting is
oceanic. Edgar, who drew and was an architect, was becoming a classicist and conservative. His formal education was exemplary; not only did
he graduate with honors in architecture from Massachusetts Institute of
Technology, win the Prix de Rome, and study in Europe, but on his
return to the United States he handled major commissions. Only one
year Williams' junior, he provided the poet with an increasingly antag-
onistic example. He proved to Williams that "classicism" could be
adapted to an "American practice," yet he illustrated the shortcomings
of the formal training that encompassed that classicism. He was not
flexible or creative—his pattern would not hold Williams. Since they
were competitive, Ed pushed Williams to the opposite pole. In the first
draft of *The Autobiography* Williams wrote, "It was in Italy that my
separation from Ed, at least for the time being, became evident." This
conflict was an important part of Williams' outlook until the late thirties. In 1921 Williams wrote to Kenneth Burke: "L'architecture c'est
poser un cailloux sur un autre. You like that? My brother handed it to
me. I wish he really knew what it means." Five months later, in a letter to
Harriet Monroe, his conception of Ed's role in his own life is more
clearly revealed.

As my brother once told me of Rembrandt: a saying of his I believe: "It takes two men to paint a picture: one to put on the paint and one to cut off the other's hands when it (the picture) is finished."[36]

In another letter Williams wrote with obvious disapproval that "My brother, for instance, thinks [Frank Lloyd Wright] a fake." Contributions that Ed might have made to Williams' books were thereafter rejected in favor of the work of Stuart Davis. Not until 1925 was there a reconciliation; then Ed designed the dust jacket for *In The American Grain*, which showed " 'The Worm' encircling the world."[37]

Though Williams gained independence in judgments about art, he never completely shook his antagonism. In the essay "The Basis of Faith in Art" (1927) an architect—clearly Ed—argues with a poet—Williams—about the relation of art to "the people." The architect is strait-laced, conservative, and narrow-minded; the poet lectures him and scores debating points that serve chiefly to underline the value of the essay as sublimation for Williams. In later interviews Williams underplayed Ed's role in his development. "My brother Ed who was later to become a distinguished architect was my first intimate," he averred to Edith Heal. "He was a year younger and bigger almost from the start."[38]

3. *A Small Group of Friends*

Returning to the United States in 1910, Williams solidified his shaky engagement to Florence Herman. She seemed a source of female "energy" in his life. "She was his wife, and served him bright colors," he wrote on a prescription blank at the time.[1] His in-laws were skeptical about the young doctor's stability, in part because of letters he wrote from Europe threatening to disappear into Constantinople. Williams' struggle to set up his practice and to prove himself entailed dropping out of artistic circles completely. He had difficulties with his father, who refused at first to allot him a portion of the house for an office. There was also the question of a residence, and "Pop" Williams forbade the newlyweds to live as well as work in his house.

Something in Williams wanted the structured environment of Rutherford. He had no real mode of internal restraints. "It can fairly be said that I choose it in order to keep myself from going too far, as a brake to the greater liberalities," he wrote.[2]

During this period his problems superceded everything else for Williams, but he did go "into the fields along the river at times to do some painting as Mr. Wilson had taught me."[3] Several canvases of this period exist, among them a landscape reproduced in Mike Weaver's *William Carlos Williams: The American Background*. This painting is a small (14" × 10") oil on board titled "The Passaic River." The handling of the subject is indeed Mr. Wilson's—a conventional pastoral. The river winds from the background into the foreground off-center to the right, according to conventional perspective. The water reflects as it flows some leafy trees executed in broad brushwork, but there are no cows, and no human figures.

On December 12, 1912, Williams and Florence Herman were married. They moved in next door to Williams' parents, where kind neighbors rented them space.

> There we had two rooms, at least our own, a large front room, where I did a little painting now and then.
> ....

I must have done a good deal of painting in those days. I really amused Floss once, I remember, with one of my works. It was painted on a narrow wooden panel knocked out of an old door: A narrow stream coursed down the length of it from right to left about which in grotesque positions nude figures of various qualities of sex and age were strewn.[4]

Williams' mother still lived, and he "painted, using her old tubes and palette . . . found in the attic." Later he said, "I know there are several oils still lying around which I perpetrated in those days," and "I once painted Flossie's portrait there." They began the life-long habit of acquiring valuable art, when it could be had reasonably. The first acquisition was an original Audubon print, which was the centerpiece of the new living room.

Novel ideas were surfacing in the New York art and literary worlds, but Williams' only vestige of his poetic career was his regard by Pound. The famous Armory Art Exhibit took place in 1913, but Williams was not there, contrary to his later assertions. Florence Williams cleared up this point in 1976. "Bill did not attend the first Armory Show, though he always insisted he did. He went to the second one, where he read along with Mina Loy and others. He wasn't himself when he swore he'd been to the first one so I gave up trying to convince him."[5] Williams' description of what he saw at the "Armory Show" does in fact describe the Palace Exhibit of 1917 perfectly. It was the latter that impressed him.

The Armory Show nonetheless must have awakened him. The newspapers of the metropolitan area ridiculed it from its opening on February 17, 1913, until its closing three months later; the New York intellectual establishment divorced itself from the "anarchy of the exhibit." Even *Poetry*, to which Williams submitted poems under Pound's guidance, was hesitant about canvases that departed so radically from the past. However, the show had a few thoughtful defenders: Joel E. Spingarn, professor of philosophy at Columbia, wrote to the *New York Evening Post*:

I confess that when I left the exhibition my feeling was not one merely of excitement; but mingled with it was a real depression at the thought that no other artists shared this courage of the painters of our time. How timid seemed our poetry and our drama and our prose fiction; how conventional and pusillanimous our literary and dramatic criticism; how faded and academic and enemic every other form of artistic expression.[6]

24

Williams must have read this letter or others like it. Less than two weeks later he wrote a harsh letter to Harriet Monroe, the editor of *Poetry*, assailing her for "fast gravitating to the usual editorial position" on art. His notion of her magazine, he said,

> was dependent on this: most current verse is dead from the point of view of art. (I enclose some doggerel showing one of the reasons why.) Now life is above all things else at any moment subversive of life as it was the moment before—always new, irregular. Verse to be alive must have infused into it something of the same order, some tincture of disestablishment, something in the nature of an impalpable revolution, an ethereal reversal, let me say.[7]

But it was not until Charles Demuth returned to the States from Paris later in 1913 that Williams actually involved himself in the New York art scene. "I had long been deep in the love of the painted canvas through Charles Demuth," wrote Williams, "Charles had been to Paris, had tried to see Gide. . . ." In fact Demuth had been almost a resident of Gertrude Stein's atelier; he had met Picasso and Braque, seen work by Matisse, Derain and Vlaminck. He met Marcel Duchamp and the other Puteaux cubists, and renewed his acquaintance with Pound, whom he knew from Philadelphia and from London. In Philadelphia Demuth had also met Charles Sheeler and his friend Morton Schamberg, who were travelling in Paris in 1912, and he introduced them to still another old friend—Marsden Hartley.

When Hartley was off in Munich, Demuth drew closer to Duchamp. According to Demuth's biographer, "the two friends shared an entire philosophy."

> It is a philosophy more Eastern than Western (reminding one that "Charles's whole appearance was at times permeated with Oriental stillness"), one which says: Let us relax and meditate on the enjoyment of living and the importance of leisure, let us sit in the shade drinking sweet wine while we watch our industrious neighbor fall off his roof.

Though their art was different, Demuth was convinced that Duchamp would paint "the greatest picture of our time."[8] Demuth, Hartley and Duchamp, in fact, became part of an extensive homosexual network that extended from Paris to Provincetown and Philadelphia. Williams was aware of this nether side of Demuth, but he was somewhat naive about it.

Two years after Demuth's return he made a house call at his friend's apartment.

> They were deep, long digs, recently scabbed over. Charley was worried about infection.
> "What in God's name happened to you?" I asked him.
> "Do you think it is dangerous?" said he.
> "No, but how did you get such digs?"
> "A friend."
> "Charming gal," I said thoughtlessly.[9]

Demuth became part of the circle of Allan and Louise Norton; in their magazine *Rogue* he published his play "The Azure Adder." Through them he became an intimate of Walter and Louise Arensberg. Since he had known and exhibited with Stieglitz before his trip to Europe, he tried to continue at 291. But his growing mastery of watercolors threatened Stieglitz' prize racehorse. "Alfred Stieglitz didn't want to carry anyone who would be in competition with John Marin," said Demuth's subsequent sponsor, Charles Daniel.[10]

To an extent few have recognized, the world that Williams decided to enter was this world that Demuth had assembled. All of the painters and many of the writers that Williams was to know in the next decade had been friends of Demuth—he became Williams' calling card. Demuth was also the source of two attitudes that mark Williams' turn toward the New York avant-garde. Before his return to the States, Demuth had written, "Pound has done a lot, but he really doesn't know about painting." And of America he said, "New York is something which Europe is not—and I feel of that something, awful as most of it is. Marcel and all the others, those who count, say that all the 'modern' progress is now up to us, and of course they are right."[11]

Nevertheless it was Pound who recommended to Alfred Kreymborg that he look up Williams. Kreymborg was a poet of the "vagabond school" who found a benefactor in Walter Arensberg, who was then building a circle of painters, writers, and critics around himself. "Around 1914," Williams said, "I began to know other poets. The *Others* movement had started, originated by Walter Arensberg and Alfred Kreymborg. Alfred lived in Grantwood, New Jersey, all year round, in a shack never meant for winter."[12] A printing press was bequeathed to them by a friend of Pound, only to be damaged in unloading. Regardless, Grantwood was convenient for Williams: he did not have to ferry to and from New York, and he met interesting people. The avant-garde had come to him.

The colony centered around Robert Carleton Brown's big, sturdy house, which rather than overlooking New York from the Palisades, more appropriately faced the Passaic River. Williams' expression on seeing it can be imagined from a self-portrait that he painted in 1914. "This Williams appears intense and on edge, so that if the bright colors and visible brushstrokes suggest something of Matisse, they most certainly remind us of Van Gogh," said one viewer.[13]

In Grantwood, Williams discovered his world. "I met Marianne Moore for the first time in the *Others* days," he said. In *The Autobiography* he waxed romantic:

> Impressionism, dadaism, surrealism applied to both painting and poem. What a battle we made of it merely getting rid of capitals at the beginning of every line. The immediate urge, which was impressionistic, sure enough, fascinated us all. We followed Pound's instructions, his famous "Don'ts" eschewing inversions of the phrase, the putting down of what to our senses was tautological and so, uncalled for, merely to fill out a standard form. Literary allusions, save in very attenuated form, were unknown to us. Few had the necessary learning.[14]

Williams gained confidence at Grantwood; even the unsolicited vitriolic "direction" of Pound helped, for it seemed to indicate that painting was showing the artistic future. Williams wrote to Viola Baxter that Pound "says he has discovered *the* coming sculptor, a Russian [sic], Gaudier-Brzeska." Gaudier-Brzeska had written his own "Vortex," which Pound sent to Williams, whom it spurred to work out his position relative to the sculptor's.

> I affirm my existence by accepting other forces to be in juxtaposition to my own either in agreement or disagreement. . . . I have no compunction in borrowing phrases from Brzeska's "Vortex," on the contrary I accept his show of force as an affirmation of my own (and insofar as I take his phrases our forces are in agreement.) . . . I am in agreement with Brzeska that time has no existence being merely the meeting place of two planes.[15]

Cubist ideas are evident in this passage, for Williams had been

27

trying to assimilate the new movements. In his "New York Letter" to *The Egoist* a year later he wrote with a sure hand about the avant-garde.

> In New York in the spring of 1915, one was feeling a strange quickening of artistic life. It seems that due to the preoccupation of London and Paris in cruder affairs, New York has taken over those spiritual controls for which no one had any time in the war-swept countries. Here was a chance to assert oneself magnificently.
>
> The weekly papers began to notice that Duchamp was with us— and Gleizes and Croty [sic]. There were even reproductions of photographs and paragraphs speaking of "New York's gain due to its little progressive colony of artists forced out of France and England."
>
> There was an exhibition of Cezanne at Knoedler's and one of young Americans, the Forum Exhibit, from which such a good man as Demuth was excluded.[16]

The tone of this piece is disingenuous. Williams condescends to those who followed the developments through the press, but that is no doubt the way he first learned of them. After Demuth's return, however, Williams began to meet the artists of the Armory Show and, as an insider, to adopt a knowing stance.

He began to visit New York galleries and shows regularly. When *Others* folded and moved piecemeal back to New York, Mina Loy's studio became the first meeting place, and excursions to exhibits were natural.

The Others Circle was more potent in New York. Arensberg, Duchamp, Man Ray and Picabia were closely involved in the planning of the 1917 Palace Exhibit. Williams got a part, although later he misremembered the occasion: "I was asked to appear at the Armory Show and I read the poem "Overture to a Dance of Locomotives." Many of the ladies in the audience left but Mina Loy said it was the best poem read that day." Williams' memories of the show were dominated by the audacity of Marcel Duchamp, who entered a porcelain urinal.

> I went to it and gaped along with the rest at a "picture" in which an electric bulb kept going on and off; at Duchamp's sculpture (by "Mott and Co."), [sic] a magnificent cast-iron urinal, glistening of its white enamel. The story then current of this extraordinary and popular young man was that he walked daily into whatever store struck his fancy and purchased

whatever pleased him—something new—something American. Whatever it might be, that was his "construction" for the day. The silly committee threw out the urinal, asses that they were. The "Nude Descending a Staircase" is too hackneyed for me to remember anything clearly about it now. But I do remember how I laughed out loud when first I saw it, happily, with relief.[17]

Williams shared the high spirits of this time with Demuth, who wrote a poem about the "Fontaine" that appeared in Arensberg's journal *The Blind Man*.

For Richard Mutt
One must say everything—then no one will know.
To know nothing is to say a great deal.
So many say that they say nothing—but these never
     really end.
For some there is no stopping.
     Most stop or get a style.
When they stop they make a convention.
That is their end.
For the going every thing has an idea.
The going run right along.
The going just keep going.[18]

Sometime in the late teens, Williams met Alfred Stieglitz, who was the center of a similar, often overlapping circle, one more concerned with photography and much more American in its composition, sensibilities and attitude. Stieglitz was deadly serious about art, alienating anyone who also held strong views—so his group was small. In his galleries—291, 391, The Intimate Gallery and later An American Place—an atmosphere of high moral purpose prevailed. He showed Matisse, Picasso and Rodin at the urging of his collaborator Edward Steichen, but he did not show Duchamp, whose work he regarded skeptically. Despite the presence of the avant-garde in his gallery, Stieglitz was restrained in his own work and taste. Williams met Stieglitz through Marsden Hartley, who participated in both groups. The date of their first meeting is unclear, though in *The Autobiography* Williams puts it after the publication of *In the American Grain* in 1925. This is surely wrong. The best evidence of an earlier date has been discovered by Bram

Dijkstra, as we have seen, but it does not seem safe to date the acquaintance before 1919, although Williams may have read Steiglitz's magazines and transected his orbit earlier.

Nor does it seem fair to impute too much of Williams' progress in this era to Pound. In 1917 they had a rupture in relations. Pound was not in tune with painting, and Williams believed that advances came from painting. He later wrote bitterly,

> I believe Pound to be as color blind as he is tone deaf. It was the great period of Picasso's supremacy, of Braque, of Juan Gris, Matisse and some of the others. Do you find any inkling of it in what Pound was writing those days? Show it to me and I'll show you that all his comments are literary banter. Picasso snubbed him. Gertrude Stein put him aside after a few words. And who among all these people do you think Pound picked as his champion? Picabia, a purely literary figure, Picabia and Leger. His war against England quickly petered out there and he had to take another jump to save himself. Ah, this time he found it.
>
> Briefly Pound missed the major impact of his age, the social impetus which underlies every effort on that front, largely through his blindness and intense egotism; he is a complete reactionary. Really he can't learn and as a result has been left sadly in the rear.[19]

It was in 1918 that Williams heard from Alanson Hartpence, who worked in the Daniel Gallery, the story of a woman who entered one day and demanded to know what was represented in the lower left-hand corner of an abstract painting. Hartpence bent over to inspect. Echoing Braque, he said, "That, Madame, is paint." It was a seminal discovery as Williams viewed it in retrospect:

> It is the making of that step, to come over into the tactile qualities, the words themselves beyond the mere thought expressed that distinguishes the modern, or distinguished the modern of that time from the period before the turn of the century. And it is the reason why painting and the poem became so closely allied at that time. It was the work of the painters following Cezanne and the Impressionists that, critically, opened up the age of Stein, Joyce, and a good many others.[20]

The publication and instantaneous recognition of T. S. Eliot stunned Williams, who was in the early stages of *Kora in Hell*. He wrote that Eliot "was writing poems as good as 'The Ode to a Nightingale.' They were effective, but we were writing poems from the dung-heap—the Ash-Can School."[21] The metaphor not only shows Williams' grasp of contemporary art and indicates his impatience, but points out the direction he would move to counter Eliot. Williams knew that the conceptual revolution made earlier in art had implications for poetry.

After the war Picabia and Gleizes, who had been leaders of the New York avant-garde, drifted back to Paris, followed by American *artistes* eager to take advantage of a favorable exchange rate. Supporting a medical practice, Williams could not leave. Not quite ready to be independent, he turned for "direction" in the crucial part of his career to a second series of men—all painters: Duchamp, Hartley and Sheeler.

Williams added Hartley's work in particular to his collection. In 1921 he bought the pastel "Mountains in New Mexico," (1919) for $105.00. Williams himself still experimented: when his grandmother died in 1920, as she lay in state, he "did a pencil drawing of her really impressive features."[22]

Williams met Sheeler in the late teens through their mutual friend Matthew Josephson. Since Sheeler, Josephson, Demuth, and Hartley had recently been to Europe, in the twenties Williams decided to make the trip, this time with his wife. In January, 1924, they embarked for six months in Europe. Their experiences, along with those of his Leipzig trip in 1910, Williams combined in *A Voyage to Pagany* (1928), for which "My brother made the design of the cover."[23]

Friendships with McAlmon, Duchamp, Man Ray, Mina Loy and others brought the Williamses a welcome in Paris. Williams had written ahead to McAlmon that he was interested in meeting the Surrealist and Dada writers, but McAlmon did not regard the movements highly and sidetracked the request. Immediately on arrival, McAlmon took Williams to the Louvre, but it was closed. Then he organized an awkward party, to which he invited Duchamp, George Antheil, Louis Aragon, Man Ray, Mina Loy and James Joyce. When he could extricate himself, Williams enjoyed walking the Paris streets, remembering the ". . . medieval Place Francois Ier, as French in its way as anything I have ever known, of that French austerity of design, gray stone cleanly cut and put together in complementary masses, like the Alexandrines of Racine." And he finally got into the Louvre.

Visited Louvre with Floss in the morning—the space usually occupied by the Mona Lisa, blank, the canvas having been cut out of the frame and stolen only a week ago. Harold Loeb went with me to the *Salon*. A few sculptured pieces (about four) were interesting, but in general the exhibit was terrible. I was surprised. The pictures the same or worse, and in Paris![24]

The Williamses saw dance—the ballet *Salade* at the Soiree de Paris—and there were more dinners "at Trianon . . . with the painter Toohey" as well as a chance to see Gaudier-Brzeska's "Faun." Finally Williams tired of it all, especially the drunken mien of the expatriates. He evaded them, "saying I wanted to see the pictures in the Luxembourg as an excuse." He "enjoyed the Impressionists, Manet and Cezanne, a few Degas there too." He saw Whistler's portrait of his mother, and attended a performance of Cocteau's *Romeo and Juliet* at the Cigale, where he apparently saw Picasso and Derain.[25]

The rest of the trip, except for a short jaunt to Venice, was spent in a small town on the Riviera. From Venice, Williams dropped a note to Marianne Moore. "St. Mark's Cathedral in Venice—have you ever seen it?—is my rich ideal of pelt and plumage." In *Voyage to Pagany* he would write: "St. Mark's . . . St. Paul's . . . Carpaccios in the Museo, stringently drawn, the Colleone and the end wall of the Hall of the Great Seal, by Tintoretto, El Greco's master, all black crooks, these were beyond comparison. . . ."[26]

In a letter to Kenneth Burke, Williams explained that by defining himself against the Paris crowd, he was working out his relationship to the classics. "I have been won over and over here," he wrote, "by the bits of wisdom that I've seen even in the museums—the statues, the whole colossal record of their oldtime fullness and our unnecessary subservience to our crippledom. We love it. That's the hell of it. We eat it, lie in it." It was a repetition, with increased awareness, of his earlier attraction to the restraining structures of Ed's classicism. Three weeks later he wrote: "They want reproductions of our paintings. They asked me if any of our men admired the newer Frenchmen, if there had been any exhibits in America! I didn't believe such questions possible."[27]

In June the Williamses set sail. The poet noted that "eastward clouds were to the north filling the sky in painter's masses, low and heavy." The discovery that Europe's literary crowd, or at least its crowd of literary transplants, was still catching up with developments in painting that he had long ago assimilated gave Williams new confidence. Cezanne, Picasso and Braque had been shown and had made their impact in New York a decade earlier, and Williams had been in on the ground floor of the movement. "He was jealous of French painting," Williams wrote of himself, "and he was backing the [Passaic] river against it." His opposition to other patterns now had a locale. "The thing that Americans never seem to see is that French painting . . . is related to its own definite tradition, in its own environment and general history," he wrote, ". . . American painting to be of value, must have comparable relationships in its own tradition."[28] That was the genesis of his program of "contact," on which he worked the next two decades.

He had resumed contact with Pound by the spring of 1926. "Things in general are picking up here, interest in painters, etc." he wrote. Williams considered himself an independent and astute judge of art, and carried this buoyant attitude on for several years. Asked by *The Little Review* in 1929 what he considered his strongest characteristic, he answered, "My sight. I like most my ability to be drunk with a sudden realization of value in things others never notice." When Ford Maddox Ford moved to New York and "tried hard to sell us one of his wife's pictures," Williams rebuked him. When his eyesight bothered him, Williams wrote to Marianne Moore, ". . . I don't like not being able to see dust flecks quite so distinctly as formerly—and the grains of pollen in the flowers."[29]

For awhile he practically disappeared from the New York scene, finding his art in Rutherford instead. "Nine times out of ten when I go into a house and have to wait a moment or two for whoever it is to appear, I find interesting [pictures] to look at, in the plainest households sometimes." But he remained an inveterate attender of openings and big shows.

> There was a grand opening at the new Museum of Modern Art in New York a few weeks ago. It really was a stampede—what a mob! Art has at last achieved its objective, it has served in America as an occasion for the rich to come out and root for it—just once, just once. The bastards. But the show is a great one and well worth repeated visits I'm sure.

Skepticism did not prevent him from accepting an invitation to read at the Museum of Modern Art a bit later. As his wife noted, it was "one of his first big time readings."[30]

Abstract expressionism, so compatible with Williams' interests, flowered without him. By the forties he was pressed to do his own work, and he had big projects planned. He wrote to McAlmon: "I used to hear something of the French gang in N.Y. a year ago but of late nothing, not interested. Peggy Guggenheim is putting her money at their disposal, I suppose through Max Ernst—I think it's Max Ernst."[31] Some of the artists close to him had died, Charles Demuth among them. Williams had bought such works by Demuth as "End of the Parade," and "Pink Lady Slippers" and written often about him. Demuth had dedicated "Machinery" and "The Great Figure" to Williams and sent him books on Matisse and other painters from Europe in 1921. Williams became more intimate with Charles Sheeler, who moved with his new wife to an upstate New York setting that the Williamses found a refreshing week end trip. The poet had aged, and he was husbanding his strength.

"For fifty years this was headquarters for them all," said Florence Williams, gesturing to her living room. "There was Marsden Hartley— that was his only pastel, over the divan there. He was broke and wanted to go to Germany, so he had an auction at Stieglitz' gallery, An American Place. Bill bought another one at the same time, an unfinished oil up in the study."

The paintings in Williams' home are of interest. Williams must have studied them often, and certainly did not hang anything that he did not like. He rarely spoke about his acquisitions, but there are descriptions in several interviews. Stanley Koehler noted a "huge, two-story painting of the Williamsburg Bridge filling the stairwell." Upstairs in Williams' study "in a corner of the room, over a filing cabinet, was an oil painting hung against a wallpaper of geometric simplicity."[32] A more thorough account was given by James Laughlin in a short story concerning his visit with "Dev Evans."

There was a lovely delicate Demuth of red flowers and green leaves—very abstract in its design and the colors subtle. And a strange Graves bird—no kind of a bird you could name but very much a bird—a dark form, only the feet and the beak drawn sharply, on a soft gray wash; it had an oriental feeling; and a Hartley, a forest scene, the logs and rocks like crude chunks, thickly painted with heavy black outlines. And over the fireplace a Marin, a view looking out over some beach that must be in Maine—those wonderful free slaps and slashes of the water-color brush, an inspired jumble of bits and patches of pure color with the white of the paper left showing between them. Evans had been friends with all these painters. He had written poems to most of them.[33]

The room housing this remarkable assembly of art, Laughlin wrote, "wasn't large, but light came in through tall windows."

Bram Dijkstra, in *A Recognizable Image*, confirms the presence of some of these paintings. The Williams' estate included Demuth's "Pink Lady Slippers," "Flowers," and "End of the Parade: Coatesville, Pa.,"; Hartley's "Mountains in New Mexico" (1919) and "Shell Contours" (1920) as well as a signed copy of "New England Sea View—Fish House" (1934); Sheeler's two "Photos of an Old Dutch Barn"; and Helene Williams' "Portrait of a Niece in Mayaguez." Flossie has also described the pieces.

> The red tulips on the wall . . . a painting by Charles Sheeler. We met him just before we sailed for Europe in 1924 at a party given by Kenneth Burke and Matthew Josephson who wrote *Robber Baron*. We liked him. He had a very dry wit. He and Bill talked right up to the time of Bill's death. They'd ring each other up on the phone. Charles Demuth painted the flower picture . . . tube roses and wild orchid and the factory study. Marsden Hartley painted the landscape . . . he was a damn good writer of essays and poems . . . the same old story . . . was never discovered . . . his paintings are quite rare. Other writers have been painters . . . E. E. Cummings. Bill could have easily; he had talent. His brother Edgar's paintings are all through the house.

Williams himself told interviewers, "I'd like to have been a painter, and it would have given me at least as great a satisfaction as being a poet."[34]

35

4. The "Others" of Walter Arensberg

"The old expressions are with us always,
and there are always others."

Arensberg

I. Grantwood

In 1913 Alfred Kreymborg got a package of manuscript titled "Des Imagistes: An Anthology" in the mail from Ezra Pound. Enclosed in it were a single poem by William Carlos Williams and a note: "Wms. is my one remaining friend in America—get in touch with old Bull—he lives in a hole called Rutherford, New Jersey." Kreymborg had heard a little about Pound from John Cournos, but nothing of Williams. Kreymborg lived at the time with Man Ray and Samuel Halpert on the sunset side of the New Jersey Palisades. Ray and Halpert were promising young painters at the Daniel Gallery, where Alanson Hartpence worked. Together they edited an experimental magazine, *The Glebe*, made forays into New York City and took turns cooking and cleaning in their $9 a month shack.[1]

Kreymborg and Williams did not meet immediately. That event was attendant on the meeting of the editors of two competing little magazines published in Greenwich Village. The chief rival of *The Glebe* was *Rogue*, published by Allan Norton to print the poetry of Walter Arensberg, Mina Loy, and Wallace Stevens, who was one of Arensberg's classmates at Harvard. When Norton arranged the American publication of Gertrude Stein's *Three Lives*, which Kreymborg proclaimed a masterpiece, the latter agreed to have dinner with Norton and his wife, even though he thought *Rogue* hopelessly sedate. It was a startling evening—Kreymborg found his poetry praised for its "naive sophistication"—and at its end Kreymborg found himself walking home with one of the guests, Walter Arensberg. Their walk took them to Arensberg's studio on Central Park West, where they talked until daylight about common interests.

> Arensberg was passionately fond of Pound and the Imagists, asked many pertinent questions about the Imagist issue of *The Glebe*, confided that *Rogue* would never do, couldn't last in any event, and what was needed in America was a poetry magazine, not like *Poetry* in Chicago, which admitted too many compromises, but a paper dedicating its energies to experiment throughout. He wondered if such a venture was feasible and whether Krimmie would join him in it. The latter was sure it was feasible, and before the evening closed, plans were already underway. Krimmie promised to get in touch once more with Pound and other poets he knew.[2]

When Pound advised, Kreymborg got in touch with William Carlos Williams, and drew him into that orbit known as "The Arensberg Circle," the sun of which was one of America's most brilliant little magazines, *Others*. Williams was unknown but welcome, because, as Arensberg told Kreymborg, "Poets as yet unknown will be asked to submit their material alongside poets of repute . . . there will be no financial inducement for contributing."[3] That was fine with Williams. Arensberg "generously assumed the responsibility of the costs of the venture," and then, since he disliked the heat of New York summers, left for a cooler climate as May rounded into June.

The newly married Kreymborg took his young bride and crossed to the New Jersey Palisades, where Man Ray had found him a cottage at minimal rent in Grantwood; there he assembled the magazine and rang up Williams. As Man Ray recalled, "Williams lived in the country about a mile from me. He was a doctor but he was becoming more and more known as a poet."[4] Very nearly the first man in Rutherford to own a car, Williams made the drive over to Grantwood whenever possible.

> I made weekly trips, winter and summer, to help read manuscripts, correct proofs. I finally edited one of the issues and probably paid for it. . . . Whenever I wrote at this time, the poems were written with *Others* in mind. I made no attempt to get publication anywhere else; the poems were definitely for *Others*.[5]

It was the innovative poet Mina Loy who put the first issue of

Others in the public eye. The opening of her sarcastic love song drew shudders even in Greenwich Village:

> Spawn of fantasies
> Sitting the appraisable
> Pig Cupid   his rosy snout
> Rooting erotic garbage. . . .

Critics deplored her topic, lack of punctuation and audacious line spacing, but Williams appreciated her innovations. Kreymborg noted that

> these technical factors not only crop up in a later poet, E. E. Cummings, to whose originality later critics attributed them, but were learned by Mina during a lengthy sojourn in Paris and Florence, where she came under the influence of Guillaume Apollinaire and F. T. Marinetti. Mina had simply transferred futuristic theories to America, and in her subject-matter had gone about expressing herself freely.[6]

The futurist aesthetic, which concerned itself with representing the speed and dynamism of modern life in art, already dominated the work of the painters in the Arensberg circle—Duchamp, Gleizes and Man Ray—and quickly became a program for the poets as well.

Loy was an important part of Arensberg's set and the foremost proponent of futurist poetry in the United States. She had been living with an English painter in Florence when Filippo Marinetti arrived in 1913. He shocked the town with his noisy proclamations and strange happenings, which intrigued Loy. She came to know him, and sent off her "Aphorisms on Futurism" to *Camera Work*. The manner in which they dovetailed with Imagism and with the push for compression in poetry makes it worth recounting a few:

> YOU prefer to observe the past on which your eyes are already opened. But the future is dark only from outside. *Leap* into it—and it EXPLODES with *Light*.
> WHAT can you know of expansion, who limit yourselves to compromise?
> THE futurist can live a thousand years in one poem.
> HE can compress every aesthetic principle in one line.[7]

In conversation Loy was fond of quoting two sayings of Carlo Carra, another futurist. "We Futurists strive with the force of intuition to insert ourselves into the midst of things in such fashion, that our 'self' forms a single complex with their identities." She liked to discuss Carra's "dynamism," an idea positing "an equation between the activity of the outside world and the activity of the mind."

A painter herself, Loy began to show the poets, through her irregular verse and unusual spacing, that they could create visual transcriptions of modern life just as the painters were creating equivalents of the sounds, sights and smells of public life. Her technique was, among other things, typographic. Her poetry aimed to clear the "fallow lands of mental spatiality" and to evoke new spaces from readers. Challenging the conventions, Loy printed her initial words in capitals to give greater force to them. She kept her whole sentence on one line, stressing the force of the final word, or she ran the sentence over so that both its final word and the initial word of the next sentence were stressed. To create the pauses—for intuition—that the futurists advocated, Loy used frequent hyphens and omitted connectives. The white space between the lines or verses, as in Cezanne's painting, was intended to connect the parts, even to stand as a metaphor for the newly freed space. That Williams was beginning to experiment with these devices is evident from his angry response to Harriet Monroe when she changed one of his poems before publishing it in *Poetry*: "It will be *physically* impossible for anyone to guess how I intended it to be read the way you have rearranged matters."[8] [emphasis added]

When Arensberg returned in the fall, he had a change of heart. Mina Loy's poetry was not what the genteel art patron had expected. "He wished to retire from the magazine, but without embarrassing Krimmie, who had committed himself to various obligations with respect to the venture. Walter generously offered to underwrite the printer's estimate for one year." As it turned out, Arensberg's support lasted considerably longer, but his apprehension that affairs had proceeded beyond polite pastimes was correct. Kreymborg, Williams, Loy and Moore formed a real avant-garde. Their demeanor was not super-subtle, as Williams' account, "The Great Opportunity," makes clear:

> But in poetry the fiercest twitching appeared. Two hundred and fifty dollars were put forward by a man, himself a poet. Kreymborg was employed to carry out his idea of a magazine free for the new in poetry. He gave up

his newspaper-writing, came out of his garret, married!, and in a little hut to which water had to be carried for washing, he started his magazine, *Others*.

There was, I think, wild enthusiasm among free verse-writers, slightly less enthusiasm among Sunday Magazine Section reporters, and really quite a stir in the country at large.
. . . .
Actually it seemed that the weight of centuries was about to be lifted. One could actually get a poem published without having to think of anything except that it be good, artistically: Kreymborg was the hero.

Every Sunday afternoon there were meetings at Grantwood. We sat on the floor, brought our own lunches, played ball in the yard and struggled to converse with one another.[9]

It was a heterogeneous lot that made their way to Grantwood on Sunday, Kreymborg remembered, and though most were calmer, "wild enthusiasm" seems an apt characterization of Williams at the time. In his autobiography, *Troubadour*, Kreymborg caught Williams' naive energy:

One man, looking like Don Quixote de la Mancha driving the rusty Rosinante, came in a battered, two-seated Ford. Though the actual place he started from was an ugly little town called Rutherford, there was enough of the Spaniard in his blood and the madman in his eye and profile to have warranted the comparison. Whenever he climbed down from the saddle, with an oath or a blessing, he disclosed the bold or the bashful features of Ezra Pound's old and Krimmie's new friend, Dr. William Carlos Williams. It was for Bill, even more than any of the others, Krimmie would steal outdoors, shade his eyes and watch for a cloud of dust along the horizon.[10]

Marianne Moore also came. Wallace Stevens came. Mina Loy came. Halpert, Ray, Hartpence, Brown and others who lived in the shacks nearby would emerge and chat in the Sunday light with Cummings or other visitors. Walter Arensberg, who made the long trip from the city out of penance, came out and brought with him Marcel Duchamp, who asked Kreymborg, "Why do you live so far from town? Is there something you do out here can't be done nearer town?"

There was, but they were shy about it. Manuscripts of poems and stories were passed, along with lunches and refreshments, to Kreymborg and his wife in the kitchen. The editor quietly removed them to the garret he had converted into a workroom and study, where he perused them later. No one was ashamed of his work, said Kreymborg, but everyone was exceedingly modest about the possible importance of his writing.

> Usually Krimmie thought more of their poems than they did themselves, and, in order to communicate this feeling, he hit upon the expedient of inducing the poets to read aloud. Williams alone approved of this scheme, but when someone challenged him to open the experiment, Bill was overwhelmed with embarrassment and to hide it chanted so savagely that the gasping sounds he emitted were unintelligible. It therefore fell to Krimmie to read aloud for Bill and the rest.
>
> . . . .
>
> They enjoyed talking shop most of all, but their discussions spread an evasive levity over the serious current of their actual thought. Like almost every other cultural activity of the new soil, the intercourse of these people was a novel experience. They had to approach it warily and grow up to the art of conversation. . . . It was not a lack of self-confidence which dictated so shy a contact, but a joyous bewilderment in the discovery that other men and women were working in a field they themselves felt they had chosen in solitude.[11]

For no one was this truer than for Williams, who lived in isolation from his peers most of the week, who used his work as "a kind of meditation" and by Sunday seethed with expression. The facts that the work was read aloud by a central reader and that the conversation built with a "painstaking, self-conscious tempo" were important to Williams' development. Not only did he incorporate the futurist tactics of Mina Loy, but he came to value immediate clarity, phrasing, speed, and a grammatical thrust that carried straight through the poem. "We were speaking straight ahead about what concerned us," he said, "and if I could have overheard what I was saying then, that would have given me a hint of how to phrase myself, to say what I had to say."[12]

The glimpse we get of Williams in this period is impressive—not the modest, sometimes reticent physician of later years, but a man of careless enthusiasm.

> No manuscripts required more reading than those of Marianne Moore and Mina Loy. However, in the almost unanimous ridicule accorded the con-

tributors, not even these ladies out-distanced Krimmie's special ally, Bill Williams. Shy though Bill was in person, blank paper let loose anything he felt about everything, and he frankly and fearlessly undressed himself down to the ground.

But such qualities made Williams valuable to Kreymborg, who noted that "among the first contributors to *Others*, no person gave as much of himself as Bill Williams."

Regardless of the many patients who required his attention in and around the gray town of Rutherford, the medico often pointed the blunt nose of his Ford toward Grantwood or wrote incisive letters to Krimmie and aided him critically in the onerous task of choosing and rejecting manuscripts. Krimmie had never encountered a more incongruous American than this artist, scientist and madman. His letters, as outspoken as his poems, attacked and applauded Krimmie in the same paragraph, and for the sake of clarity many a goddam was thrown at the editor—and thrown back in rebuttal. At the close of such an exchange of civilities, Bill would laugh, turn on himself—another favorite pastime—and subject the patient to a surgical operation in which no phase of the raw spirit was spared. Groans would issue from the defenceless ego, and then someone had to treat him like the adolescent he was at such times. Shyness, bravado, imagination, scientific accuracy, childishness were constantly at war in this son of a Porto Rican woman . . . and an Englishman. One had to develop many shades of responsiveness to cope with the medico's changeable moods and melodies. Krimmie learned the dance so effectively that Bill often charged him with hypocrisy and diplomacy. Then words would fly once more and Bill would go back to castigating himself on paper. A fiery verse or two would be posted from Rutherford to Grantwood.[13]

All the new developments in art, to Williams' amazement, presented themselves immediately there above the Passaic. "Grantwood was the focus of all these events," Williams wrote, "I was hugely excited by what was taking place there. . . . on every possible occasion, I went madly in my flivver to help with the magazine which had saved my life as a writer." The residents, permanent and part-time, were soon to be in other places though. "Malcolm Cowley lived there for a while and Man Ray, looking suspiciously about, getting ready to quit for Paris. I'll not forget my rather awed delight at meeting Duchamp, the great Marcel," said Williams. "I'd sneak away mostly on Sundays to join the gang, . . .

show what I had written and sometimes help Kreymborg with the make-up."

> We'd have arguments over cubism which would fill an afternoon. There was a comparable whipping up of interest in the structure of the poem. It seemed daring to omit capitals at the head of each poetic line. Rhyme went by the board. We were, in short, "rebels," and were so treated.[14]

"Cubism," as Williams uses the term, means simply "the new." As a French scholar of Williams' work has pointed out, cubism hitch-hiked over the Atlantic on futurism's appeal:

> A l'influence cubiste est venue en effet s'ajouter celle de futurisme, mouvement d'origine italienne . . . qui cherche à représenter l'object en relation dynamique avec son milieu. . . . Sans doute en raison de dynamisme et de la mobilité de leur milieu, les jeunes artistes américains ont été encore plus sensibles à l'influence du futurisme qu'à celle du cubisme.

Charles Demuth was painting in Bermuda with Marsden Hartley while Williams was in Grantwood, the scholar adds, but the range from Sheeler to Demuth shows the painters were "plus sensible à l'influence de futurisme dont les fameuses lignes-forces." Duchamp, she notes, told Kreymborg that even Picasso was not a cubist.[15]

This created a tension, unsuspected at first, between futurist and expressionist elements in the circle. It was a split, moreover, that mirrored Williams' central dilemma: futurism focused on the appearances of things, and lent itself to a formulaic approach. It had all the faults of programs allied with classicism. The expressionists, on the other hand, insisted on so much freedom that they approached artistic antinomianism. Any constraint, any structure, they saw as an infringement on their emotions. The group embodied the same problem with which Williams was struggling.

For Williams the most promising poetic syntheses in the group were those of Moore and Loy. Moore's style seemed to him sometimes cubist, but mainly futurist. "Mm. Moore has taken recourse," he wrote, "to the mathematics of art."

> Unlike the painters the poet has not resorted to distortions or the abstract in form. Miss Moore accomplishes a like result by rapidity of movement. A

poem such as "Marriage" is an anthology of transit. It is a pleasure that can be held firm only by moving rapidly from one thing to the next. It gives the impression of a passage through.[16]

Williams had an unreserved admiration for Mina Loy, a futurist with Matisse's appreciation of light. It is clear that he observed her closely.

> When she puts a word down on paper it is clean . . . . The essence of her style is her directness in which she is exceeded by no one. Her metaphors, when they can be detected, are of the quality of sunlight, they sparkle. There is no dimming of the light. What she sees and she sees everything that goes on about her, directly. [sic] Her lines are short. There is no inversion of the phrase for effect or to keep an imposed order. You cannot find a single instance of a measure retained to complete a conventional stanza or indeed a set pattern of any sort. The light, as in the impressionists of her period, is reflected from all surfaces.[17]

Williams' passion for poetry and for *Others* carried him through the Grantwood phase of the Circle without any resolution of his tensions. In 1916, when at Pound's behest he wrote a piece for *The Egoist*, he was uncritically cheerful about everything his group represented.

> Good verse was coming in from San Francisco, from Louisville, Ky., from Chicago, from 63rd St., from Staten Island, from Boston, from Oklahoma City. At least it was verse one could print.
> New-comers to the city if they were alive to artistic interests in their own parts naturally drifted into the crowd.
> *Others* was commented on in *The New Republic, The Boston Transcript, The Literary Digest, Life* and who knows what other magazines of importance. This little magazine was said to be the sun of a new dawn—in its little yellow cover! America had at last found a democratic means of expression! It was free verse! Even the papers went so far as to make extensive mockery of the men and the movement in their funny columns. We were elated at our success![18]

"Bill developed tremendously in that period," said his wife later. Yet a break-up of the group was imminent. *Others* got too big—it needed management, as Williams saw.

> The weekly meeting went on. A stock company was proposed. *Others* was to be managed by a committee. We were to have a clubhouse—above 42nd

St., oh, yes, it had to be above 42nd St.—that much was certain. We could have a large room for exhibits of pictures, silk goods, sculpture, etc. Here we could have our social meetings—Stevens would like that—with a little dance afterwards. Then again we could use the same room for plays and readings. In the same building would be rooms for rent and at least two apartments where you and I and our families could live and edit *Others* and keep a book store and—that was a fine dream!

If there was a trace of bitterness in Williams' apprehension that the center of the group was moving farther away geographically, it was sweetened by the fact that the last issue of *Others* was left in his hands. The dissolution thereafter was slow, but inevitable.

It seemed that the painters and the poets didn't get along very well together, perhaps that was why we couldn't get things said which we were all aching to say.

Well, let's meet next time without the painters.

Next time it was the women who interfered. The women agreed to stay home. Six men met one evening and had a bully good time discussing the news and affairs in general in a reasonably intelligent way. This was the high water mark.

It was mid-winter by now. *Others* was wabbling [sic] badly. Subscriptions came in slowly. Kreymborg had to move to the city. A few poems of doubtful moral tone made enemies. Kreymborg insisted on keeping his hand on the tiller and anyway it began to be doubtful if there was going to be much gain, either financially or artistically, connected with the enterprise. One began to hear obscene murmurs. Fine! Now, at last, we were to get down to real values!

This piece was written in 1916; it shows a markedly different Williams from the man Kreymborg described in 1914. If Williams was depressed by the migration of the group back to New York, he had nevertheless gained his own confidence and credence. His fires were now stoked privately, incessantly. He and Florence threw a party for the principals of *Others* at their Rutherford home, hoping to close the final issue on an up-beat.

We fed 'em and wined 'em all day long. They were under the cherry tree when the snapshot was made of the Arensbergs, M. Gleizes, Marcel Duchamp, Kreymborg, Sanborn, Man Ray, Hartpence and Bodenheim. In another picture were their wives and sweethearts, Gertrude Kreymborg among them. There were besides Ferdinand Rhyer and Skip Cannell leaping upon the trunk of a car.[19]

"At last the movement is dead," summarized Williams. "Now for the advance." As it turned out, that was a prescient conclusion.

II. New York

The *Others* group did not end at all: it was "relocated" by its Maecenas, Walter Arensberg, who found the Sunday journey to New Jersey arduous. During his summer sojourn in California, he had decided that he could accomplish more by concentrating his time, effort and money. He had become relatively less interested in poetry and, under Duchamp's tutelage, more interested in avant-garde art, chess and his own research on Francis Bacon. He considered the circle that rose in Grantwood to be his own creation, however, and he wanted it to continue—closer to home.

Expense presented no object. Walter and Louise Arensberg were awash in money. His wife came from a wealthy family, and Arensberg was heir to a fortune. A family glass works and ceramics refractory supported Arensberg and two of his artistically inclined brothers in comfort until the Great Depression. He graduated from Harvard in 1900, where he was a classmate of Wallace Stevens. They had written together as undergraduates and proceeded to serve a stint on the *New York Evening Post* between 1900 and 1903. Then Stevens enrolled in law school, and in 1907 Arensberg married Louise Stevens (no relation). Her interest in modern music complemented his own taste for contemporary poetry, and she had income from a textile fortune. They decided to "travel." Having met the Steins in San Francisco, they called on Gertrude in Paris, admired the art on her walls, and decided they would become collectors. Stein took them to see painters, but they postponed any purchases until they returned to America. Back home they bought a sketch of Puteaux by Jacques Villon, one of Duchamp's brothers, from the 1913 Armory Show. Then they expanded into the more legible synthetic cubists.

Arensberg wrote poetry and contributed prose pieces, some clearly inspired by Stein, to Allan Norton's *Rogue* during this period. His first book of poetry, *Poems*, (1914) had been derivative of French symbolism and of Mallarmé particularly. Shortly after its publication, the Arensbergs moved to a large apartment at 33 West 67th Street, where works from the Armory Show, no longer so shocking, began to adorn the walls. They bought Matisse's "Portrait of Mlle Yvonne Landsberg" in 1914, the same year they began collecting Picasso and Braque. In particular they sought works by painters who had outraged the public: Picasso, Matisse, Picabia, Gleizes, and Duchamp.

When Duchamp arrived in June, 1915, the Arensbergs met him at the boat and whisked him off to a luncheon at their apartment. He stayed for some time in "a small studio that adjoined the upper level of the Arensbergs' apartment by a short hallway," and later moved downstairs to a studio.[20] Eventually over one third of the Arensbergs' art collection came through his quiet efforts. The most immediate result of the new friendship was a change in Arensberg's poetic direction: rather than symbolist poetry, which Duchamp convinced him was out-dated, Arensberg focused on futurism and an incipient form of dada. He polished and published his second book, *Idols*, in early 1916, then finished off his responsibilities to *Others* after the summer in order to have more time to explore Duchamp's ideas.

By this time the Others were all in New York. His original collaborator, Kreymborg, was divorced and living on Bank Street, where he had taken in an obstreperous Chicagoan named Maxwell Bodenheim. Wallace Stevens, in Hartford, was more likely to come to New York than to New Jersey, as was E. E. Cummings. Marsden Hartley had arrived from Berlin; the rest of the important painters, Ray and Halpert excepted, already lived in the Village.

The task of commuting did not give Williams pause; his participation in the group actually increased during this period.

> Along with everything else I was going into the city, Mondays, Wednesdays and Fridays to the Pediatric Clinics, first to the Baby's, then the Post-Graduate Hospitals, for advanced training. . . . On Fridays, which was my day off, I'd stop over for a party or to drop in on Hartley or somewhere. The group often met somewhere on the second floor of a small 14th St. apartment, most often at Mina Loy's—that Vestal of the arts, a devout believer in the community of the arts—narrow quarters where anyone might on occasion turn up.[21]

But Loy moved and next, as Flossie recalls, "they used to meet in New York at Lola Ridge's. She had a big, barn-like studio." It was a good place to stage the plays that Williams, Kreymborg, and Loy were then writing. "It was tough, but somehow I got in to rehearsals from Rutherford three nights a week after office hours," wrote Williams. Then Lola Ridge moved, and when Williams curtailed his playwriting—Kreymborg lost his prize manuscript—he turned to the alternative offered by the painter's world. He felt the need to re-establish contact with avant-garde ideas, and Arensberg decided that Williams, unlike Loy and Kreymborg, was acceptably genteel. In his adamantly American manner, Williams called them "parties."

> There were parties, mostly of painters, at Arensberg's studio. These were of a different sort from the usual "broke" goings on. Arensberg could afford to spread a really ample feed with drinks to match. You always saw Marcel Duchamp there. His painting on glass, half-finished, stood at one side and several of his earlier works were on the wall, along with one of Cezanne's "Woman Bathers," the work of Gleizes and several others. It disturbed and fascinated me, I confess I was slow to come up with any answers.[22]

In the view of Marcel Duchamp, it was a "salon," as select a gathering of artists as Paris could offer. All descriptions of an evening at the Arensbergs' confirm that the paintings and sculpture were exceptional, the food was plentiful, and no expense was spared. Beatrice Wood, the paramour of H. P. Roche and later of Duchamp, said, "Drinks were served at midnight, and Lou would also bring out trays laden with chocolate eclairs for those who did not drink."[23] Gabrielle Picabia-Buffet, a painter welcome at any Parisian salon, described the Arensbergs as

> amateurs et mécènes éclairés et généreux chez lesquels on était sûr de trouver à toutes heures de jour et de nuit des sandwiches, des joueurs d'échecs de grande classe et une ambiance libre de préjugés traditionnels ou sociaux. . . .
>
> J'ai gardé le meilleur souvenir des soirées passées chez les Arensbergs dans leur studio. . . . [24]

On the other hand, she wrote, only a few painters "se groupaient autour d'Alfred Stieglitz dans sa galerie. . . ." The reasons for the shift were various, according to Stieglitz' biographers: "After 1913 [and the Armory Show] . . . he gradually lost enthusiasm for his task and assumed a more passive role in the New York art world. . . . his supporters were drifting away from him." Stieglitz closed his gallery in June, 1917, and stored his canvases in an unheated studio, where he lived. He had no gallery to serve as a meeting place until 1925. The flow to Arensberg's salon was natural, writes one biographer: "Arensberg was . . . less domineering and self-assertive and more interested in listening to the opinions of others. He was an unusual figure to find at the center of an artists' group and his friends were as exceptional as he was."[25]

Charles Sheeler and his roommate Morton Schamberg took pictures of the Arensberg living room in 1918 that, coupled with records of his loans to exhibits, give some idea of the painting that Williams saw. The photos record the work of Picabia, Duchamp, Gleizes, Crotti, Schamberg, John Covert (Arensberg's cousin) and Walter Pach. It is known that Arensberg also owned over a dozen Picassos and Braques, five of Juan Gris' major paintings, including "The Man in the Cafe," and thirteen Klees, including "Magic Fish." Arensberg owned six of Brancusi's important sculptures, not counting the phallic "Princess X," which he had lent to the 1917 Independents Show. Juan Gris' "Still Life: The Table," one of the first *papier colles*, was prominently displayed. Nor were Americans unrepresented: Arensberg owned several works by Hartley and Demuth and so many of Charles Sheeler's paintings that he became the major donor to the first Sheeler retrospective in 1939. Williams was a perspicacious and excited observer.

> Everything was not by any means reflected upon [the] surface. Here was my chance, that was all I knew. There had been a break somewhere, we were streaming through, each thinking his own thoughts, driving his own designs toward his self's objectives . . . I had never in my life before felt that way.[26]

The 1916 Forum Exhibit, at which Williams and Loy read, and the 1917 Independents Show, were both organized in Arensberg's living room. The sponsoring body was the Society of Independent Artists, an American version of the French group that promoted the first no-jury, no-prize salon in Paris in 1884. Duchamp, Crotti and Roche worked with Arensberg, Pach, Covert and Man Ray to stage the exhibits. Arensberg was the managing director, his cousin Covert was secretary and Duchamp was chairman of the hanging committee. The meetings were open, although irregular, since the Arensbergs' apartment was open from the early afternoon until two or three in the morning. Williams was present frequently enough to find himself with a significant part in the 1916 exhibit, and to rally in support of the pseudonymous Richard Mutt in speech and print in 1917.[27]

Duchamp's urinal led to even more outré events, such as the Society's sponsorship of a lecture by Arthur Craven to a group of society matrons. Craven's subject was supposed to be modern art, but he arrived drunk and began to take off his clothes. He was arrested, and only Arensberg's bail money and subsequent intervention kept him from being prosecuted.

This ebullience had a counter-balancing, but less evident, reflective component back in Arensberg's studio. "The emphasis on discussion, on cerebral puzzles, the stress on the intellectual rather than the aesthetic are all characteristic," writes one scholar, "as was the tranquil avoidance of the political and social issues that preoccupied" similar groups in Europe at the time.[28]

Although he had blamed the painters for the breakup of Grantwood, Williams now saw them as the embodiment of his own struggle to balance form and emotion, classicism and romanticism. The poets, he wrote, "were *restless and constrained*, closely allied with the painters." In the Arensbergs' salon, Williams sought another, newer form of the constraints that Pound had introduced from afar into the poetry of Grantwood. The "form" of the Imagists had become passé; it "was not structural—that was the reason for its disappearance." Williams needed a new way to form his emotions.

As he had planned, Arensberg established himself as the chief reference point of the group. Demuth and Zorach might be writing plays, Ray and Dove domesticating futurism, and Williams scoring the libretto of an opera, but Arensberg was everyone's guide. He bought pictures, sponsored magazines, and made emergency loans. Everyone tested his or her best, freshest ideas against him, for Arensberg had cultivated a taste comparable to Gertrude Stein's. He exemplified the New York avant-garde so much that Tristan Tzara later called him "le vrai Dada." In *Kora in Hell*, which is Williams' vault into the front rank of this salon, his association with Arensberg is highlighted.

Once when I was taking lunch with Walter Arensberg at a small place on 63rd St. I asked him if he could state what the more modern painters were about, those roughly classed at that time as "cubists": Gleizes, Man Ray, Demuth, Duchamp—all of whom were then in the city. He replied by saying that the only way man differed from every other creature was by his ability to improvise novelty, and since the pictorial artist was under discussion, anything in paint that is truly new, truly a fresh creation, is good art.[29]

Williams sought Arensberg's opinions not only on painting. As a poet, Arensberg had earlier developed ideas about modern poetic technique. He continued and deepened Williams' interest in typography, first stimulated by Loy and Moore. Arensberg was also attentive to the mechanics of reader interest. He acknowledged the first revolution in modern art to be what J. Hillis Miller calls a "return to the facts of immediate experience." But Duchamp had convinced him that the "merely retinal" was useful only to indicate an intellectual, imaginative world existing beyond the canvas. Arensberg tried through typography to reveal the noumenal potential of the subject. As the following example shows, he wanted to erect a conceptual structure in the reader's mind and then to de-construct it. The poem emphasizes its own construction rather than mimesis.

On a sheet of paper
    dropped with the intention of demolishing
    space
    by the simple subtraction of a necessary plane
draw a line that leaves the present
    in addition
    carrying forward to the uncounted columns
        of the spatial ruin
        now considered as complete
    the remainder of the past.
The act of disappearing
    which in the three dimensional
    is the fate of the convergent
        vista
is thus
    under the form of the immediate
arrested in a perfect parallel
    of being
    in part.

This is a kind of exercise spun out on the reader's good will, calling for mental assembly on his part that leads nowhere; once penetrated, the theme is banal. What is interesting are the instructions, the way the reader is *told* to read the poem: "draw a line . . . Carrying forward . . . the act of disappearing . . . under the form . . . arrested." In another example, the directions are not so pronounced, but the content is important—Arensberg attempts to handle emotions in this manner.

> For purposes of illusion
> the actual ascent of two waves
> transparent to a basis
> which has a disappearance of its own
> is timed
> at the angle of incidence
> to the swing of a suspended
> lens
> from which the waves wash
> the protective coloration.
> Through the resultant exposure
> to a temporal process
> an emotion
> ideally distant
> assumes on the uneven surface
> descending
> as the identity to be demonstrated
> the three dimensions
> with which it is incommensurate.[30]

It is not a good poem, but it is possibly the paradigm that Williams had in mind years later when he wrote "Descent." Williams saw what Arensberg was attempting in these poems, but his own experiments, grounded in the clarity and syntactic thrust gained at Grantwood, avoided the heavy-handedness of Arensberg's verse. Williams did not believe in disappointing the investment of good will that the reader brought to the poem. He eventually found that a poetics highlighting the deceptiveness of appearances and the multiplicity of viewpoints usually forfeits some clarity.

Arensberg had also adopted Duchamp's interest in "new grammars." The rules of these hypothetical grammars were to be based on relationships of sound rather than of sense.

Ing? Is it possible to mean ing?
Suppose
      for the termination in *g*
         a disoriented
         series
      of the simple fractures
             in sleep
             Soporific
      has accordingly a value for soap
                   so present to
                   sew pieces.
And suppose the *i*
            to be big in ing
            as Beginning.
                        Then Ing is to ing
as aloud
      accompanied by times
and the meaning is a possibility
               of ralsis.[31]

When dada succeeded futurism. Arensberg was its foremost exegete. His prose poems, such as the following section of "Vacuum Tires," were undoubtedly among Williams' models for *The Great American Novel* and parts of *Kora in Hell.*

If, however, the showcases are on trolleys, bottles must be corked for the make-up of negroes. Or if a goitre appears in the elevation of the host, a set of false teeth, picked for the high lights by burnt matches, must be arranged at once in three acts. For the first provide electric fixtures that are tuned to cork tips. For the second consideration is flour, third being a key that is rarely advertised. Notwithstanding the thermometer into which the conductor spits, the telephone meets in extremes. A window will change the subject for standing room only.[32]

Apparently, E. E. Cummings learned much about the technique of "dislocating" objects or reactions from their appropriate contexts from Arensberg's poems. So well known was Arensberg as a proponent of each new movement that Francis Picabia answered more questions about him than about his own work when he moved to Barcelona in 1918.

Around 1920 this continual quest for the new began to wear thin with Williams, and by 1923 the physician had put a comfortable distance between himself and the New York obsession with the "cutting edge" of culture. Williams took what he wanted and left the ridiculous, somehow without insulting his friend. Of one of Arensberg's later ventures, Williams wrote

> Such things as *The Blind Man* are very useful, very purgative, very nice decoration, even very true. Its sponsors are rather glad to be in a state of decay. It is rather naive, I think . . . Oh, chaos! Oh, yes, but chaos is somewhat overdone.[33]

In 1921 the Arensbergs moved abruptly to Hollywood, without telling anyone why. It was commonly assumed, even by such friends as Charles Sheeler, that they had tired of the eighteen-hour-a-day commotion in their home. But Beatrice Wood, who became an intimate of Louise Arensberg, indicates a different reason. "Walter had gone through a fortune, his, and possibly some of Lou's, was drinking heavily, loaning money to anyone who asked for it, so finally Lou read a riot act," said Wood. "Either he stopped the philandering and went West with her, or she would leave him."[34]

Like several other American members of the group, with whom he was discovering common interests, Williams had extracted all he could from the avant-garde. Williams, Demuth, Sheeler and others thought "chaos" a fine purgative, but they had an eventual destination in mind. "We looked on the French with a certain amount of awe," said Williams. "And yet we were repelled, too. There was a little resentment in all of us against the success of the French. The time had come for us to think on our own terms."[35]

5. *Three Painters of the 67th St. Salon*

I. Marcel Duchamp

By all accounts Duchamp, the expatriate painter who had become a celebrity after the 1913 Armory Show, was the centerpiece of the salon and Arensberg's personal seer. When he immigrated to the United States in 1915, the delighted art collector found him a studio and began to consult him on purchases. Duchamp's bags could hardly have been unpacked when Williams heralded his arrival with a "Spring Letter" to *The Egoist*. "The weekly papers began to notice that Duchamp was with us," wrote Williams, thumbing his nose at Europe and Eliot and counting, it seems, on the prospective eminence of *Others*. Williams and Duchamp were to develop a special relationship, though not a markedly social one—it was the sort of awkward, contentious, but respectful relationship that often characterizes artistic circles.

Williams' account of Duchamp in *The Autobiography* is the best known anecdote about the group, and focuses on a cut the painter carved into the poet at the Arensbergs' studio one evening.

> Seeing on Arensberg's studio wall a recent picture by Duchamp showing five heads, in pastel shades, the heads of five young women in various poses and called I think "The Sisters" (I think it was a picture of his own sisters), I wanted to say something to him about it. He had been drinking, I was sober. I finally came face to face with him as we walked about the room and I said, "I like your picture," pointing to the one I have mentioned.
>
> He looked at me and said, "Do you?"
>
> That was all.
>
> He had me all right, if that was the objective, I could have sunk through the floor, ground my teeth, turned my back on him and spat. I don't think I ever gave him that chance again.[1]

The date of this incident would be valuable, but Duchamp never wanted to talk about it and Williams' chronology is miasmic. Just before his flight to Buenos Aires in 1917 to avoid the American draft, Duchamp was dissipated, rude, a libertine, and a clown; at one point he was ejected from a theatre for perching at the end of a cantilevered flagpole inside. If he and the largely temperate Williams fell out, it is understandable. Clearly the snub occurred some time after Arensberg moved the *Others* group to his studio.

By all accounts in the first two years Duchamp was quiet, retiring and easy to approach. His young lover, Beatrice Wood, remembers him as "the gentlest, kindest man I have ever met."[2] In the rural, intimate surroundings of the Grantwood colony, where the artists numbered only a dozen, Williams and Duchamp no doubt came to know each other fairly well. It was only after the group moved to New York and Duchamp became a "figure" that he became truculent.

It is true, too, that Duchamp adopted a certain straight-faced silence to avoid artistic argument, to camouflage his reticence and his unpracticed English. Arensberg served him at first as explicator. If anyone wanted to buy a Duchamp, or to engage the artist in a project, he went first to Arensberg. Williams clearly wanted to understand Duchamp:

> . . . according to Duchamp, who was Arensberg's champion at the time, a stained-glass window that had fallen out and lay more or less together on the ground was of far greater interest than the thing conventionally composed *in situ*. . . . We returned to Arensberg's sumptuous studio where he gave further point to his remarks by showing me what appeared to be the original of Duchamp's famous "Nude Descending the Staircase." But this, he went on to say, is a full-sized photographic print of the first picture with many new touches by Duchamp himself and so by the technique of its manufacture as by other means it is a novelty.[3]

Many of the Frenchmen present had a better grasp of Duchamp's ideas, but no American could explain him so well or make his projects seem so compatible with American realities. Arensberg, in fact, understood Duchamp well enough to back him into difficult theoretical corners; the photographic copy of the "Nude" that Arensberg commissioned, as Duchamp later confessed, was "not the work I'm proudest of."

Unlike some of the other Americans, Williams spoke and understood French. Of the Frenchmen only Roche was fluent in English, although Beatrice Wood reports that Duchamp's English was good and there are letters in English from him to Arensberg as early as 1916. Having heard Arensberg's explanations, Williams probably listened in on the conversations of the French. He asked questions: was such an effect intended? how could the success of a work be determined? Having known them before the "salon" moved, Williams probably felt that he was more their equal than the other recently arrived guests. Nevertheless, Williams had worked himself up that evening to express admiration for "Yvonne et Magdaleine déchiquetées" (1911), and he did not drop compliments in an off-hand way. Williams understood what he liked now, and why. Having digested Duchamp's oeuvre, he wanted to talk about it, the way he talked with Pound or Ed.

The snub "filled me with humiliation so that I can never forget it," wrote Williams. But in the meantime, "watch and wait . . . I wasn't up to carrying on a *witty* conversation in French with the latest Parisian arrivals."

The talk at Arensberg's was itself an art form. "It was a true salon," said Duchamp, "a remarkable thing." Among the French, conversation was extremely literary, as Duchamp recalled.

> The amusing thing about the literary people of that time was that, when you met two authors, you couldn't get a word in edgewise. It was a series of fireworks, jokes, lies, all untoppable because it was in such a style that you were incapable of speaking their language; so, you kept quiet. One day, I went with Picabia to have lunch with Max Jacob and Apollinaire—it was unbelievable. One was torn between a sort of anguish and an insane laughter.[4]

Linked to this verbal milieu was Duchamp's artwork, which was hung in the Arensbergs' apartment and Duchamp's studio for inspection. Arensberg owned a dozen of Duchamp's pieces and those that he didn't own, he was trying to buy. The first things Williams would have noticed about Duchamp's works were the titles, because Duchamp had "discovered" the title as part of the art object. "For me the title was very important," he said. "There is something like an explosion in the meaning of certain words: they have a greater value than their meaning in the dictionary." Duchamp's titles were arresting, as in "Jeune Homme Triste dans un Train," of which he had said, "The young man is sad because there is a train that comes afterward."

Hanging next to this canvas was "The King and Queen Sur-rounded by Swift Nudes," whose final words Duchamp first wrote as " . . . Nudes at High Speed." "It was literary play," he said. "The word 'swift' had been used in sports; if a man was swift, he ran well." Also conspicuously mounted was a work Katharine Drier had commissioned, "Tu m' . . . ." "It was a sort of resumé of things I had made earlier," said Duchamp, "since the title made no sense, you can add whatever verb you want, as long as it begins with a vowel, after tu m' . . . ." Actually the title is pointed, and a French speaker such as Williams would know that. "Tu m' . . ." is a contraction for the collo-quialism "tu m'emmerdes" (you bore me), a sentiment referring to the tedium of such a recapitulative art work and to the person commission-ing it.

Other clever titles of Duchamp's included "Apolinere Enameled" (1916), an advertisement for Sapolin Enamel in which the wording is altered to allude to the French poet. Williams recalled several of these works fondly: "In Advance of a Broken Arm," the 'ready-made' snow-shovel of 1914; "Fontaine," the R. Mutt urinal of 1917, and "The Pas-sage from Virgin to Bride." But the most important was the salon's cen-terpiece: "The Bride Stripped Bare by her Bachelors, Even." "Titles in general interested me a lot," said Duchamp,

> and the bringing together of words to which I added a comma and "even," an adverb which makes no sense, since it relates to nothing in the picture or title. Thus it was an adverb in the most beautiful demonstration of adverbness. It has no meaning. . . . In English too, "even" is an absolute adverb; it has no sense. All the more possibility of stripping bare.[5]

Williams and Marianne Moore, sleuthing about the studio, were not long in discovering the peculiarity of Duchamp's titles, which led them to reconsider the role of the title in the poem. Williams became confident enough of his re-evaluation to write to Harriet Monroe.

> Isn't the art of writing titles, as all art is, a matter of concrete indirections made as they are in order to leave the way clear for a distinct imaginative picture? To directly denote the content of a piece is, to my mind, to put an obstacle of words in the way of the picture.[6]

Williams began to use his titles as poetic tools. He found that titles could recast the context of the poem, lifting the reader to a new framework. This is the case in "Tract," "Overture to a Dance of Locomotives," and "To a Solitary Disciple." In other poems, such as "Sea Elephant," "All the Fancy Things," and "The Attic Which Is Desire," Williams seizes the reader's attention in the title and snares him by continuing that syntax into the first line of the poem. Williams' titles ceased to rest benignly above his poems when he saw how Duchamp had put them to work.

As Duchamp indicated, the punning and word-play proceeded among the French like Chinese firecrackers. Williams appreciated, even admired, their facility with language. Duchamp was, said one friend, an accomplished "interlingual pun artist." Among his creations was the persona Rrose Sélavy, which derived from a canvas that Picabia asked all his friends to sign; Duchamp had written "Pi Qu'habilla Rrose Sélavy" (for Picabia sex is life). Another of his high jinks was his remodeling of the "Mona Lisa," on which he had drawn a goatee and appended the acronym L.H.O.O.Q., which when sounded out in French leads to "Elle a chaud au cul," the vernacular equivalent of "She's a hot piece." The chess players in the salon chuckled over his ready-made "Trebouchet" which sounds like the chess term "treboucher," meaning to "stumble over." There were others: "Fresh Widow," a pun on the French window; a curious condition called "incesticide"; and such silliness as his statement that "by condescension . . . a weight is heavier when it descends than when it rises."

Williams disliked the precious and sexual slant of Duchamp's word play, yet these verbal gymnastics showed him the plasticity of language and the need to pay attention to the sounds as well as the sense of his words. Words could be bent, molded, cut and spliced. That much was good: he felt freer to break lines where he wanted, to enjamb words, and to supercharge them with meaning. But he also began to realize how closely the contexts of the words had to be watched; dictating the circumstances of the words, in fact, was the greater part of the poem.

One of Duchamp's major works in 1917 was an experiment with a "new language," a project certainly in the air at the Arensberg's apartment. Inspired by Raymond Roussel's *Impressions d'Afrique*, Duchamp began to search for a language of absolute precision. He sought irreducible words, the meanings of which could never be misunderstood. First he created an alphabet, the letters of which were dots, lines, circles and squares; the meaning of these signs would vary with their position. As part of his study he made the "Three Standard Stoppages," which was prominently displayed in Arensberg's living-room. Appearing at first to be a kind of military map, the "Stoppages" are actually, in Duchamp's words, "canned chance." He let a "straight horizontal thread one meter in length fall from a height of one meter onto a horizontal plane while twisting *at will* to give a new form to the unit of length." The lines so formed were fixed, transferred to glass, and served as the prime measures of the new "language." By establishing a new measure, Duchamp illustrated how arbitrary all the old ones were—a discovery that Williams saw was significant for the poetic line as well.

Duchamp came to a dead end on this level, but his inventiveness found several outlets on the syntactic level. He published a number of puns and "sentences" in *391* when Picabia was editor. These reveal that Duchamp next exploited the *sound* of the word in his quest to renew language. "What you want is a grammatical rule: the verb agrees with the subject in consonance; for instance, le nègre aigrit, les négresses s'agrissent ou maigrissent, etc."[7] He also improvised punctuation, occasionally using an entire line of ellipses in the middle of a poem, as in "SURcenSURE", or isolating a phrase amid elipses (" . . . which he commands . . . ."). In a 1917 poem, "Speculation," Duchamp ends lines with triangles of periods, similar to the "therefore" sign in symbolic logic. At another point, he uses a comma and a colon in conjunction to produce a very strong, but not quite full stop. Williams tried these forms out in *Paterson*. The case for his having seen "Speculation" is strong because the content of the poem—shop windows, their reflections, the effect on passersby—is similar to a section of Williams' "Notes in Diary Form."

> The wind blowing, the mud spots on the polished surface, the face reflected in the glass on which as you advance the features disappear leaving only the hat and as you draw back the features return, the tip of the nose, the projection over the eyebrows, the cheekbones and the bulge of the lips the chin last.[8]

Williams also had the opportunity to read the "notes" that accompany "The Bride Stripped Bare by her Bachelors, Even," for these were secreted in a box near the work. The last of these, written as a poem,

contains peculiar word arrangements designed to intensify or diminish
the impact of selected words. There are similarities between Williams'
triadic line and Duchamp's technique, as two sample lines show:

> more
> The term "indefinite" seems to me   accurate
> ···
> the chief of the 5 nudes) it will be very finite in width,
>   etc.
> thickness   ,   in order little by little[9]

When Williams mentions Duchamp so many times, the question
of inspiration naturally arises: did Williams write any poems based directly on Duchamp's work? Probably not, for the Duchampian effect
was itself literary, and contingent on a contrast between art and literature to which Williams had less access. Duchamp's use to Williams was
principally intellectual. But there are traces, allusions to Duchamp that
pop up unannounced in Williams' work. The most obvious is in Williams' short poem "El Hombre" and Duchamp's sketch "Encore a cette
Astre." The poem is short:

> It's a strange courage
> you give me ancient star:
> Shine alone in the sunrise
> toward which you lend no part.[10]

Arensberg owned Duchamp's sketch, which illustrated the poem "Encore a cette Astre" by Jules LaForgue. LaForgue was popular among the
avant-garde, and his work appeared regularly in *The Little Review*,
where Williams helped with the translations. LaForgue's star is "sun-
like" and ends up alienated, "scorned by the heartless stars." Both poems
place the lone individual in opposition to the mass, but Duchamp's
sketch, more to the point, shows a figure climbing up stairs toward a
sun.

Duchamp figures prominently in the aesthetic of *Kora in Hell*,
too. The "prologue" features him, and the book itself is an experiment
with "canned chance" and other Duchampian notions. *Spring and All*,
Williams' subsequent book, explores the possibilities of the verbal
"ready-made": what is a poem, and what is not? Williams weaves poetry

and prose together without titles or markers to help the reader, highlighting what he calls the "radiant gist" of poetry. And Duchamp's influence can be discerned in *The Great American Novel*, although this book owes much to Arensberg.

It is to Duchamp's ideas that one turns to understand his importance to Williams' poetry. He produced few actual "works" after his arrival in the United States at the age of twenty-five. He painted three canvases, executed a few glasses, and selected a number of "readymades." The tenor of this production was theoretical and, by explaining it to Arensberg, Ray, Dove, Hartley and other American artists, he changed the fundamental assumptions of American art.

"The spectator makes the picture," said Duchamp. It is generally agreed that he viewed art as a completely cerebral reaction, solely in the mind of the viewer. As Harold Rosenberg put it, he was "Valéry's emissary to New York." There were, for Duchamp, no objects that were "art" *intrinsically*. The artist, in fact, did not exist without his complementary viewer. Usually he was unaware of the real significance of his work, and the viewer, who judged it, supplemented the creation by interpreting it.

> I believe very strongly in the "medium" aspect of the artist. The artist makes something, then one day, he is recognized by the intervention of the public, of the spectator; so later he goes on to posterity. You can't stop that, because, in brief, it's a product of two poles—there's the pole of the one who makes the work, and the pole of the one who looks at it. I give the latter as much importance as the one who makes it.[11]

The embodiment of these ideas is "Why not Sneeze, Rrose Sélavy?" (1921), which consists of a small bird-cage filled with 152 lumps of marble cut into sugar cubes. The spectator lifts the cage, feels the strange weight, then notices the title, which is written on the bottom of the cage and reflected in a mirror on which the whole creation rests. Thrown off guard, the viewer/participant is transfixed. The "art" happens to him, precisely as Duchamp envisioned it.

Williams wrote less than Duchamp of the viewer's role in the art, but in one of his workbooks, he made the following note to himself:

> . . . always in a work of imagination, leave a large part of the thing to the imagination of the spectator; this to arouse, also to give him work to do.

For that is the prime destiny of the thing produced: to have the beholder *take part* in it thus completely. Thus and only thus to complete it.

By this, by this fulfillment art liberates us from the tyranny of sex.[12]

Williams was more often explicit about the *shared* consciousness of art: "A work of art is important only as evidence in its structure, of a new world which it has been created to affirm." But the stress he laid on the *craft* of writing is what indicates that he always had the reader's attention in mind. "A poem is a small machine made out of words," he wrote. "A poem is an organization of materials. As an automobile or kitchen stove is an organization of materials."[13]

Duchamp stressed this same aspect: "the word 'art' interests me very much. If it comes from Sanskrit, as I've heard, it signifies 'making.' Now everyone makes something, and those who make things on a canvas, with a frame, they're called artists. Formerly, they were called craftsmen, a term I prefer."[14] None of the other major influences on Williams—not Keats, not Pound, not Loy—spoke in these terms.

Nor was this "making" to be produced by resorting to "inspiration" or to other spiritual forces. In Duchamp's view it was the result of "newness" created by intellect and craft. The "act of selection" was all important, and the most effective selection employed *displacement*. Either the object, or its logical function, could be displaced from context. For example, Duchamp could physically change the angle from which an item was seen. In "Bicycle Wheel" (1913), the fork of the bike is upside down and attached to a kitchen stool—the dynamics of this common object are now seen from a novel vantage point. The process is repeated in the 1914 "Bottle rack" (hung from the ceiling), the 1917 "Hat Rack" (also on the ceiling), and the 1917 "Trébouchet" (a coat-rack nailed to the floor). Williams saw all of these projects and was struck especially by those which achieved displacement by renaming: "In Advance of a Broken Arm," the snow-shovel Williams remembered as a "pick-axe"; and "Fontaine," the 1917 R. Mutt urinal.

Dislocation became one of Williams' important techniques. "*Lifting* to the imagination those things which lie under the direct scrutiny of the sense, close to the nose," wrote the poet, "It is this difficulty that sets a value upon all works of art . . . ." Many of Williams' poems in this period attempt to displace their subjects from the ordinary physical or logical context. Every reader has his favorite example:

"Smell," that surprising paean to the nose; "Pastoral"; or "Flowers by the Sea," in which the chicory and daisies trade places with the sea.

Equally valuable to Williams was the way that Duchamp solved his problem of intellectual "consistency." "Not to be engaged in any groove is very important for me," Duchamp asserted, "I want to be free, and I want to be free for myself, foremost."[15]

Duchamp's ideas on this subject were complex. He reasoned that perfect consistency with oneself in all circumstances led to intolerance or fanaticism; therefore inconsistency was a positive virtue. Since contradictions *did* exist in this world, at least as the senses and emotions perceived it, inconsistency was a way of recognizing them. A virtuous man was the sum of his consciously held uncertainties, Duchamp maintained, and holding on to them was his only rational mode of behavior. In practice "inconsistency" meant not to choose, not to categorize, but rather to *affirm* contradictions. No contradiction, he reasoned, ever disappears; it simply gives rise to a new contradiction. Duchamp exalted contradictions. A friend said he showed "a humorous but firm refusal to acknowledge the laws of immediate causality."

In *Kora in Hell* Williams assumed Duchamp's reasoning. "The poet takes advantage of [contradictory events] to send them on their way side by side without making the usual unhappy moral distinctions."[16] He does so because "You cannot hold spirit round the arms but it takes lies for wings, turns poplar leaf and flutters off—leaving the old stalk desolate."

Employing one of Duchamp's distinctions, that of "drawing neither from the left nor the right," of refusing to recognize *opposite* categories, Williams writes that "A poet witnessing the chicory flower and realizing its virtues of form and color so constructs his praise of it as to borrow no particle from right or left." Elsewhere in the volume one finds Duchamp's ideas presented piecemeal:

It is chuckleheaded to desire away through every difficulty.
. . . .
The instability of these compositions would seem such that they must inevitably crumble under the attention and become particles of a wind that falters. . . .
. . . .
Thus a poem is tough by no quality it borrows from a logical recital of events.

In one of the first improvisations Williams even employs the word "stoppage" to describe his desired effect.

> Between two contending forces there may at all times arrive that moment when the stress is equal on both sides so that with a great pushing a great stability results giving a picture of perfect rest. And so it may be that once upon the way the end drives back upon the beginning and a stoppage will occur.[17]

Inconsistency led Duchamp to focus on the near universal tensions that precede all sexual and other consummation: that point before any problems of consistency arise. This for him was the primal moment of art, but suffering our common fate, Duchamp did choose, did consummate. Immediately, however, he separated himself from his choice by irony. Little of his work demonstrates a commitment to a position, material, message, or mode because in the execution Duchamp bathed it in the irony that he thought all acts of choice deserved.

Irony and sarcasm were the aspects that Williams remembered Duchamp for in *The Autobiography*. As Williams soon realized, however, this was only his defense against those who adulate fixed positions, as Williams had appeared to do in praising "Yvonne et Magdaleine." That the two artists never found a social channel of communication in the later phase of the salon, though an impediment, scarcely prevented the rebuffed poet from comprehending the uses to which Duchamp put irony.

Kora in Hell makes this debt explicit, especially in its sixteenth and eighteenth sections, in which Williams calls himself "a fool ever to be tricked into seriousness . . . an owl of irony fixes on the immediate object of his care as if it were the thing to be destroyed, guffaws at the impossibility of putting any kind of value on the object." In a note among his unpublished papers, in fact, Williams explicitly links Duchamp, the techniques of displacement and irony, and the putative failings of Ezra Pound.

> Marcel's color machine that invents sentences or cutting paper into what is cut—is to say that: a thing makes the machine that makes the chance sentence—quite clearly we are not chance (since we invent machines that accurately make chance. . . .)

> But nothing has a context, we hold it, we shape it. We are not out
> of it, we have no relations in it. It does not concern us.
> 　　Ezra Pound and his clear undying style. It is very difficult for Ezra
> to make because he is too fond of what he makes it of.[18]

Plumbing Duchamp's "affirmation" of the "inconsistent," one
suspects that his real subject was eroticism—and this is true. Eroticism is
not hidden or desexualized in his work, but defended intellectually.
Many of his works that the uninitiated have trouble deciphering are
thoughtfully constructed bulwarks against the concretization of the sen-
suous: a fleet allusion to incest Duchamp would have found erotic, but a
photograph of genitalia would have offended him. Duchamp defined as
"pornographic" the latter state of "reification." Intelligence, he maintained, was the great aphrodisiac. The place of eroticism in his work was
"enormous. Visible or conspicuous, or, at any rate, underlying."

> . . . a closed in eroticism, if you like, an eroticism which wasn't overt. It
> wasn't implied either. It's a sort of erotic climate. Everything can be based
> on an erotic climate without too much trouble.
> 　　I believe in eroticism a lot, because it's truly a rather widespread
> thing throughout the world, a thing that everyone understands. It re-
> places, if you wish, what other literary schools called Symbolism, Roman-
> ticism. It could be another "ism," so to speak.
> ·
> It's really a way to try to bring out in the daylight things that are constantly
> hidden. . . . To be able to reveal them, and to place them at everyone's
> disposal—I think this is important because it's the basis of everything and
> no one talks about it. Eroticism was a theme, even an "ism" which was the
> basis of everything I was doing at the time of the Large Glass.[19]

The "Large Glass" consists of two panes, the upper representing
the Bride, the lower her Bachelors. The Bride is organized around the
mechanical equivalent of a uterus. Within a few mechanical steps she
produces a "gas," or "blossoming" as Duchamp termed it. The Bachelors, however, sustain a system of interference, sublimation and repression that distances them from their "end-product desires." All their defense mechanisms are represented mechanically and no doubt owe
something to the popularity of the Rube Goldberg. This work was
under construction before Williams on a daily basis for several years, and
embodies nearly all of Duchamp's theory of eroticism.

The major obstacle to Duchamp's "art," then as now, is making the spectator participate in this special state of mind. At this point in his theory there is a great emphasis on craft that is important to Williams. Rather than a "reifying" influence that would contradict the vagueness of eroticism, Duchamp intended his "craftsmanship" to be anti-scientific. The "precise and exact aspect of scientific materialism," said Duchamp, could be used to tease the viewer of art into states of mind that were purely cerebral and formless, disproving the determinism to which science pretended.

The common notion of Williams, one suspects, is that he wasn't interested in such esoteric theory. Those who thus dismiss him miss the import of much of his early work. Duchampian eroticism linked Williams' feelings about sex to his poetry. Passion is a topic Williams wrote about in his first two volumes, where his treatment was redolently Georgian. Following his inclusion in the "Others" group, he experienced, as Kreymborg recounted, personal embarrassment in "undressing himself to the ground." But soon he was writing poems like "Danse Russe." He was learning from Duchamp how to put craft into the service of the erotic—how an emphasis on materials and craftsmanship could make his belief in the "dance" of life clearer.

By 1954 it probably seemed to Williams that this strain in his work was and had always been wholly his own, and sitting down to write *The Autobiography* he remembered a foreigner whose value to the Americans in the Arensberg Circle had been one of shock, of rude awakening. But the untangled facts of the liaison seem to place Duchamp and Williams in the kind of tense, inquisitive clash that typified the poet's relationships with Pound, Hartley and Ed—fractious embraces that led to some of his best work.

II.   Marsden Hartley

Marsden was one of the best men of the group; his small Dresden China blue eyes under savage brows made him look as if he were about to eat you, which he would have liked, I suppose, to have done.

Williams

Few people have had better insight into Williams than Marsden

67

Hartley. The two became close friends immediately on meeting and never in their twenty-year friendship did Hartley disguise his warm feelings for Williams. The poet, on the other hand, disliked being fawned over, and later tried to put Hartley in his past. Perhaps some of the "serious citizens" that Hartley recognized in Williams feared that they would be eaten, too. This attitude has obscured an interesting cross-fertilization between poetry and painting, and diminished the significance that should be attached to Hartley's role in Williams' career.

Williams first met Hartley around 1916 at the Arensbergs' apartment. Hartley lingered on the fringes of the crowd—he was on the fringes of many crowds. Stieglitz had been his first sponsor, but the photographer's influence was declining, and Arensberg's emphasis on the new in art seemed to offer a broader scope to Hartley's talent.

A man who painted *and* wrote poetry, as Hartley did, automatically interested Williams, who was spending his spare time browsing in galleries. It turned out that they both knew Ezra Pound—Williams from college, Hartley from Europe. They also shared an interest in the "egoism" of Dora Marsden's journal *The Egoist*.

Williams was just then emerging as a poet, but Hartley was a painter of reputation; an essayist for several magazines; a cosmopolitan from Paris and Berlin, and an acquaintance of Picasso and Kandinsky. "A granddaddy to us all, male and female," Williams called him. "Men like Marsden Hartley joined our parties. He made many friendships in those years, but seems to have been satisfied to leave the group centered around the French of those years—and one of the most productive and delightful groups that ever came to the fore in France—more or less alone. It is to me at least as if he had said to himself that that sort of thing was not what he was primarily interested in. That was French and he, you could almost hear him say, was American. That is what drew us together. Because it was at that time that I began to know him."[20]

Williams was hearing American in 1916, feeling native with everyone he encountered—anchored by a family and medical practice to Rutherford, N. J., he had little choice. But Hartley's "localism" had developed through exposure to the world, largely under the tutelage of Stieglitz and Gertrude Stein, and it accounted for his return to the United States. This sense of free aesthetic choice was something Williams lacked with a hunger.

Though he was young, Hartley had traveled fast. Born in the

Maine factory town of Lewiston, he moved to Cleveland with his widowed father when he was seven. Frail and insecure, he received a scholarship to the Cleveland School of Art, where he so impressed a trustee that she gave him a five-year stipend to study in New York. He went East before graduation and was "discovered" by Stieglitz, who gave him a one-man exhibit at "291" in 1909. Stieglitz saluted Hartley in his journal *Camera Work* as a painter with unusual technical acumen, a distinct personality and brilliant potential as a colorist. With the aid of Arthur B. Davies and two sponsors, Hartley went to Paris in 1912. There he lost no time gaining entrance to Gertrude Stein's Saturday evening salon: he introduced himself as a friend of a friend, which he was not, and promptly met Picasso and Braque. In Paris 27 Rue de Fleurs became his second home, a place to talk art and to meet other gay men. After imitating the styles of several French schools, Hartley became absorbed in the German Expressionists, particularly Franz Marc, to whom he wrote. Marc invited him to come and exhibit with the Blaue Reiter group, though he had not seen any of Hartley's work. With his close friend Arnold Ronnebeck, a German sculptor, Hartley went to Munich, where his extended stay was made possible by aid from Paul Haviland. Hartley and Ronnebeck read the *Blaue Reiter Almanac* and Kandinsky's *Über das Geistige in der Kunst*, which so impressed them that Hartley wrote about Kandinsky to Stein, Stieglitz and others. "I know that what I have to express coincides perfectly with his notion of Das Geistige in der Kunst," wrote Hartley after visiting Kandinsky in his studio. Dissatisfied with what he considered French intellectual dandyism, Hartley abandoned Paris and began to show his work in Berlin and Munich; the more mystic program of the Germans suited his intuitive nature and led him to feel more American in Germany than he had felt in America. In fact, he compared his talks with Kandinsky to the discussion of Emerson and Whitman about *Leaves of Grass* on the Boston Common.[21]

Visitors from New York tried to check up on him, and one, in a letter to the *Little Review* in 1914, mentions his living a very private life, tucked away in "the garden house, up three flights, at number four Nassauishe Strasse." He was not oblivious to the rise of fascism, though his neighbors thought him an American Indian, and in 1915 he decided to leave.

He asked Stein to write an evaluation of his work. Since he had exhibited with the expressionists in Berlin in 1913, where his intensity and technique led one critic to compare him to Munch, and had shown with Marc and Kandinsky in the Blaue Reiter group, Stein took him on those terms:

> In his painting he has done what in Kandinsky is only a direction.
> . . . .
> He is the only one working in color, that is considering the color as more dominant than line, who is really attempting to create an entity in a picture which is not a copy of light. He deals with his colors as actually as Picasso deals with his forms.[22]

Back in New York Hartley was within a year seen in the salon of Mabel Dodge, who labeled him "that gnarled New English spinster-man"; at the Liberal Club; at the Societe Anonyme; and at the Arensberg's. Stieglitz gave him exhibitions in 1916 and 1917, but their relations cooled. Williams remembers incorrectly that Stieglitz "dropped Hartley." In fact, when "291" closed in 1917, Hartley was without a place to exhibit, and the Arensbergs had begun to collect him in a small way.[23]

Williams and Hartley liked each other because they were outsiders, because they sensed the potential for a *native* modern art in America. From the start Williams was interested in and highly critical of Hartley's paintings. Hartley's Berlin paintings seethed with agitation, said Williams: "It was a prediction of the war in the work." Hartley was attracted by Williams' ideas on localism, and by the way he used his medical practice and home life as "a kind of meditation": for Hartley, who had neither, it was an attractive stability.

They began, casually enough, with a mutual interest in shaking free of Ezra Pound, who contended that an American art was impossible. Williams was at work on the prologue to *Kora in Hell*, where he was attacking "Pound's early paraphrases from Yeats and his constant later cribbing from the Renaissance and the modern French." Hartley had met Pound at parties in Paris, and disliked the critical stance that Pound and Edgar Jepson had assumed:

> Jepson's appreciation of T. S. Eliot is hardly borne out by the poems that follow him in the *Little Review*, though we know that T. S. E. has done far better things. These in hand will hardly bear out Jepson either for fine Americanism or for fine construction. . . . I suffer for "Little lamb

who made thee, dost thou know who made thee" in the presence of the Pound-Eliot phraseology.

Hartley's letters in the *Little Review* also dished out Pound's special brand of vitriol.

> Pound makes us wonder with his incessantly tedious schoolmaster whip-pings. Naughty boy, my countryman, not to know so much! . . . . I should be humblest and proudest of all, for Pound once asked me to write for *The Egoist* an elaboration of a preface I wrote for one of my exhibi-tions. I appreciate this still and hope one day to rise to the distinction. Pound has stated himself clearly further over in the issue on the value of savantism and literacy. I congratulate E. P. on knowing a genuine lot.[24]

Hartley concluded this letter by touting the superiority of Wallace Gould, "The Maine Poet," over T. S. Eliot.

Gould was the first "project" undertaken by Williams and Hart-ley. Williams always attributed the "discovery" to Hartley: "The L. R. began to print the poems of a man from down East, a find of Marsden Hartley, named W- G-." Hartley apparently met him on a visit to Lewis-ton, his hometown. "A huge bear of a man, weighing 300 pounds ac-cording to Marsden," wrote Williams; this was in 1917, but not until 1918-19 did they get Gould into print. "Gould despises art and that is becoming of any real artist," explained Hartley in the *Little Review*, where Gould became the subject of a debate between Williams and Hart-ley, and editors Margaret Anderson and Jane Heap. The point of the controversy was not Gould; it was to allow Williams and Hartley to advance a program of criticism to counter Pound, Jepson and Eliot, and to see if the literary world accepted it. The editors caught on fast:

> Mr. Hartley has simply made up words about Wallace Gould. Almost nothing that Gould has written justifies any of Mr. Hartley's praise. Wal-lace Gould is a writer who has not yet learned how to write. [July, 1919.]

> There are some of us to whom everything Hartley writes is propaganda to establish himself as an artist. [Oct., 1919.][25]

Fortunately, they had another "discovery" waiting in the wings. Rex Slinkard was a Saugus, California, rancher, whose prose about painting has admittedly radiant and stunning passages. Williams began to boost his stock:

> What is it I see in Rex Slinkard's letters? . . . evidence of the man's criti-cal attitude toward his art of painting. There is an abundance of fresh color but presented without the savage backbite of a Degas using pinks and blues. It is all very young, this man's writing about his painting; it is what I recognize as in some measure definitely and singularly American.

This is closer to the truth: Williams and Hartley praised Gould and Slinkard in hopes that the readership would recognize in the critics the masters of the native tradition.

Winning their freedom from Pound, Williams and Hartley staked out the domestic turf, then attempted to prove it cosmopolitan. The avant-garde programs of Duchamp and Picabia—first futurism, then Dada—threatened to usurp the New York scene, but Hartley called on his knowledge of Kandinsky to subsume them. The "local" was the only possible "universal," as Williams later proved via Kandinsky in the prologue to *Kora in Hell*

> Every artist has to express himself.
> Every artist has to express his epoch.
> Every artist has to express the pure and eternal
>   qualities of all men.

Hartley dropped a note to Williams on August 27, 1920, saying that he particularly liked this "spiritual" quality in the Improvisations.[26] They also valued the way Kandinsky's ideas linked the "local," the emotional, and the classic contours of art in a way that neither doted on the past nor succumbed to "formlessness," which was Williams' personal demon.

They began a new campaign in the journals, this time praising each other for "localism" and the theory of "contact." "I agree with Williams," wrote Hartley, "The London office should be returned to native soil. That is to say a nice little visit from E. P. would do so much for village life in this country."[27]

Hartley was also publishing poems, some of them good and many similar to Williams' work. The subjects both men chose grew out of their concern with localism, but they also shared a number of tech-niques. Both employed arresting line breaks, neologisms, single-word lines and ellipses. Hartley, unlike Williams, broke lines on prepositions, articles or conjunctions, regardless of the line rhythm. Sometimes he achieved a fresh effect, but more often not.

> there is no doubt but that he discovers the
> same image as the child, who remarks the
> radiant glint of his marbles on the top spray
> of the wave he once played with,
> or as the fringed lace on the dress on a
> Titan's wife—
> the inwash cooling at least the eye with
> a something exceptional white or green or
> blue, too pale almost to mention, if[28]

And so on. In the compounding of new words, though, Hartley had as models Pound's "translations" of Greek and Chinese, and Waley's renderings of Li Po in the *Little Review*. Hartley echoes them when he writes of "go-down of sun," "Sudden-gusted air," and "sun-crisped fields."

Hartley early adopted the practice of isolating a single word on a line, and he never let it go. But he lacked the syntactic command that lay behind such poems as Williams' "Spring" or "Young Locust." His efforts were more abstract.

> To
> spin
> a rapture
> high
> is
> solar
> sanctity.

Hartley, too, had profited from the lesson in ellipsis offered by Pound and the Imagistes.

> Singular how look of death in squirrel's face
> can seem so reverent; but this is one of
> many little comedies,
> claws folded as hand of violinist, as in
> peace, with thanks for the lovely party
> which now—forbid—is over,

no chance to know again guile
of spring love,
wealth of nut, sweet smell of bayberry
and dry cloves.[29]

Hartley's poems have a prosaic quality at odds with the simple, vibrant expressionism of his painting. He never discovered how to deliver verbally the emotion inherent in the large color masses and centered compositions of his painting.

The subject matter of Hartley's poems often suggests shared interests with Williams. His poems use sparrows as metaphors for the aged; he employed Lincoln and the red man as examples of indigenous genius in *Adventures in the Arts*. His poem "Park Avenue Baby" gives a baby's eye view of the world before Williams' *White Mule* and *The Buildup*. His "Dialogue" between garbageman and ice-man on art anticipates Williams' dialogues on art in "Love Song" and "The Basis of Faith in Art."

Hartley's personal life was difficult. Williams recalled that in one of Hartley's garrets his bed hugged a wall behind which the "subdued conversation" of young lovers was "close to his ear" as he slept. "His whole life had been a similar torment which painting alone assuaged."[30] The way in which loneliness is celebrated and turned into a positive power in Williams' "Danse Russe" represented an ideal for Hartley, who set forth his feeling of irremediable isolation in "The Lonely Return to the Lonely."

The lonely—the Divine
are they explicit one
to each?
Does each teach its own reach
to other;
that one is shadow, one is gleam—
one the wave length
one the stream?

Feeling so desperately alone, Hartley permitted his sexuality to flow an unnervingly general course, as had his idols Blake and Whitman. He could be a lady's man, but he was also attracted to Duchamp, to

Robert McAlmon, to Hart Crane and to the doctor from Rutherford. And he wore his hunger on his sleeve.

> Some take their walks at night
> And that's exciting,
> you see the lovely world at its best
> when it is fighting
> in the act of making love
> without the prettiness of plighting—
> raw love just off the spit
> such are accustomed to it.[31]

He ended by repelling most people. He was physically an ugly man; rejection hurt him, and he retreated into the kind of voyeurism latent in the poem above and into cynicism about the heterosexual world. His friendship with Williams went through a strained period; the *coup de grace*, Williams reported in the final version of *The Autobiography*, occurred one day as they sat on the cot in Hartley's garret. The painter propositioned Williams:

> I felt sorry for him, growing old. That was the moment he took for his approaches. I, too, had to reject him. Everyone rejected him. I was no better than the others. One of our finest painters. He told me I *would* have made one of the most charming whores of the city.

This happened in 1920, but the final draft is somewhat different from the first draft.

> One of our finest painters. A cheap requital. I kissed him goodbye at the street door. He told me I would have made one of the most charming whores of the city. We were close friends until his death.

This precedes another incident, deleted entirely, in which Williams describes Hartley's clumsy attempts to seduce Djuna Barnes, after which Williams concludes, "God knows he called me names enough. I really loved the man, but we didn't get along together."[32]

Something has been elided here, something painful. The quarrel between Williams and Hartley was more complex and was tied—at least in Williams' mind—to his rejection of advances by an eccentric known as "The Baroness." Hartley responded in a letter to Williams' flip account of how he had dismissed the Baroness:

> I'd rather not have known the Baroness story because it brought up the worst word in the vocabulary of the anglo-saxon mind, viz [illegible]. I disclaim it because it has the quality of apologies in it for me as a social being. How can you assume anything so much as to put forward a sentence like "has been hung on you to a startling extent." What you hate is your own problem. But the inference is immeasurable.
> . . . .
> . . . That's why I object to the fag end of your letter. I shall learn to be rough and say it holds cheapness for me because it holds assumption. You cannot know anything until you are [illegible] yourself. Any outside knowledge or information that is dragged in is irrelevant.
> . . . .
> It means that you suspect that the only way I can be approached is by "SPECIFIC" experience.[33]

The fight was traumatic for Williams as well. He worked out some of his feelings in an unpublished essay, "The Baroness Elsa von Loringhoven."

> My light-heartedness has become suspect by my friends. It has seemed juvenile very often or at best incomplete. I have suffered bitterly from slights too immaterial to be of visible consequence but curiously important to me. They have come from friends who believed me a liar in deed since I did not carry my "spring" through, that I stopped there.[34]

Despite this break, Williams and Hartley continued to be friends: the importance of the emotional and intellectual connection that they once had prevented each from cutting the other off. Williams helped get Hartley's poems into print, first in *Contact* and later in the *Little Review*. In the latter Hartley also published long letters and two poems of homosexual theme. Williams' interest in Dada in the twenties was in turn spurred by Hartley, who called it the "first joyous dogma I have encountered which has been invented for the release and true freedom of art."

"We published some fine poems by Marianne Moore, Hartley and others," Williams later wrote of the *Contact* days. Hartley introduced him to his co-editor, Robert McAlmon, later in 1920; but McAlmon soon married an heiress. At the wedding Williams appeared with a cluster of rare orchids, and it was "good old Marsden, the most wonderful of party men . . . spoke the perfect comment . . . POETS PAWING ORCHIDS."[35]

A stipend from a benefactor allowed Hartley to spend many of the following years in Taos, a New Mexican town discovered by Mabel Dodge and adopted by Georgia O'Keefe. There Hartley became interested in the Indians and their lore. He wrote "Tribal Esthetics" for *The Dial*, laying great stress on the coherency and balance of the Indian's culture as opposed to that of the white man. But he was not sentimental: "We will not know them," he wrote, "for their cultural extinction is inevitable." These reports interested Williams, who was planning *In the American Grain*. Hartley's descriptions of the harmony between man and land figure in the chapters "DeSoto and the New World," "Pere Sebastian Rasles," and "The Discovery of Kentucky." The chapter on "Abraham Lincoln" was probably suggested by Hartley's poems and paintings of the president. While at work on the book Williams wrote to Hartley, "You will see how heartily I am in agreement with you when you damn the Spanish Conquistadors and how little you need fear treading on my toes in anything you say."[36]

Hartley continued to push "contact" as an artistic program and as a journal. In 1921 in *The Nation*, he wrote that "Art is a matter of direct contact which we have to consider. There can be no other means of approach." Hartley's collection of essays, *Adventures in the Arts*, also appeared in 1921. Suddenly he was an important figure, for Waldo Frank was making Americanism respectable. A number of Hartley's subjects and themes dovetailed with Williams' work of the period, soon to be published as *In the American Grain*. Hartley wrote:

> There will be no magic found away from life. It is what you do with the street-corner in your brain that shall determine your gift.

> It is the redman who has written down our earliest known history, and it is of his symbolic and esthetic endeavors that we should be most reasonably proud. He is the one man who has shown us the significance of the poetic aspects of our original land.

> The phrase that brings together these two strikingly different personages in art is the one of Cezanne: "I remain the primitive of the way I have discovered"; and that of Whitman, which comes if I am not mistaken from

'Democratic Vistas,' "I only wish to indicate the way for the innumerable poets that are to come after me."[37]

Several chapters dealt with acrobats, vaudeville and circus performers, an interest Hartley had picked up in Paris from Picasso and then translated into an American theme. In 1923 in *The Great American Novel* Williams took his own shots at the subject.

> Drown me in pictures like Marsden, make me a radical artist in the conventional sense . . . . O very great men of America please lend me a penny so I won't have to go to the opera. Why not capitalize Barnum?
> . . . .
> The imagination will not down. If it is not a dance, a song, it becomes an outcry, a protest. . . . Men and women cannot be content . . . with the mere fact of a humdrum life, must give it splendor and grotesqueness, beauty and infinite depth.
>
> America . . . goes now and then en masse, by Gosh, to the circus to see men and women and animals perform exquisite and impossible feats . . . [38]

Hartley won his own literary credentials with the printing of *Twenty-Five Poems* in 1923. Williams said nothing of the volume, but the poems and Hartley's other prose met with more receptive editors; his paintings began to be prized. He wanted to go to Europe, and persuaded Stieglitz to hold an auction of his unsold works. Williams went with an eye toward purchasing bargains, but found himself priced out of the market. It was the first in a bitter series of reports.

> I always wanted to buy a picture or two from him fresh from his palette, but he had to keep his prices high in order to live, too high for my pocketbook . . . Finally at an auction at the Anderson Gallery, when even his good friend Stieglitz had no longer a place for him in his gallery, I was able to buy a canvas or two—one of them unfinished—but NOT one of the flower pieces I wanted.

When Hartley returned to the United States, he moved to Maine, intent on living his old age there as simply and inconspicuously as possible. He wrote to Williams now and then, often asking for news of the New York art world. "I can't tell you anything of the happenings among the painters in New York, for I seldom go into the city these days to see the shows," Williams wrote back, and offered to send *In the American Grain* and *White Mule*. He added, "The health of your views about art is still sticking by me."[39]

In 1936 Hartley gave Williams a quality reproduction of "New England Sea-View: Fish House," one of the canvases that Williams had coveted. The poet in turn could be a perceptive reviewer of Hartley's work.

> The colors and shapes he painted (are) for the most part seen close to the eye and positively, even crudely, painted, boldly and with aggressive simplicity. Their outlines whether it was two white birches broken off leaning together in the woods were distinct, dramatically conceived what it was obviously to mean . . . an inescapable tragedy to which the whole canvas pointed and nothing marginal. A mountain torrent dashing itself to pieces on the rocks was no less dramatically centered, or it might be a boulder standing alone, a split boulder with the two halves eternally separated.

But in 1937 their relations cooled further. Williams wrote Stieglitz a long, critical letter about the Hartley exhibition then in his gallery.

> This was the strangest show of Hartley's I have ever seen. It taxed the good will of the spectator pretty hard because of the monotonous tone of the pictures and the similarity if not identity of the sizes, one next to the other along the wall. It was a tough session. I don't know. All I seemed to see was black. Some seemed not to have come off at all. Others were so full of mannerisms that the good of them seemed buried . . . I could not understand the heavy black outlines to the forms—as paintings that is. It seemed to me too much for the effect desired. After all, death is not sad. It's life that's sad. Is that what is meant? . . . [40]

On Hartley's rare excursions to New York, Williams tried to make him feel at home. He wrote to McAlmon that he had thrown a party for Hartley and that "Marsden and my new Scotty pup . . . were the heroes. Hartley was well primed by my son Bill and a pal with good Gordon gin so that he positively glowed. Haven't seen him so young and happy in years." More often Hartley remained in Maine, where he became almost a member of the family with which he boarded. Williams disapproved of hermitage; the Hartley pastel that he had purchased, "Mountains in New Mexico," he began to call "Marsden's Breasts."[41]

Perhaps the bitter note crept in because Hartley had the grit of his own independence. His death came as a surprise and Williams, writing of it to McAlmon, reveals a trace of remorse.

> Floss always . . . looks at the obituary notices. Yesterday she found the name of Marsden Hartley. The *Times* gave him 3/4 of a column, a brief summary of his accomplishments. I was going to send you the notice but what's the use. I went in to see his last show. There were some florid, formal flower pieces, a mountain or two, some fish, a group portrait of a man kneeling on 5th Ave. or thereabouts in front of the Rockefeller Church, a ten foot man in overalls, scrawny, pathetic. So what? Why do we live? Most of us need the very thing we never ask for . . . I'm afraid Marsden was stuck—in his own mind, in his technique obsessed with fears—and unwilling to use the good eyes he had and think. This is an ungracious and ungenerous attitude to take before the spectacle of a man dead. There it is.[42]

But it is not there—not the tense, inquisitive friendship of their early days together, nor the faithful aesthetic alliance of their middle years that led each man to artistic success.

III.   Charles Sheeler

It is strange that William Carlos Williams did not really know Charles Sheeler, who had been on the fringes of the Arensberg Circle, until both were mature artists. But in view of Williams' collaboration with painters in whom he found an echo of his interests, that is the proper way for it to have happened. "One night I particularly remember," wrote Williams, "at Mat Josephson's place, I met Charles and Katharine Sheeler." This seems to have been in 1919. Josephson had just returned from Europe and recounted that "I wanted to arrange for my older friends, William Carlos Williams and Charles Sheeler, to meet each other; and so we had a Dutch treat dinner in a speak-easy, after which Williams, Sheeler and their wives returned to our house, each guest bringing his own bottle of wine. We all sat on the floor not out of any Bohemian affectation, but because we had no chairs."[43]

Like other expatriates Josephson had returned from Europe because he perceived a new locus of artistic progress in New York. Sheeler, who had been a guest of the Arensbergs since 1917 and had photographed the art in the apartment in 1918, shared this view. His biographer reports that:

> Arensberg, a poet and astute patron of the arts, became an especial friend. The Arensberg home was a rare American manifestation of the salon. Sheeler was a member of this unstructured club of intellectuals until the Arensbergs, finding the crowds pressed too hard upon their privacy, escaped in the early 20s to residence in California.
> ·
> In these days, or nights, the free association of ideas was not taken as steam rising from the subconscious, but as the very hot breath of genius. . . . The Arensbergs bought, collected, listened, invited, and served rice pudding and fruit at midnight.

Sheeler himself was rather aghast at the way the Arensbergs lived amid constant activity. "Arensbergs' was like the upper level of Grand Central Station," he said. "The Arensbergs moved to California to get away from all that. It went on after dinner until six a.m."[44]

Despite his interest in the art and painters of the salon, Sheeler never stood at the core of the group.

> He had a prim attitude about glib foreigners whose conversation, usually in French, which he did not understand, rarely included him: his relationship with them was, at best, tenuous ("They didn't know I existed!") Only Duchamp seems to have taken some polite interest in the young American's work, and if Sheeler never comprehended the mysteries of Dada, he was at least mildly intrigued by the Frenchman's cryptic "readymades."
> . . . Sheeler, an archetype of the provincial American painter, remained on the sidelines of the international discussions at the Arensbergs'.

Sheeler had begun his career, like several of the European cubists, as a draftsman—an industrial art student. But a chance glimpse of Thomas Eakins at work and a trip abroad changed that. "I was taken to see Michael Stein and his wife," he said "and saw the Stein Collection. I couldn't go back where I'd left off. It was a tadpole period when you have two hind legs and a tail before you finally become a frog."[45]

On his return to the United States, Sheeler moved into a country house with his friend Morton Schamberg. Both earned a living in photography, Sheeler finding a field for himself in Philadelphia photographing newly finished houses for their architects, who wanted the prints mainly as records. The buildings were boxy, unpleasing hybrids, but Sheeler transcribed their masses with revealing honesty, an aesthetic that ran parallel to his preoccupation with structural form in painting. It was as though by looking hard at these simple forms, by photographing them honestly, he could make them live and glow.

In 1912 Arthur B. Davies befriended Sheeler and invited him to send six canvases, including the Cézannesque "White Tulips," to the 1913 Armory Show. Arensberg saw the paintings, and although he bought no work at that time, he soon began to acquire Sheelers from Marius De Zayas. Sheeler met the dealer when he started photographing the African art in De Zayas' Gallery for books and catalogs, and he became quickly the master of this specialty. Apparently he met both Demuth and Hartley in the gallery also. De Zayas mounted shows of Sheeler's photographs in 1918 and 1925, and showed his paintings in 1917 and 1920. Sheeler never exhibited elsewhere, not even with Stieglitz, until after 1930.

In 1917 Sheeler showed two paintings at the Independents Show, both of which John Quinn bought. He also met the Arensbergs, who invited him to their apartment. Arensberg's sponsorship of Sheeler for the next twenty years testifies to the catholicity of his taste: the shy American was diametrically opposed to futurism in topic and technique. Like De Zayas, he was interested in Chinese art and philosophy, especially the teachings of Lao Tzu. He sought to suppress the flamboyancy of personality in his work. His favorite adage, recorded in the "Black Book" that was his personal Bible, was the well known Zen parable that "To a man who knows nothing, mountains are mountains, waters are waters, and trees are trees. . . ."

For the new viewer, this mystic intent is often difficult to discern. Sheeler painted with crisp edges, tidy proportions, subtle juxtapositions, and unusual sympathy for the non-human—a new world way of seeing things. "Americans had a way of seeing hard facts with sharp edges in the light of reason," wrote one of his critics. Sheeler knew that his countrymen focused on *things* and that these things had an earned value and price. He offered them nothing of atmosphere and he resisted symbol and confession. The *evidence*, he offered, however, was so intense as to be religious.

This "precisionist" style, as it came to be called, was basically a conservative, scourging style. It offered an alternative to the romanticism of American realism and regionalism represented by Sloan, Glackens and Henri. Yet for all its absorption of the abstracting and classicizing elements of European painting, it did not depart from the American scene: Sheeler painted the cityscape, the farm theme, the dignity of industry—all with an emphasis on utility and simplicity. As such, it was a mature style; it had arrived, and would not change substantially. It was the kind of artistic analogue that Williams, his great poetic innovations now underway, sought as a stabilizing influence. In Sheeler's work was the bewildering clarity Williams was catching and fixing in the images of "The Red Wheelbarrow" and "Young Locust."

Williams and Sheeler became fast friends. References to "visiting the Sheelers" in Connecticut, or later at their Irvington, New York, cottage are common in Williams' correspondence after 1919. He even told his publisher, Laughlin, to drop in on them. In *A Novelette* (1921–31) there is an entry, "Nothing would please me better than to run up to Westchester and see S." Biographer Constance Rourke notes that Sheeler read the chapters of "In the American Grain" that were published in *Broom* in 1923 and was "warmly enthusiastic about them." She adds that Williams,

> who [already] knew some of Sheeler's work, felt that he had "looked at things directly, truly. It was a bond. We both had become aware of a fresh currency in expression, and as we talked we found that we both meant to lead a life which meant direct association and communication with immediate things."[46]

Occasionally the friends collaborated, as in their 1925 attack on H. L. Mencken in *Aesthetic*, Josephson's journal. Williams denounced Mencken as a "third rate intellectual," and Sheeler contributed the picture of a skyscraper on the facing page. Later Williams introduced Sheeler to his second wife, an expatriate Russian dancer; so pleased was Williams in his matchmaking role that he wrote that Sheeler "is as happy as a man can well be. . . . He has money now and lots of work to do at top prices and she is a decoration."[47]

Called upon to write introductions for the catalogs of Sheeler's exhibits, Williams set down some of his most cogent analyses of painting, yet there is usually a bit of waffling in his summations. Williams always pointed to the positive: "I think Sheeler is particularly valuable because of the bewildering directness of his vision, without blur, through the fantastic overlay with which our lives so vastly are concerned, 'the real,' as we say, contrasted with the artist's fabrication.''[48] Yet in his later review of Sheeler's work, Williams confessed to a fear that photography had arrested the painter's style, that he was "stuck" in the way Hartley had been. Williams acknowledged the problem, but put a good face on it.

> Is he going to change in his style or go on developing it as before? As a man grows older we ask of him not so much the new but how he has served the gift he originally possessed. Does he see to it that he paints always better pictures?
> . . . .
> Charles Sheeler has lived in a mechanical age. To deny that was to lose your life. That, the artist early recognized. In the world which immediately surrounded him it was more apparent than anywhere else on earth. What was he to do about it? He accepted it as the source of material for his compositions.
>   Sheeler made a clean sweep of it. The man found himself impressed by the contours of the machine; he was not impressed by the romantic aspects of what the machine represents but the machine itself.[49]

Sheeler was far less critical of Williams. Having seen the evaluation quoted above, he wrote to Arensberg:

> They are giving me a very handsome catalog with about twenty-six illustrations and a piece by William Carlos Williams. I know that my recommendations in literature carry no more weight with you than my recommendations of chocolate ice-cream with Lou. Nevertheless I venture the opinion that several prose pieces recently published by Williams are among the outstanding literature of this day. He continues as a source of encouragement to me in the example he shows of what one can produce in spite of obstacles which would frustrate the less determined. I look forward with pleasure and impatience to the opportunity of presenting Musya to Lou and you sometime in the near future.[50]

The discovery that Williams makes through Sheeler's art is, in a sense, his last lesson in the Arensberg Circle. The dizzying revolution in styles that Duchamp and Arensberg began and continued had caused Williams to seek artistic restraint, to search for a new principle of classicism. Sheeler, independently, had done the same. But despite the wit that he brought to all his painting, Sheeler's sense of form had become fixed and invariable. His vision and his subjects won Williams completely, but he was beginning to repeat himself—Duchamp's cardinal sin— through an inability to create new forms.

This is not to imply that Sheeler's artistic use to Williams was entirely admonitory: several of Sheeler's paintings, such as "Chrysanthemums" (1912), "Pertaining to Yachts and Yachting" (1922), and "Classic Landscape" (1930), evidently provided the inspiration, or artistic analogues, for poems by Williams ("Chrysanthemums," "The Yachts," and "Classic Scene").

More important, however, was the "nativeness" and rehabilitation of the American locale that Sheeler personified. In *The Autobiography,* when Williams wanted to explain the significance of Charles Olson's essay on projective verse, he turned for an analogy to Sheeler's life, which he perceived as the embodiment of Olson's theory.

> The poem is our objective, the secret at the heart of the matter—as Sheeler's small house, reorganized, is the heart of the gone estate of the Lowes—the effect of a fortune founded on tobacco or chicle or whatever it was.
>
> The poem (in Charles's case the painting) is the construction in understandable limits of his life. That is Sheeler; that, lucky for him, partial or possible, is also music. It is called also a marriage. All these terms have to be redefined, a marriage has to be seen as a thing. The poem is made of things—on a field.
>
> The poem, the small house (gray stone, a wisteria vine big around as a leg, the association of the broken-down estate peopled by the perfect trees) has been seized by Charles difficultly, not easily, and made into an expression—as well as he can, which he paints—as well as he can! (Not realistically.)

"Nothing can grow," concluded Williams, "unless it taps into the soil."[51]

6. Sheer Paint, Sheer Poetry

"L'exactitude n'est pas la vérité."

Matisse

I. The Intuitionalists

Throughout his life Williams delighted in telling the story of the woman who asked Alanson Hartpence about the painting in his gallery. Hartpence's reply—"That, madam, is paint"—became Williams' synecdoche for a revolution in perception. "It was the secret meaning inside the term 'transition' during the years when the painters following Cezanne began to talk of sheer paint: a picture a matter of pigments upon a piece of cloth stretched on a frame," he said.

But the Hartpence story is the sort of anecdote one approaches with caution. How much of the revolution in painting did Williams really understand? How deep was his background? If painting was as influential in his work as Williams maintained it was, there must be attitudes, techniques and subjects that he transferred to the world of poetry. From his letters, notes and essays one can apprehend what Williams was seeing in the painters. Though he did not study them by period or historical order, his intuitional handling of them reveals the artist's eye—he divided them into two general groups that would have pleased an art historian. The way he worked with these groups, furthermore, reveals what he borrowed for his technique, and how that technique was internally organized and how it operated.

Williams founded his approach on Cezanne, whom he understood to occupy a position in painting analogous to that of Whitman in poetry. In the opinion of Williams and Hartley it was "Whitman and Cezanne who have clarified the sleeping eye and withheld it from being totally blinded . . . both Whitman and Cezanne stand together in the name of . . . freedom from characteristics not one's own."[1] Like art historian H. H. Arnason, they saw that Cezanne represented a brilliant juncture of opposing directions.

> Cezanne's unusual combination of logic and emotion, of reason and un-reason, represented the synthesis that he would seek in his paintings.
> . . . Painting itself from the seventeenth to the nineteenth century had increasingly become a power struggle of drawing versus color; in the seventeenth century the Poussinists against the Rubenists; in the nineteenth century the neoclassicists against the romantics, Ingres versus Delacroix.[2]

It seems unnecessary to recapitulate Cezanne's technique at length, but it is important to underscore that he did more than simplify form, clarify the palette, and discard renaissance perspective. His innovations resulted from Cezanne's fidelity to the eye: he painted in small, independent snatches, each section of canvas viewed from a different angle, a tiny picture in its own right. The recent research on vision reported by Rudolph Arnheim and others confirms Cezanne's intuition.[3]

Little in Williams' background prepared him for Cezanne, but he gravitated to him immediately. "There was an exhibition of Cezanne at Knoedler's," wrote Williams in his report to *The Egoist* in the spring of 1916. Presumably he attended, for it was that period of his life in which he was "getting to know" other poets and artists.

Nor was it the first showing of Cezanne in this country. Before 1913 Edward Steichen had sent a few Cezannes to Stieglitz for display at "291," and in the Armory Show of 1913 an impressive display of Cezanne's work was hung. Thirteen canvases and five lithographs were mounted, and a dozen of these were sold: Arensberg bought a lithograph for the bargain price of $40.00.[4]

That Williams understood the notion of a "new reality" in Cezanne is revealed in some of his essays. In "The Beginnings of an American Education," he explains that when a student has completely absorbed the lessons of a master such as Cezanne, he realizes that the chief accomplishment of the master has been to go beyond his teachers. Therefore, the student must break with his masters: "A painter like Cezanne or Titian, or a statue as good as some by Phidias, is a complete triumph to the learned, and worth nothing whatever" to the ambitious artist.

More tributes to Cezanne came later. In his *Autobiography* Williams referred to Cezanne as the cornerstone on whose work rested the triumphs of Joyce, Stein, Picasso and Matisse. He reiterated this view in the sixties: "I was tremendously involved in an appreciation of Cezanne. He was a designer. He put it down on the canvas so that there would be a meaning without saying anything at all. Just the relations of the parts to themselves."[5]

After Cezanne, art historians agree that there were two principal lines of development: the one rational, highly structured and leading to cubism and its progeny; the other more intuitive, sensual and lyric. Williams also discerned this parting, which was seen as early as 1910 by Roger Fry: "In opposition to Picasso, who is predominantly plastic, Matisse aims at convincing us of the reality of his forms by the continuity and flow of his rhythmic line, by the logic of his space relations, and above all, by an entirely new use of color." In fact, this statement comes from a book in Williams' library.[6]

Matisse is certainly the greatest figure among those schools—the fauves, the orphists, the Blaue Reiter—whose interpretations of Cezanne are antithetical to those pioneered by cubism and futurism and their progeny. But beyond a common lyrical, "pastoral," intuitive approach they do not share so much in common as the more "disciplined" schools following cubism; in fact, the development of this "position" is the history of lone, inspired men: principally Matisse and Kandinsky.

The work of Matisse arrived in America in 1905, much earlier than that of any of the other new painters. He had shown at the Salon d'Automne his "Joie de Vivre," which was bought by Gertrude and Leo Stein and became the centerpiece of their collection. A few days later the four Steins—Gertrude, Leo, Michael, and Sarah—were browsing at the Automne when they were taken with "Woman with a Hat" and bought it. Returning home to inspect the damage of the San Francisco earthquake, Sara Stein took these pictures and showed them—the first Matisses in America.

A small group of Matisse's drawings was exhibited in New York in 1908. Bernard Berenson wrote a laudatory essay for the *New York Post* that would have caught Williams' eye. In February, 1910, Steichen brought over a larger selection for a second exhibit, and James Hunecker, the critic, saw in the paintings "the truth and magic of their contours. . . . In a word, an amazing artist, original in observation and a scorner of the facile line."

Gertrude Stein, whose work and criticism Williams later followed closely, became Matisse's principal explicator in America. She wrote two pieces, one on Matisse, the other on Picasso, for special issues of *Camera Work* in 1912. Williams was interested in the high value that Matisse placed on intuition. "If the inventive imagination must look as I think," he wrote, "to the field of art for its richest discoveries today, it will best make its way by compass and follow no path."[7]

In 1912 there was an exhibit of Matisse's sculpture at "291" that Williams apparently attended. But he saw the Matisse that impressed him most in 1915. It was called "The Blue Nude." Michael and Sarah Stein had purchased "Tableau No. 111" at the 1907 Paris Independents show, at which point Matisse renamed it "Blue Nude (Souvenir de Biskra)." The painting was lent by the Steins to the Armory Show; it was seen there by the wealthy lawyer and art collector John Quinn, who was interested in, but uncertain about, Matisse. It has been erroneously assumed that Williams saw the canvas at this show and that Quinn purchased it there. In fact, the Steins lent "Blue Nude" and "Music" to a 1915 show at the Montross Gallery in New York, which Williams attended. This prompted his famous essay "A Matisse." After the show John Quinn bought both paintings.[8]

In the years that followed there were many shows of Matisse in New York. Marius De Zayas mounted a show in December, 1920, and some scholars think Williams' essay was written then as a polemic. But since Williams had several earlier opportunities to see the "Blue Nude," his essay seems to be a retrospective appreciation. More importantly, the essay begins "On the french grass, in that room on Fifth Ave. . . . " The Montross was located at 550 Fifth Avenue, but the De Zayas Gallery was on a cross street.

From any vantage, the essay is one of Williams' best pieces of art criticism. His opening line assimilates Matisse into the American scene: "On the french grass, in that room on Fifth Ave., lay that woman who had never seen my own poor land." What follows is not a description of the canvas but a recreation of it in prose. Williams imagines how the model came to her pose, the attitude of the painter toward her: "The dust and noise of Paris had fallen from her," he wrote. "So too she lay in the sunlight of the man's easy attention. His eye and the sun had made day over her." Just as Matisse recasts the reality that he sees, Williams recasts the canvas. Rather than holding "a mirror up to nature," he imitates Matisse's creativeness; he imagines a train whistling "beyond the hill" in the background. Three times in the first paragraph, as if groping for a way to express the purely visceral nature of the scene, Williams repeats "There is nothing to be told." There is no plot, only his intuition of the physical facts leading to the painting. In the woman's mind he posits the thought "Nothing is to be told to the sun at noonday."

By painting, Matisse becomes the spirit of the sun for Williams: "The sun," he writes, "had entered his head in the color of sprays of flaming palm leaves." One searches the "Blue Nude" in vain for such foliage—Williams invented it. "They had been walking an hour or so after leaving the train . . . he had painted her resting, with interest in the place she had chosen." Williams invents the context of the picture, endows Matisse with his own sensual interest in female ways and, always, almost unconsciously, returns to *place*. Why, he asks, did she choose this place? When the model disrobes, as Williams saw hundreds of his patients do, he wonders that "when they have worn clothes and take them off it is with an effect of having performed a small duty." An effect such as this cannot be caught by the painter—it is one of the *poetic* triumphs of the essay, as is the next phrase, which relates women to light: "They turn to the sun with a gesture of accomplishment." Finally Williams ties all the various themes together in three neat, diminishing paragraphs, the last of which tactfully reminds the reader of the opening of the essay:

> It was the first of summer. Bare as was his mind of interest in anything save the fullness of his knowledge, into which her simple body entered as into the eye of the sun himself, so he painted her. So she came to America.
>
> No man in my country has seen a woman naked and painted her as if he knew anything except that she was naked. No woman in my country is naked except at night.
>
> In the french sun, on the french grass in a room on Fifth Ave., a french girl lies and smiles at the sun without seeing us.[9]

If this is polemic, it is enjoyable and subtle.

Williams' love for Matisse never diminished. In a 1930 letter to Marianne Moore, he wrote: "It is strange, nothing whips my blood like verse. . . . Often though I get the same feeling from the work of others. The best of French painting does it. Matisse does it." Matisse was a synonym for "the best," and Williams wanted no less than the painter's intuitive genius in himself, as he revealed in a short, unpublished poem.

"The Fault: Matisse" appears to concern "The Moroccans," a Matisse displayed in New York often.

> See what there is
> and interested in what you see
> to a fault.
>
> look by look and each look
> an emerald
> a grid, a blue
> as it strikes, stays, never moves
> even though in movement
> more than a lemon
> or a tree, that is, the light
> or a fresh plucked
> branch of lemons
>
> fragrant as flesh and careless
> as a thigh. Everything
> is a picture
>
> to the employing eye
> that feeds restlessly to
> find peace.[10]

The "employing eye that feeds restlessly" is a characteristic shared by Matisse and Williams. It is a way of seeing that casts the seen world into satisfying sequences: Roger Fry maintains that the ability of Matisse to communicate intuitively is due to "an astonishing sense of linear rhythm, a rhythm which is at once continuous and extremely various, that is to say it is capable at once of extraordinary variations from the norm without loss of continuity."[11] This is the same quality that we find in Williams' verse, in his triadic line and his "variable foot." Both artists possessed an unusual sense of visual rhythm; they could execute a wide range of variations on and show how extremely elastic was the basic "master-beat" that the eye or ear apprehended.

Art historians, writing about Matisse, tend to link him with Kandinsky. Alfred Barr, for example, writes that "the singing color of the 'Joy of Life' opens the way to Kandinsky." "Matisse," writes Jacque Lassaigne, "resembles [Kandinsky] in so many ways." The criterion at work is the dichotomy between line and color, reason and unreason.[12]

Kandinsky could have been a brilliant fauve or cubist—he had total visual recall—but he realized that those were not solutions for him. His impetus to paint came from something other than a love of surface texture. His theme was "the Absolute in the seriousness of its world-creating play." His work was spiritual, and Williams recognized and accepted it on that level. In 1910 he wrote a small book, *Concerning the Spiritual in Art*, which had a remarkable impact on Williams.

In its time Kandinsky's little book represented a new viewpoint. Its first section is a long meditative passage in which the painter opposes the idea of art for art's sake and denounces forms of creativity that concern themselves with "means" alone. Kandinsky proclaims the freedom of art from means, from all materialistic doctrines, and urges artists to press forward in a visionary, prophetic manner. He strikes the same chords that Elena struck for Williams. "The artist sees what will be, and makes it seen." In opposition to scientific materialism, he lauds the artistic experiments of Wagner, Debussy, Maeterlinck, Schonberg and von Webern; the neo-impressionists; the painters attracted by the shadowy and unsubstantial, such as Rossetti and Boecklin; the work of Cezanne, for its revelation of the inner essence of things; and that of Matisse and Picasso, whom he considers the greatest of his contemporaries. These artists are the leaders, standing at the apex of a triangle that Kandinsky uses as a metaphor for society. The harder the apex pushes upward, the more the mass of humanity is pulled along; all artists should be pushing, attempting to reunite humanity with spirit. Williams used these ideas as the basis of his essay "The Neglected Artist," which expands on his 1906 letter to Ed.

The second part of the book is a theory of color, line and form. Colors, he wrote, have at first a purely physical effect of short duration on viewers. After longer viewing, however, "one acquires a kind of inner resonance in response to color. . . . Vermillion has the charm of flame . . . keen lemon yellow hurts the eye; each color produces a different spiritual vibration. Colors are inherently rough or smooth, sticky or uniform, wet or soft or dry. They produce a scent and a sound." Color became the dominant sensual trait of Williams' poems in the late 1910s.

Colors in turn are conditioned by lines and shapes, with which they have a symbiotic relationship. "Form alone has . . . a power of inner suggestion," Kandinsky wrote. The more abstract the form, the "more clear and direct its appeal" to the spirit. Horizontal lines are inherently peaceful, while vertical lines connote a sense of action or emotion. Certain shapes likewise dictate feelings; he uses as examples the rhomboid and the triangle. This emphasis on the triangle became important to Demuth and Hartley, and hence filtered into Williams' poetic vision, appearing variously as the prow or the attic or the steeple. Williams used the shape, like Matisse and Kandinsky, when seeking to give form to an inexpressible absolute. He also adapted the rhomboid for his own use. In a 1955 letter to Henry Wells he remarks, "Many years ago I was impressed with the four-sided parallelogram . . . I found myself always conceiving my abstract designs as possessing four sides. That was natural enough with spring, summer, autumn and winter always before me."[13]

The final section of Kandinsky's book delivers two sets of maxims important to Williams. In accord with his triangular paradigm of society, Kandinsky postulated that the artist/prophet must serve three functions. He (1) needs to express himself, (2) is impelled to express the spirit of his age, and (3) has to help the cause of art. "Every work of art is the child of its age, and in many cases the mother of our emotions. . . . It follows that each period of culture produces an art of its own which can never be repeated. Efforts to revive the art principles of the past will at best produce an art that is stillborn." Williams quotes this program almost verbatim in his "Prologue" to *Kora in Hell*.

> . . . and Kandinsky in his *Ueber das Geistige in der Kunst* [sic] set down the following axioms for the artist:
> Every artist has to express himself.
> Every artist has to express his epoch.
> Every artist has to express the pure and eternal
> qualities of the art of all men.[14]

The second set of ideas, which Kandinsky illustrated using his own work, is a codification of creative methods. First there is "simple composition," which is melodic and consists of a few elementary forms arranged in simple fashion. It resembles the lyric impulse. Then there is "complex composition," in which many forms of varying complexity exist in "symphonic" arrangement. This mode breaks down into three types. There are "direct impressions," typified by the work of the impressionists. These are based on external reality, and form the classical conception of art. Second, there are "improvisations," which originate in the artist's soul and are spontaneously produced. This is the romantic impulse. Third, there are "compositions," in which "such stress is laid on construction that only the determinant structural elements remain." These works are formed slowly, dictated by deep inner emotions; they mediate between the two impulses.

Williams adopted this system as a working format for several years. He titled *Kora in Hell: Improvisations* so pointedly that little argument seems necessary. A second book, *The Great American Novel*, is constructed according to Kandinsky's idea of improvisation, and the painter is mentioned in it twice. In the first instance Kandinsky is noted, insightfully, as the product of German expressionism: "Expressionism is to express skillfully the seething reactions of the contemporary European consciousness. Cornucopia. In at the small end and—blui! Kandinsky!" A page later Williams raises an aesthetic problem for himself and wonders if "a great artist, say Kandinsky" would solve it the same way.[15]

Though Williams certainly knew about Kandinsky from Hartley late in the decade, there is a fair case to be made that he learned of the German artist earlier: *Über das Geistige in der Kunst* was reviewed in the June 20, 1914, issue of *Blast* at a time when Pound was acting editor. The section of the book that Williams quoted in *Kora* is prominent in the review, and as Gail Levin notes, Williams appears to have copied the spelling of "Über" as "Ueber."[16]

II. The Structure of Cubism

Though Williams left his heart with the intuitionalists, he learned the lessons of the cubists well. The popularity of cubism among the avant-garde in the United States contributed, for the cubists had important "trans-Atlantic" connections. In 1904 when Picasso moved into the Bateau-Lavoir in Montmartre, among his neighbors were Guillaume Apollinaire, the poet, and Max Jacob, the critic, both of whom were soon to visit the United States.

In his important work of this period Picasso asserted that the human figure and face could be subordinated to his requirements of the total painting. It was *all* plastic. "It could be distorted, cut up, transformed into a series of flat-color facets essentially indistinguishable from comparable planes composing the environment in which they existed," writes Arnason.[17] This meant that a painting could exist as an independent organization of lines, shapes, planes and colors related to one another on the surface of a canvas.

In exploring this avenue, Picasso abandoned Cezanne's emphasis on the unity, or gestalt, of the picture. He shifted point of view at will. He saw noses, eyes and mouths from below, from above and simultaneously; and tables and other props frontally or serially. Picasso did not "walk around" the subject in order to provide this multiplicity of viewpoints, but it is undeniable that he elicits a sense of movement in space from the viewer. He created a new kind of pictorial space in which perception is supposed to be plastic, moving through various viewpoints and yet always at the same place. The series of "independent snatches" that Cezanne saw was not sequential, said Picasso, but simultaneous.

Accompanying this multiplicity of viewpoints was a massive and crude remodeling of the human body. The decisive influence on his thinking was African sculpture, the examples from the Ivory Coast and other French colonies that he saw at the Trocadero Museum and in the shops of second-hand dealers. Or perhaps, as he claimed, it was early Iberian figurines. The interest in African art soon spread to the United States. First imported by Marius De Zayas, a friend of Williams, the sculpture was important variously in the work of Hartley, Dove and O'Keefe. Charles Sheeler was hired by De Zayas to photograph the exhibits.

What all these artists found fascinating in African art was the way it suggested the same "new reality" toward which Cezanne had pointed. "The way in which these Negro craftsmen had succeeded in recreating nature without copying it," said one, "in particular their knack of representing the human face and body by methods that, while utterly unlike those of the traditional sculpture of the West, were, plastically, no less valid." That Williams understood this validity is evident in his essay "Picasso Breaks Faces."

> Picasso's struggles are taking place in my blood—and not as a Spaniard but as a man facing a common world.
>   What is a face? What has it always been even to the remotest savagery? A battleground. Slash it with sharp instruments, rub ashes into the wound to make a keloid; daub it with clays, paint it with berry juices. This thing that terrifies us, this face upon which we lay so much stress is something they have always wanted to deform, by hair, by shaving, by

every possible means. Why? TO REMOVE FROM IT THE TERROR OF DEATH BY MAKING OF IT A WORK OF ART.[18]

Most of Williams' references to Picasso are ambivalent or negative; they belie the important lesson the poet learned. As noted earlier, Picasso appears briefly in *A Voyage to Pagany*. The protagonist, Dev Evans, is at a performance of Cocteau's "Romeo and Juliet" at Le Cigale, when he sees "Picasso, Derain—and many more, all the lights."[19] Williams associates Picasso with Derain, a fauve who later adopted cubism, again in "French Painting" (1928).

A Voyage to Pagany also contains two references to a fictitious French painter named Pichat, which may be a pseudonym for Picasso. "Every now and then someone bursts out like Pichat with design. And takes the shape of the moment. But America is off the track completely." At another point Evans is prompted to wonder,

> what effect all this had had upon the mind of that modern French genius of whom New York had been ecstatically talking just at the outbreak of the war; that fine painter whose pictures had been so admired and ridiculed— and whose influence on several of Evans' painter friends had been so great.[20]

Around 1928 Williams wrote *The Embodiment of Knowledge*, a book that includes the essay "French Painting." The piece opens with a paragraph showing substantial comprehension of Picasso's work,

> It is, in paint, an effect of this plain problem: How shall the multiplicity of a natural object, impossible to detail or completely encircle, be represented by pigment on canvas. Plainly it is not to trace it as it stands for that intelligence is impossible, repetitious and uncalled for. . . . It is to represent some phase of this object that the schools point. Each pose caught being a success.

In another essay on the prescience of artists, Williams writes of "the prediction of war" in the paintings of Picasso in Paris.[21]

During the late twenties and early thirties Williams did not write much or well of Picasso, for all of his energy had turned toward an "American" poetry. This may account for the marginalia of that period turned up recently: "Picasso will not leave Paris because he has the brains to know that if he came to America he would have to be affected by it and paint that way—and he doesn't want to at his age." Williams' regard for Picasso continued to ebb, judging from a 1932 letter to Kay Boyle.

A poet should take his inspiration from the other arts too. Picasso? Which line is significant? Damned if I know. Maybe there is something running through it all. But he seems so intent on proving that he just doesn't have to work after any particular mode that I have lost interest in him.[22]

But in the early 1950s Williams wrote a short essay on Picasso for *The General Magazine and Historical Chronicle*. One paragraph has already been quoted. The remainder acknowledges Picasso's creation of "new reality," though Williams dissents from his techniques.

Last winter in Paris seven pictures were shown in the Picasso exhibition, all representing an attack upon the human figure—limbs, body, and face, an attack showing the struggle that continued unabated throughout the "occupation years" in France.
. . . .
This Picasso understands better than anyone living in the world today. He is a Hercules holding us back from destruction. He is not the only hero, but he is one of the greatest now alive. Do we understand that? The confusion of the past has been that "character," the character of the face, even in a portrait by a Titian or a Michelangelo, was anchored irretrievably in a meat of set color and contour. In these seven pictures we see a progress in the attack Picasso has been making upon that face. We may humanly disagree with his tactics but with his strategy we cannot disagree. His success has been phenomenal.
Paris attracts genius because it offers a man its body to do with as he will. For that, an artist seeks to give in return his own very blood. Nothing is held back, either way. Picasso healthy as a pot, Spanish as the sun itself, has been a grateful lover. He is more Catalan than one from that windy north that ran in the veins of El Greco from about Burgos. His figures rest upon the earth, well-bottomed. But they are, for all that, Spanish in that their spirit transcends the flesh. What is a face? What is a torso (toro)? Something to kill, that out of it may rise something greater, upon which the whole world hangs breathless. Will it arise? Can it be? Shall we accept the tawdry defamations fed to us as tenet and party or BELIEVE that we can, in fact upon this earth, witness a ghost lift from a body that had been stabbed to the heart?

This is the war that Pablo Picasso wages for us, besieged as we are, in the guise of paint and canvas.[23]

There were two other "cubist" painters, in a strict sense of the term, who drew Williams' attention: Braque and Gris. Georges Braque, who worked closely with Picasso, was responsible for the emphasis of cubism on the immediate and local. After this pair decided they wanted to paint always within fifty miles of Paris, Braque "began to concentrate on the still life," and soon so did Picasso. Still life and the local were important to Williams, who wrote,

All poems can be represented by
still-lifes   not to say
watercolors   the violence of
the Iliad lends itself to an arrangement
of narcissi in a jar.[24]

Braque was incorporating into some of his pictures letters from labels and other printed matter, as Apollinaire explained to America, "because label, notice and advertisement play a very important aesthetic role in the modern city and are well-suited for incorporation into works of art."

Braque also made the first statements in print about cubism, and these were published in the May, 1910, issue of *The Architectural Record*, a periodical published in New York to which Williams' brother may have subscribed.[25] Williams still wrote regularly to Ed, and if Braque's statement was passed along, his comment on painting the nude would have caught Williams' attention: "I couldn't portray a woman in all her natural loveliness. I haven't the skill. No one has. I must, therefore, create a new sort of beauty, the beauty that appears to me in terms of volume, of line, of mass, of weight, and through that beauty interpret my subjective impression."[26]

Williams may also have made an acquaintance with Braque through Hartley, who had translated into English in 1913 Roger Allard's essay concerning Braque and Picasso, "What is Cubism?" Williams paid a tribute to Braque in *A Voyage to Pagany*:

And still he stood and looked at the low gray houses ranged around in an hexagonal symmetry and, feeling broken down, low, pleasant-plain, he put a pear, which he had just bought, again to his lips. . . . Was it an *aisle*? As far as he could tell it said Braque. It linked completely with the modern spirit. It was France, cold, grey, dextrous, multiform and yet gracious.[27]

In later life he was fond of telling how "Braque would take his pictures out of doors and place them beside nature to see if his imitations had *worked*." Not to copy the appearance of nature but to drink its creative juice—this was the point that Williams learned from Braque. In his later essay on French painting, Williams saw Braque as the ultimate artist in the French drive toward concreteness: "Facing it, realizing that it is pigment on a surface, French painting went as far as Braque," who "remains the pivot for an appraisal of its continued activity." The painter had pointed out to him what writers must do: "It is the same question of words and technique in their arrangement—Stein has stressed, as Braque did paint, words."[28]

Juan Gris, the third cubist favored by Williams, differed from Picasso and Braque in a fundamental way. While the latter gave more thought to the qualities of the subject than to the actual structure of the picture, Gris subordinated the various elements to a rigorous architectonic scheme. He took extreme care to assemble each element in the picture into a unified whole, usually a very readable one. He created a system in which oblique parallel rays of light define simple, clean-cut forms of rigid appearance, yet his technique does not hamper a delicate, poetic imagination.

The rays of light that Gris employed became "ray-lines" or edges, similar to the "lines of force" developed by the Italian futurists and employed by Demuth. Gris had studied light striking bottles and other objects and noted the play of broken gleams and reflections. He developed these edges into a network that overlaid the canvas evenly, always paying attention to their composition as well as that of the larger picture.

Williams probably encountered Gris in print first, for Gris' statements on cubism appeared frequently, and he took pains to be clear. His dealer, Daniel Henry Kahnweiler, was a tireless publicist for Gris, calling attention to the "linear rhythm" in Gris' work, an idea Williams admired. "No sooner has the painter drawn a line on this space," said Kahnweiler, "no sooner has he introduced a form, than a *rhythm* is established between the proportions which are thus created. It is this rhythm which constitutes the law peculiar to the newly created object, which is forever unique."

Gris stressed two other points that Williams liked. Be of your own age, he advised: the work of a great artist "has a personality stamped with the period in which he lived. His works could not be dated either before or after the time at which they were created." That fit in with Kandinsky's advice. The second point was that "in all great periods of art one senses the desire to represent a *substantial and spiritual* world."[29] [emphasis added]. Gris attempted, like Williams, to link form and spirit, or "drawing" and "impressionism," the classicism of Ed and the romanticism of Elena that were always a concern of the poet.

References to Gris sprinkle Williams' writings between 1919 and 1935. Many of the fragments and anecdotes about Gris in *A Novelette* (1928) were probably written much earlier.

> . . . he thought again of "Juan Gris" making a path through the ice. That was the name of the approaching tugboat. I have always admired and partaken of Juan Gris. Singly he says that the actual is the drawing of the face—and so the face borrowing of the drawing—by lack of copying and lack of a burden to the story—is real.

Gris' theory of creation is contrasted at one point to the "single monotonous repetition like the one hill of Eze" [Ezra Pound/Ezekial], the latter a method without wit. At one point, taking exception to the contemporary opinion that Hemingway created "lifelike" conversation, Williams created a conversation according to the hints Gris offered.

> —It must have no other purpose than the roundness and the color and repetition of grapes in a bunch, such grapes as those of Juan Gris which are related more to a ship at sea than to the human tongue. As they are.
> —As you by becoming pure design have become real. In the singleness of this epidemic which is like the singleness of Juan Gris.[30]

Conversation on a par with Hemingway's this is not, but it shows the impression Gris made on Williams, and the poet's enthusiasm for his techniques.

Williams also mentioned Gris in *The Embodiment of Knowledge*; in letters to Kenneth Burke and Kay Boyle; in *The Autobiography*; and in *Spring and All*, where he describes Gris' painting "The Open Window," and writes about the collage "Roses."

The other two cubists whose work influenced Williams began as futurists. Fernand Léger was attracted to futurism because it had established itself as the most aggressive artistic movement of its age in the least amount of time. It demanded that art be a representation of the sheer force of modern experience, in particular of speed, power, machinery, conflict and change. The first manifesto of the Futurists demanded the destruction of libraries, museums, academies and other conservatories of the static and traditional in art, an idea Williams pursued in Book Two of *Paterson*. The second more technical manifesto of 1910 proclaimed:

> The gesture which we would reproduce on the canvas shall no longer be a fixed *moment* in universal dynamism. It shall simply be the dynamic sensation itself (made eternal). . . .
> Indeed, all things move, all things run, all things are rapidly changing . . .
> A profile is never motionless before our eyes, but it constantly appears and disappears. On account of the persistence of an image upon the retina, moving objects constantly multiply themselves. . . . Thus a running horse has not four legs, but twenty, and their movements are triangular! . . .[31]

Léger's work and views were made known in America through Gertrude Stein and Walter Pach. Léger also belonged to the "Puteaux Group," with Duchamp, Picabia, and Gleizes.

Williams and Ezra Pound went to see Léger during the Williamses' 1924 trip to Europe. In early work Williams often mentioned Leger favorably. But in *The Autobiography*, the poet records that he

> went with Pound to visit Fernand Leger at his studio, a very businesslike person with little to say. His picture on the easel did not move me, looked wooden, too much the actual figure, blunted for some purpose or design, of course. I was at a loss to appraise it. I remember saying, awkwardly, that "one thumb of one hand of one figure looked dislocated. . . . Was that what he intended?"[32]

There are several other brief references to Leger in Williams' work, but none throws any light on this ambivalent assessment.

The other "painter" influenced by futurism—Duchamp—moved in a direction opposed to Leger's. Duchamp did not want any painting that was "merely retinal" or "olfactory," that seduced the viewer by his sense of sight or smell (linseed oil, turpentine). He wanted to "break up forms—to decompose them much along the lines the Cubists had done. But I wanted to go further—much further—in fact, in quite another direction altogether."[33]

Duchamp had painted in swift succession the two versions of "Nude Descending a Staircase," "The King and Queen Surrounded by Swift Nudes," "The Passage from Virgin to Bride," and finally the "Bride"—works that are static representations of dynamic action. He wanted to exhibit these in the Parisian shows in 1912, but they were considered heretical to cubism, which fast established itself as an orthodoxy.

While Duchamp's interest in movement at first seems due to the emphasis on dynamism by the futurists, this is not quite the case. Duchamp wanted to use the pictorial formula of futurism and the theoretical bent of cubism. He intended to use kineticism as the point of departure for his intellectual musings.

> I was interested in ideas—not merely in visual products. I wanted to put painting once again at the service of the mind. And my painting was, of course, at once regarded as "intellectual" and "literary" painting. It was true I was endeavoring to establish myself as far as possible from "pleasing" and "attractive" painting. That extreme was seen as literary.

One has to read his notes on Kandinsky, of all artists, to catch Duchamp's deeper drift, his concern with creating a new boundary for the emotional forces inside himself. "In tracing his lines with ruler and compass," wrote Duchamp, "Kandinsky opened to the spectator a new way of looking at painting. It was no more the lines of the unconscious, but a deliberate condemnation of the emotional: a clear transfer of thought on canvas."[34] His art often seems cold, but Duchamp had compassionate, almost communal intentions.

When he arrived in New York in 1915, Duchamp concurred with the futurists in the use of dynamism and on the worthlessness of all preceding painting, but he stood for an intellectuality that was diametrically opposed to the concern with surface that Williams was learning from other European art. His impulse was the same sensuality, but he intended to show that such a state was essentially cerebral. Williams took from him important parts of his own aesthetic, and learned incidentally that there were no secure way-stations on the avant-garde route: only constant innovation succeeded.

References to Duchamp dot Williams' papers. The first is in that "New York Letter" to *The Egoist* in 1916. There are passing references to him in letters, for Duchamp belonged to the Grantwood group, as a photograph of him at the Williamses' picnic documents. He appears in the "Prologue" to *Kora in Hell*; in *The Embodiment of Knowledge*; and in *The Autobiography*. With Arensberg's help, Williams interpreted Duchamp's theory as an increased emphasis on technique, on eroticism *and* on the unconscious, rather than as the abandonment of the overtly sensual and suppression of the unconscious. Even Arensberg's presence could not clear up much of the aesthetic confusion about Duchamp's work, the success of which depended on everyone's uncertainty.

III.   The Lesson for Poetry

"When Williams breaks a line, it is physically broken."

Hugh Kenner

In the early twenties Williams summed up his experiences with French art, and art generally, in the process of deciding what to retain and to discard if he were going to create a truly American poetry. He was attempting to emerge from "transition" into "sheer paint," and the essay "French Painting" helped him along. Comparing painting and literature, Williams found four criteria that, producing French excellence in painting, should produce American excellence in poetry.

First, the Frenchman works "with the material before him," neither limiting nor cosmically expanding his vision or subject. In his materials, he is "a kind of laborer—a workman—a maker in the plain sense."

Second, he takes his locale *de facto* as suitable for creating art. France is therefore not a magic locale, and there is no need for Americans to run off to it.

Cosmopolis is where I happen to be. The virtue of Paris is not that it is a world capital of art. Facile nonsense. It is that Paris is a French city, dominated by French ideas . . . None more local than the French: its vigor. It is the local that is the focus of work—available everywhere.

Third, only through concentration on this locale can the artist discover the purity that is universal.

In painting, the pure is design. It is painting itself. For a hundred years in France it has been predominant. It has uncovered endless "means" "borrowed" by Industrial art. But art itself exists distinct from that. It is not a dray horse carrying something for an alien purpose.[35]

Fourth, the local tradition, if it exists, is important. If depleted, it replenishes itself by attracting outsiders and by borrowing from other cultures; but it is never uncentered from itself. "The thing that Americans never seem to see is that French painting . . . is related to its own definite tradition, in its own environment and general history. . . . American painting to be of value, must have comparable relationships to its own tradition."[36]

In this context, the painter's or poet's problem reduces finally to "what to represent and how." French painting is important to Williams because "I believe it to have been for a hundred years one of the cleanest, most alert and fecund avenues of human endeavor, a positive point of intelligence from which work may depart in any direction."

Facing it, realizing that it is pigment on a surface, French painting went as far as Braque, it became a surface of paint and that is what it represented. It went to this extreme to free itself of misconceptions as to its function. . . .[37]

Williams insists that "all painting is representation and cannot be anything else." The object of the hundred years of revolution in painting was not to escape representation, but "to escape triteness, the stupidity of a loose verisimilitude." But painting was no longer illusion either; it no longer disguised its materials. It was struggling to find a new form, just as poetry was.

Williams thought that two basic, opposed forces ran through both: "One is closely clipt with ascertained bounds while the other runs away, going along from point to point, like a child picking flowers under a hedge." As the metaphor indicates, Williams recognized the second "romantic" impulse as the basis and final justification of art. It is, he continued, "the sensual thing itself in its full length and breadth . . . *earthly love,* in its own right (Paolo and Francesca) . . . celebrated to the full—free to the winds."[38] But if he gave himself over to this impulse, in Williams' case, a paralyzing muteness resulted:

> Terrible nevertheless when the wordless, emotional certainty wells up and obsesses one—driving off friends and brothers—parents and perhaps women—sometimes a whole youth of delight. It is tyrannic, obsessing— mandatory—and nothing emerges . . . this has been fled from as the destruction instead of the creation behind all . . .

The trick was to coax the "earthly love" out and yet not allow interference at this early stage. The impulses of "the sensual thing itself" had to be teased out.

> Sit down blind and start to fling the words around like pigments—try to see what nature would do under the same circumstances—let 'em go and (without thinking or caring) see where they'll lead you.[39]

Despite its irrational nature, the "sensual thing" given free rein did not necessarily result in the poetic equivalent of a de Kooning painting. The impetus contains its own principles, and by study of Matisse, Kandinsky and others, Williams learned how to work with them. When Williams, in an early letter, wrote to Pound, "I can't write fiction. All I do is try to understand something in its natural colors and shapes," he was indicating his first intimations of how to form this force. Color and shape are the first and most important areas of control that painting revealed to him. Color for Williams was an almost chemical reaction to experience. "Of any work," he wrote, "the important thing to ask is: What are its contacts? One may almost say there is nothing else of importance to be asked. There will be established thereby—what? *Color;* something in any case ponderable in the experience of other men."[40] "Color is light," wrote Williams in a late review of American naive painting. "Color is what most distinguished the artist: color was what these people wanted to brighten the walls of their houses, color to the last inch of the canvas." In this lay their admirable vitality and also their error, for their color "ran, mostly, to the very edge of the canvas as if they were afraid that something would be left out, covered the whole of their surfaces." Covering all, it diminished all, said Williams.

Color is controlled by the forms that it fills; and from such masters as Matisse and Kandinsky, Williams learned that although form was primarily a "stop" on the romantic impulse, it could also be approached from the inside—employed in the putting down to create "rhythm" or measure.

> . . . there is a tendency expressed in all the masters when their early and later works are compared to become more simple or as I believe more abstract, more general. That is he sees not trees and fence rails but horizontal and perpendicular lines, not an apple and a human face but crimson and a faint green shadow. But beyond that there are laws, even more abstract, that one rarely discovers, which may, in general, be classed as of that rhythm which bespeaks life.[41]

This rhythm, could best be gotten through a kind of contraction, a reduction without loss of essentials. This compactness was a kind of visual or poetic shorthand: "Picking out a flower or a bird in detail that becomes an abstract term of enlightenment." To include only relevant details, and to make every detail tell—as Matisse did—is the essence of compactness. These defined details, often in the foreground of both the painter and the poet, act as visual avatars of the "sensual reality" behind them.

This apprehension that form was not anathema to earthly love showed Williams where Cezanne had succeeded and where Whitman had gone astray. "The understanding of Walt Whitman is after the same nature. Verse is measure, there is no free verse. *But* the measure must be one of more trust, greater liberty, than has been permitted in the past. It must be an open formation. Whitman was never able fully to realize the significance of his structural innovations." Williams wanted, however, to protect the impulse abiding in Whitman from the neo-classical forces he saw in Eliot and Pound.

> And so about a generation ago, when under the influence of Whitman the prevalent verse forms had gone to the free verse pole, the countering cry of Order! Order! reawakened. That was the time of the new Anglo-Catholicism.

The result was predictable. Slash down the best life of the day to bring it into the lines of control.[42]

Williams' defense against overly rigid "lines of control" was a close study of futurism, from which he learned how to obtain "selection," or measure, without calcification.

After the initial ferment had occurred, Williams said a "calming" took place, during which time the recalcitrant impulse was put into form. "The grossly active agent of the moment . . . tries to break the artist from his complete position to make him serve an incomplete function," effecting a sloppy rhythm:

> This is very bad, this looseness, according to one of the major tenets of art, conscious restriction of prescribed form, and very good according to another—unconfined acceptance of experience. Close order makes for penetration. Looseness is likely to prove weakness, having too little impact upon the mind. But it is wise, always, to beware of that sort of order which cuts away too much.[43]

Thus the classical force that keeps art "closely clipt" within bounds is brought to the fore. It can be employed to prevent the "looseness" that leads to "little impact upon the mind."

This idea of the creative process is fairly traditional. But in the process of mediating between the closely clipt and "the sensual thing itself," Williams takes new steps. First, he moves the mediating process closer to the moment of "the sensual thing." Since this force most often comes to Williams through the eye, a minimum amount of time may elapse before he sets down what the eye saw, how it saw, in what order it saw, and what connection between the parts it saw. The "forming" process must occur close to the moment of vision or of imagination, so as not to lose the uncanny selection and logic of vision. Williams wrote his poems on prescription blanks, scraps of newspaper, anything at hand.

Second, new ways of "clipping" the impulse into "close order" must be invented. All "close orders" in art, Williams noticed, were based on *measures*: time in music, visual rhythm in art, and meter in poetry. All great artists, in effect, *re-measured* their arts. They showed that the old measures were dead by introducing new ones that made the subject suddenly live again. Williams proposed to "measure" his poetry from a position nearer "the sensual thing itself"; and painting suggested to him that the rhythm could be visual rather than auditory.

Those painters whom Williams admired, such as Gris (who said his art was mathematically based), measured their subjects in ways that made them more "readable," more immediate and more visceral.

> It is a multiplication of impulses that by their several flights, crossing at all eccentric angles, might enlighten. . . . it is really distressingly broken up. But so does any attack seem at the moment of engagement, multiple units crazy except when viewed as a whole.[44]

The "whole" is created by the rapid movement of the eye between parts or sequences. Just as the white of Cezanne unites the entire canvas while lending discreteness to its parts, the sunbeams of Gris and ray lines of Demuth in their "crossing and converging establish points" where the "apprehension perforates."

How could Williams do the same thing in poetry? He looked, as these artists did, to the tributary stream of futurism. The arrival of Mina Loy in Grantwood in 1916 put a poetic futurist on Williams' doorstep; the influence was magnified by Marcel Duchamp's arrival a year earlier. Williams grasped the lesson for poetry: "It grows impossible for the eye to rest long upon the object. . . ." he wrote, "Here is an escape from the old dilemma. The unessential is put aside rapidly as the eye searches between for illumination."[45]

In an essay on his Grantwood friend Marianne Moore, Williams identifies syntax as the rhythmic key. Just as the eye sees without transition, Moore "occupies the thought to its end, and goes on—without connectives," and yet "the purely stated idea has an edge exactly like a fruit or tree or a serpent." In this "occupation" of the thought until its dismissal, Williams and Moore part with Duchamp, whose futurism was intended to allude to the extensive off-canvas world of the intellect.

Williams apparently asked Moore at Grantwood how she achieved her poetic effect. "The only hint I ever got," he reported, "was that she despised connectives." He noticed when she read, however, an equalitarian attitude toward subject matter and an emphasis on speed: "A swiftness that passes without repugnance from thing to thing." And he deduced from the way speed was measured into lines an important psychological trick: ". . . one always finds her moving forward ably.

. . . Her own rhythm is particularly revealing. It does not interfere with her progress; it is the movement of the animal, it does not put itself first and ask the other to follow."[46] Rhythm, he declares, is not imposed by the poet but is an attribute of the subject, or of the poet's apprehension of the subject. Like the brushstroke of the Japanese *sumi-e* painter, it must not be interfered with by logic. This is not to say it is completely the product of the subconscious: the *sumi-e* painter spends years learning about the consistency and characteristics of his inks, learning how to produce with his brush the effect he desires. But when he is creating art, his focus is not on technical expertise but on what chance and the moment give him—false starts, drips or imperfections in the paper—and he works spontaneously with these.

Williams worked in much the same way. As close as possible to the point of their perception, he translates his visual impressions into words and lines. In keeping with his belief in strong color and in simple shape, he writes of discrete objects and solid colors whenever possible. His nouns are simple and visual, his adjectives strong, and his prepositions serve to locate objects visually. He forms his lines out of words much as Cezanne formed his scenes out of brush strokes: by painting snatches that lean on the whole for intelligibility. In their mutual dependence, his lines keep the eye moving from thing to thing, and each word seems new.

This process can be described largely in Williams' own words. "Get into the fluid state," he advises again and again, "for unless you do, all you say will be valueless."

How does one take to the imagination? One may recognize its approach in that its first stages are like those of falling asleep—which any one may observe for himself. It is likewise governed by the conditions of sleep.

At first all the images, one or many which fill the mind, are fixed. I have passed through it and studied it for years. We look at the ceiling and review the fixities of the day, the month, the year, the lifetime. Then it begins; that happy time when the image becomes broken or begins to break up, becomes a little fluid—or is affected, floats brokenly in the fluid. The rigidities yield—like ice in March, the magic month.

The flow begun, and the mind incorporating almost unconsciously the rules that it has learned, the trick is not to procrastinate, not "to involve the mind in discussion likely to last a lifetime and so withdraw the active agent from performance. The answer is, an eye to judge.—When the deer is running between the birches one doesn't get out a sextant but a gun—a flash of insight with proof of performance—and let discussion follow. If the result is a work of art the effect is permanent." The hand writes down, in the measure that practice and the impression of the subject dictate, what the eye *sees*, when, how and in the order that the eye sees it. The arrangement of the words and lines reveals the fidelity of the poet to his vision; Williams said that the lines "have a character that is parcel of the poem itself. It is in the small makeup of the lines that the character of the poem definitely comes—and beyond which it cannot go."[47]

The balance achieved in this way between "earthly love" and "closely clipt" form is precarious, Williams admits. By attending to the measuring qualities too strictly he risks losing the informing sensuality; giving himself over to the latter he fails to communicate. But this precarious poise is the only creative state for Williams. If maintained, it gives the whole poem "the impression of a passage through." It synthesizes the "closely clipt" technique and the "sensual thing itself," showing that "poetry is not limited in that way," as Williams said at the end of the essay on Moore. "It need not say either Bound without/Boundless within."[48] Like Hartpence's painting of sheer paint, it can become a poem of sheer words.

7. *The Apprentice Work*

> *"Nothing grows in the shade of great trees."*
>
> Brancusi

I. *Poems* (1909)

An anonymous reviewer for the *Rutherford American* welcomed Williams' first book, *Poems*, into the established order of verse by noting how traditional it was.

> We are reminded of that Dr. Williams of an older generation in Rutherford, whose graceful verse won Queen Victoria's praise, and, although no tie of relation exists, we can imagine how proud that gentle soul, long passed away, would have been of a Rutherford boy who is also a poet.[1]

"I'm afraid I *was* a rather sanctimonious young man," Williams later conceded. And a thoroughly Victorian one. *Poems* opens with an ode to "Innocence" and follows with another "To Simplicity." In succeeding poems the poet pursues happiness, love, and a better self. Subsequently he asks protection against "Loneliness," "Preoccupation," "Bewilderment," and "Age." He closes with a "Hymn to the Spirit of Fraternal Love" and a "Hymn to Perfection." Manifest as its faults are, this volume does at least intend to present a sequence of idealism tempered by experience.

Serious readers of Williams have generally ignored *Poems* because technically it is indistinguishable from thousands of other imitations of Keats, and Williams is considered a poet distinguished by his technique. This is to overlook that Williams' technique evolved from his mediation between his close clipt and formless selves; as wanting as the volume may be, it introduces these life-long concerns. "I appear to be stating my case right from the beginning," Williams said. "The first line in the first poem read, 'Innocence can never perish.' I really believed that then, and I really believe it now." The second poem of the book—on simplicity—is not only a theme and a characteristic but a mode of action, one Williams develops in his poetry. "And I still care about simplicity," he added, "I try to say it straight, whatever is to be said."[2]

Other poems, such as "The Folly of Preoccupation," give evidence that even in this Keatsian period Williams was inclined to look to the imperfect and the local for his inspiration; and to find there an "all pervading all perfection."

> And beasts there be with cloven nostrils born,
> And birds that tear their young, and eyeless things;
> But man more curst, more twisted, ruthless torn,
> For each of these a shriveled thousand brings.

> Yet to man's eyes, He who, all these can see,
> Constrained to throb in just apportio..d space,
> Should all-pervading all perfection be.

But the diction and technique of these poems later embarrassed Williams, who preferred to pretend that such poems as "Innocence" had never existed.

> Innocence can never perish!
> Blooms as fair in looks that cherish
> Dim remembrance of the days
> When life was young, as in the gaze
> Of youth himself all rose-yclad,
> Whom but to see is to be glad.[3]

Not until 1958 did Williams speak of this book:

> The poems are obviously young, obviously bad. I took the only form I knew, rhymed couplets, learned from Milton. The poems should be classified as sonnets, not the Shakespearian sonnet, but the sonnets of Keats and other romantic poets. There is a definite Elizabethan influence; I loved the songs in *As You Like It* and I can see plenty of echos of them in these early poems. My, but I was proud of the fifth line in "Innocense" [sic] "Of youth himself all rose-yclad"—and what a devil of a time the printer had setting it.

Other poems in the volume repeat these inversions, the 19th century diction, and the classical references: a good example is "To Simplicity."

> Thou first born nymph of any woody dell,
> Thee have I lost, O sweet Simplicity,
> All in the crooked shade and cannot tell
> Where thou art hidden; but when lacking thee
> I care no more to live; how sad, then, sad a youth am I.[4]

But there are, here and there, a few hints of Williams' later technique. In "To His Lady" Williams mixes lines phrased in standard accents with lines of rhythmic speech. This is part of a trend discerned by Linda Wagoner among the unpublished material of the 1910–12 period that shows "Williams replacing conventional stanza patterns with structures that grew from combinations of individual lines. Length of line appears to be determined by unit of thought."[5] Bits of diction also stand out. In "June," Williams' personified subject is "tricked out in loose attire," reminding the reader of Elsie. "The Quest for Happiness" contains a clever sacrilegious echo of the Lord's Prayer: "That which is to do / That will be done." The use of catalog appears in two other poems. "To His Lady" opens with a command, which although oratorical here, will later become a favorite directive tool of the poet.

Hints of Williams' imminent use of painting are less apparent. Several poems evince a strong fear of passion, carnal and emotional, however, which will later be sublimated through techniques drawing on Duchamp's ideas. In "July" Williams is attracted by the "lusty sinews primed / For deeds of passion." The natural fecundity of summer entices him, but he immediately warns himself against "thine own reckless humors." "Halt afar!" he commands July, for the month portends "mad excess." The reason Williams gives for his fear—"many a scar / Quick fancy sees there aptly pantomimed"—may reflect his shattered love affair with Charlotte Herman, or indicate a more general fear of hurt. Williams' rationale is that he prefers not to be "choked and weighted down" with passion, but to walk where "Action's brazen helmet solely shines." Further evidence that it is the hurt of passion that repulses Williams is offered by "Love," in which he declares that "Love is twain, it is not single / . . . Passion 'tis, and pain which mingle."

This tendency to dichotomize the emotions appears again in "To

My Better Self." Williams addresses his "Good, honest part" and implores it to "bestir thyself" lest "thy brother Cain surpass thee." Unable to accept some of his traits as part of a single personality, Williams seems to have struggled to subdue sensuality to platonic love, to turn his romanticism into classicism, to fit his formless emotions to social norms. These dangerous impulses, which he associated with his mother, Williams saw as an impediment to his career as a poet.

Even in 1909 Williams connected this loss through passion with Ed, with emotional restraint, and with classical forms. "Hymn to the Spirit of Fraternal Love," one of the concluding poems, was clearly written for Ed, and besides the classical equipment—shepherds, pyres, Egypt and Galilee—it equates sibling love with the cleansing effect of winter wind.

> But leave me rather bare, with crooked arms outspread
> Into the breath of winter, writhing neath her sting.[6]

One faculty Williams rates highly in *Poems* is *vision*. "A Street Market N.Y., 1908," is set in Williams' immediate environment, and although it shows no conception of how to present the visual excitement of its subject, it gives itself over in abstract language to the "Kaffir and Jew" who "Commerce for bread and brew."

> Eyes that can see
> Oh, what a rarity!
> For many a year gone by
> I've looked and nothing seen
> But ever been
> Blind to a patent wide reality.

A second poem repeats this concern with the appearance of things. "The Bewilderment of Youth" seeks to discern a noumenal unity beneath the phenomenal multiplicity of life.

> Man perplexed by detail in his youth
> O'erstares his world; views forms which myriad seem,
> Distracting here, there, each with changing gleam,
> Like fireflies pointing midnight's curtain smooth.

Thereafter, the poet develops the contrast between youth and age, but he concludes on a transcendental note that presages a riper Williams.

> But with his age at length he finds this out;
> That these but aspects are of scant things true;
> And as he ages more, more few and few
> Becomes this late engrossing, formless rout;
> Until he sees, when life is almost done
> These final few go mingling into one.[7]

All in all, however, the public must be forgiven if it bought only four copies of *Poems*, providing the author a gross income of one dollar.

II. *The Tempers* (1913)

"It was Ezra Pound who arranged for the publication of *The Tempers*," said Williams. "I paid $50 to Elkin Mathews, the English publisher, and there was a mix-up. For at least five years they kept billing me for the $50." Pound was not only the agent for, and the principal influence behind, the book, but the sole critic to take notice of it.

> God forbid that I should introduce Mr. Williams as a cosmic force. . . .
> Mr. Williams may write some very good poetry. It is not everyone of whom one can say that.
> Mr. Williams has eschewed many of the current American vices: I therefore respect him. He has not sold his soul to editors. He has not complied with their niminy-piminy restrictions.
> He apparently means what he says. He is not over-crowded with false ornament.[8]

Pound's compliments cloak the extent to which this volume embodies his influence. Pound's classical learning and precocious technical skills seemed to Williams harmonious with the feelings he had expressed to Ed in 1909. If Pound's criticism says nothing of passion, constraint or vision in Williams' work, it is because these were concerns extraneous to Pound's revolution, in which he had enlisted Williams. One expects and finds in *The Tempers* a dilute imagism, less archaic diction, more straight-forward phrasing, and some purposeful line breaks and typographical effects. Contrary to some scholarly opinion about it, this book shows progress; the advance is slight but that does not justify ignoring it.

The poems of *The Tempers* clearly show increased attention to the *sound* of the words. Williams said of *Poems* that he had been impressed by Shakespeare's songs. In this subsequent volume, he employs the lyric pattern repeatedly. "Peace on Earth," "The Fool's Song," and "The Birth of Venus" contain lyric refrains that are repeated in every stanza. Some of these are quotidian, but "Peace on Earth" startles the reader.

> The Archer is awake!
> The Swan is flying!
> Gold against blue
> An Arrow is lying.
> There is hunting in heaven—
> Sleep safe till to-morrow.
>
> The Bears are abroad!
> The Eagle is screaming!
> Gold against blue
> Their eyes are gleaming!
> Sleep!
> Sleep safe till to-morrow.

Williams' notions about the opposite title of this poem were the subject of his letter to Harriet Monroe, which was mentioned earlier.

Vernacular diction makes its first appearance in Williams' "Mezzo Forte" of this volume.

> Take that, damn you; and that!
>   And here's a rose
> To make it right again!
>   God knows
> I'm sorry, Grace; but then
> It's not my fault if you will be a cat.[9]

Playful and domestic, this poem seems closer to the later Williams than anything he had yet written. The interjections, contractions and colloquial language mask a strict scheme of rhyme and meter, however, that is an excellent example of Williams' ability to handle traditional forms.

"Portent," "Mezzo Forte," and "Ordeal" show an increased willingness to experiment with typography. The first verse of "Portent" runs:

Red cradle of the night,
   in you
     The dusky child
Sleeps fast till his might
   Shall be plied
Sinew on sinew.[10]

Unfortunately archaisms prevent other verses from being as evocative as they might.

These small advances can probably be attributed to Pound's vociferous, pestering letters. But two of the main faults of the book are also attributable to him. His hand is evident in "The Death of Franco of Cologne: His Prophecy of Beethoven," a dramatic monologue that defames Browning and Keats by combining the techniques of both. This three-page, trochaic hexameter poem even personifies musical notes as "Precious children, little gambollers!" There are also six pages of "Translations from the Spanish, El Romancero," which Pound apparently encouraged as a classicism consonant with Williams' heritage. By engaging him thus, Pound stalled Williams' process of self-discovery. Spanish was for Williams the language not only of romanticism, but of his mother, his guiding muse. "I had not yet established any sort of independent spirit," Williams said, ". . . this was a period of finding a poetry of my own. I wanted order, which I appreciated. The orderliness of verse appealed to me—as it must to any man—but even more I wanted a new order. I was positively repelled by the old order which, to me, amounted to restriction."[11]

In *The Tempers* one catches Williams at this inchoate stage. The battle that he launched against passion in *Poems* continues, but "thy brother Cain" seems to gain ground during the lulls. Obscure as it is, the poem "Ordeal" is about the inroads made by passion "Because of love's whim sacred!" Williams prays for the salamander, which according to medieval legend could live in fire, to "Swim / the winding flame / Pre-

destined to disman him [the poet] / And bring our fellow [better self]
home to us again." The winding flames represent emotion; the salamander, a mode of rescue.

"Con Brio" also deals with passion, but veils its subject in allusions to Arthurian legends. The poet broods over Lancelot's behavior in
"the high time of his deed with Guinevere."

> But, by the god of blood, what else is it that deterred
> Us all from an out and out defiance of fear
> But this same perdamnable miserliness,
> Which cries about our necks how we shall have and less
> Than we have now if we spend too wantonly?
> Bah, this sort of slither is below contempt!
>
> In the same vein we should have apple trees exempt
> From bearing anything but pink blossoms all the year,
> Fixed permanent lest their bellies wax unseemly . . .[12]

Williams decides that "Lancelot thought little and rode off," like Action
in his shining helmet, leaving the reader feeling that despite his desire to
deplore emotional miserliness, Williams doesn't quite dare to defy the
social norms. The problem for the young poet is that he lacks a form or
method of clarifying his mind when passion clouds it, but he does not
want to admit confusion. Williams faces this indecision in "Postlude,"
where in spite of classical allusions, odd elisions, and metaphysical con-
ceits, the final verse turns the poem to the present—with great impact.

> But you there beside me—
> Oh how shall I defy you,
> Who wound me in the night
> With breasts shining
> Like Venus and like Mars?
> The night that is shouting Jason
> When the loud eaves rattle
> As with waves above me
> Blue at the prow of my desire.

This technique of using the final lines to "frame" the preceding material marks Williams' apprehension of multiple points-of-view in painting. His advances become technical, as he begins to bring the painter's
techniques over into poetry.

"Certain poems in *The Tempers*," Williams said, "or perhaps just certain lines in some of the poems, show that I was beginning to turn away from the romantic. It may have been my studies in medicine; it may have been my intense feeling of Americanism; anyhow I knew that I wanted reality in my poetry and I began to try to let it speak."[13] *The Tempers* catches Williams in mid stride. Only about half of his poems are rhymed, but he still uses capital letters. He introduces strong colloquial speech, but he still makes bows to classical learning. His emotions and personae are too fluid for his own comfort, but the first crystals in the solution have appeared.

III. *Al Que Quiere!* (1917)

Williams did not publish another book until *Al Que Quiere!* in 1917. Most biographers believe that between *The Tempers* and this volume, Williams suffered the crisis he described as "a sudden resignation to existence, a despair—if you wish to call it that, but a despair which made everything a unit and at the same time a part of myself. I suppose it might be called a sort of nameless religious experience. I resigned, I gave up."[14] Forsaking his Keatsian manner, he tossed a fat sheaf of earlier poetry into the furnace.

He was contacted by Alfred Kreymborg in 1913 and invited to Grantwood, where he met Marianne Moore and later Mina Loy. The focus of these poets on form, and the influence among them of futurism, brought Williams' attention to that aspect of his own work—he needed a form to express the new "unity" he felt.

When I came to the end of a rhymthic unit (not necessarily a sentence) I ended the line. The rhythmic unit was not measured by capitals at the beginning of a line or periods within the lines. I was trying for something. The rhythmical unit usually came to me in a lyrical outburst. I wanted it to look that way on the page. I didn't go in for long lines because of my nervous nature. I couldn't. The rapid pace was the pace of speech, an excited pace because I was excited when I wrote. I was discovering, pressed by some violent mood. The lines were *short*, not studied.

Williams' poetry underwent great changes in the next three years, some with such rapidity that the sequence of innovation has remained unexplored. The result was *Al Que Quiere!*, but the poems that com-

prise the book were published earlier in *The Egoist, Poetry,* and *Others.*
Close attention to these poems and the order of their publication reveals
Williams working jaggedly but persistently to create a poetry that
"made everything a unit and at the same time part of myself." "From
this time on you can see the struggle to get a form without deforming the
language," he said.

The foundation of Williams' innovations was imagism, which
had begun as a movement around 1909, but had no impact on him until
its general popularity around 1913. It was in Grantwood, Williams
noted, that "We read Ezra's famous 'don'ts.' " His contributions to *The
Egoist* begin to show this influence in the August 15, 1914, issue, and
more expressly in the December 1, 1914, issue. Some poems of the earlier
number—"At Dawn," "A La Lune" and "The Revelation"—attempt
to strike a compromise between the old Keatsian mode and the new method, as though imagism were simply a kind of conciseness. And that may
be how Williams initially saw it: "Another characteristic of all art is its
compactness," he said. Later he explained his interest in imagism as the
consequence of his interest in painting: "I was interested in the construction of an image before the image was popular in poetry. The poem
'Metric Figure' is an example. I was influenced by my mother's still-
lifes."[15] He wrote a number of still-lifes, or imagist poems, that are read-
ily identified; but then his focus changed.

In the second set of poems (December 1, 1914), Williams published "Aux Imagistes," which rather than an imitation is an adieu. It
reveals Williams' growing distance from imagist concerns.

> I think I have never been so exalted
> As I am now by you,
> O frost bitten blossoms,
> That are unfolding your wings
> From out the envious black branches.
> Bloom quickly and make much of the sunshine
> The twigs conspire against you!
> Hear them!
> They hold you from behind!
> You shall not take wing
> Except wing by wing, brokenly,
> And yet—
> Even they
> Shall not endure for ever.[16]

The "frost bitten blossoms" is a traditional metaphor, nicely visualized for two stanzas and explained didactically in the third. Though the diction is straight-forward, the lines are all broken at the ends of the phrases and are mostly end-stopped. "The greatest problem was that I didn't know how to divide a poem into what perhaps my lyrical sense wanted. Free verse was not the answer. From the beginning I knew that the American language must shape the pattern."[17] Williams is not really concerned about imagism as a technique here. He sees it as part of the eternal cycle of revolt, like spring, against the more durable forces of death and conservatism—represented by the tree and its enmeshing twigs. Not as a group, but individually, will the imagists liberate themselves from traditional poetics, a view that draws on the ideas of Cézanne and Kandinsky. Eventually a new poetry may become easier because the old poetics appear likely to die off. Since progress is always made by individuals, Williams writes, he prefers to fight his own battle.

During this period Pound declined as Williams' mentor, largely because he was not attuned to the visual arts. When cubism and futurism were flooding New York, he adhered to a *fin de siècle* idea of painting that drew on Beardsley and classicism ("Il Cortegiano").

> In general one may say to the uninitiated curious that cubism is an art of patterns. It differs from the pre-Renaissance Italian patterns, and from the Japanese or from the pattern of art in Beardsley in that these arts treat a flat space. They make a beautiful arrangement of lines or colour shapes on a flat surface. Their first consideration is the flat space to be used.
>
> Cubism is a pattern of solids. Neither cubism nor these other arts of pattern set out primarily to mirrour natural forms. Thus one is removed from Andrea del Sarto and Carlo Dolce and from the discussions of art in Il Cortegiano. . . .[18]

The new artistic schools that Williams came into contact with all emphasized construction; Pound, after his earlier overhaul of poetic technique, now offered only classical learning. As Williams later wrote, "I was looking for a metric figure—a new measure. I couldn't find it and I couldn't wait for it. I was too impatient; I had to write."

But Pound had put Williams in touch with the chief local innovator in phrasing and rhythm, Alfred Kreymborg, who asked him to join his efforts in *Others*. Kreymborg suggested that Williams allow his line to open up, that he write out his poems in sentences and cut them into lines if necessary. Williams later noted that his poems of the ensuing

period were "written in conversational language, as spoken, but rhythmical." He said "Gulls" was an example, and added that he intended it
to be a "study in sheer observation," like the poems painted after his
mother's still lifes. In the confluence of these two intentions the reader
will see several hallmarks of Williams' mature style.

> My townspeople, beyond in the great world
> Are many with whom it were far more
> Profitable for me to live than here with you.
> These whirr about me calling, calling!
> And for my own part I answer them, loud as I can,
> But they being free, pass!
> I remain! Therefore, listen!
> For you will not soon have another singer.
> First I say this: you have seen
> The strange birds, have you not, that sometimes
> Rest upon our river in winter?
> Let them cause you to think well then of the storms
> That drive many to shelter. These things
> Do not happen without reason.[19]

This is also the first instance in which Williams addresses his neighbors.
The avant-garde movements he was sampling led him to rethink his idea
of his audience. No longer could he apostrophize to truth and beauty, as
Keats had done, before an imagined audience of like-minded fellows.
His inclusion in *Others* led him to feel distinct from the world of Rutherford, and yet profitably part of its "real world." Address to the
"townspeople" hereafter will mark such poems as "Invitation," "Slow
Movement," "A Confidence" and "Tract." In more serious poems,
though, he still addresses, either implicitly or overtly, his grandmother
/muse, who is the guiding spirit of "The Wanderer," "March," and
"January Suite."

Less obvious but more important is the prosy quality of "Gulls,"
the "opening up" that Kreymborg urged. The sentences run as long as
three or four lines, forcing Williams to use the line break as a tool. To
break lines at the ends of phrases or sentences is derivative of metered
verse, in which the end-stopped phrase is planned. Williams could no
longer ignore the line break as a tool of spontaneity, and in "Gulls" he
experiments, sometimes without success ("That sometimes/rest upon"),

and once to produce the desired crispness ("These things / Do not happen without reason").

The prosiness of his "opening up" also forced him to search for new ways of imparting energy. Direct address was his first major resort; he used commands and a tone of absolute confidence to give his lines an aggressive, driving quality. "Therefore, listen! / For you will not soon have another singer," Williams orders. He is certain that "These things / Do not happen without reason."

Williams came to know the poetry of Walter Arensberg, which introduced him to the controls, stops, and holds he could place on his expostulating drive. He cut his lines short, and piggybacked the energy of the command on sentences that continued for many lines. "Tract," which *Others* published in the fall of 1916, is a good example of Arensberg's influence.

> I will teach you
> my townspeople
> how to perform
> a funeral—
> for you have it
> over a troop
> of artists—
> unless one should
> scour the world—
> you have the ground sense
> necessary.
> See! the hearse leads
> I begin with
> a design for a hearse.

An example of his mature use of this technique is "Chicory and Daisies," in which he addresses the flowers:

> Lift your flowers
> on bitter stems
> chicory!
> Lift them up
> out of the scorched ground!
> Bear no foliage
> but give yourself
> wholly to that![20]

Just as he incorporated imagism into his own concern for the visual, Williams digested Arensberg's concern with directive and line break. The poetry that resulted from this advance is impressive chiefly for its energy, its insistence, and its prepossessing sense of self.

At this point Mina Loy played an important and underestimated role in Williams' poetry. She showed him how to develop that quality which Kreymborg hinted was so important to Williams: "the art of conversation with a painstaking, self-conscious *tempo*." Hearing Loy read, and then reading what she had written, Williams saw that the impression of speed, imparted by syntax, was the base of it all. Once this sensation was established, the poet could order a pause, strike off at a new angle, introduce an opposed image, or make a parallel, while the massed momentum of the verse carried the reader through the changes. Williams' command of futurist tactics is shown by "Dawn," first published in *Al Que Quiere!*

Ecstatic bird songs pound
the hollow vastness of the sky
with metallic clinkings—
beating color up into it
at a far edge,—beating it, beating it
with rising, triumphant ardor,—
stirring it into warmth,
quickening in it a spreading change,—
bursting wildly against it as
dividing the horizon, a heavy sun
lifts himself—is lifted—
bit by bit above the edge
of things,—runs free at last
out into the open—! lumbering
glorified in full release upward—

                            songs cease.[21]

As Williams noted in a letter about that time, "My liking is for an unimpeded thrust right through a poem from the beginning to the end, without regard to formal arrangements." The omission of capitals, the minimal punctuation, and the use of a series of parallel participles are techniques that Loy popularized in the *Others* group. These characteristics do not appear in Williams' work until the publication of "Dedication for a Plot of Ground" and "Touché" in *Others* in 1916. In the second poem, Williams attempts to keep the sense of physical energy present by attributing it to the subject, "the murderer's little daughter."

Her skinny little arms
wrap themselves
this way then that
reversely about her body!
Nervously
she crushes her straw hat
about her eyes
and tilts her head
to deepen the shadow—
smiling excitedly.

This poem ends when the poet asks himself,

Why has she chosen me
for the knife
that darts along her smile?[22]

The lack of punctuation in this poem is particularly important. Williams had discovered that verbs controlled the sense of motion, and that parallelism could be used to channel it, but most of his lines were syntactically end-stopped, ignoring the potential that continuous enjambment offered. In some poems, however, he began to use end-stopped lines to portray events in a series, and enjambment to depict those happening concurrently. "He forces meaning to continue by placing conjunctions at the ends of lines and by separating subjects from verbs, objects from prepositions," remarks Linda Wagoner.[23] But even scholars who appreciate this advance in "Touché" denigrate the ending as a "tag." This is to ignore a major structural change in Williams' poetry.

In the period preceding 1913, Williams was a dedicated and tireless sonneteer. He testifies in *I Wanted to Write a Poem* that the bulk of the poems he committed to the furnace flames were sonnets and imitations of Keats. He was looking for a form and as he said, "The greatest problem was that I didn't know how to divide a poem into what perhaps my lyrical sense wanted." The sonnet was the form in his repertoire with which Williams again and again synthesized his experiments. His use of imagism, his commands to the reader, and his adaptations of futuristic innovations were all grafted on the stock of the sonnet. His steps are easily traced in "Offering," which appeared in *The Egoist* on the eve of Williams' involvement with *Others*.

> *As* the hedges, clipt and even,
> That parallel the common way—
> And upon one side the hedges
> And upon one side bare trees—
> *As* these hedges bear the dried leaves
> That have fallen from spent branches,—
> Having caught them in mid air—
> And hold them yet awhile
> That they may not be so soon
> Jostled about and tramped on—
>
> The red, the yellow, the purple—blues—
> *So* do my words catch and bear
> Both leaves and flowers that are fallen—
> In all places before the feet
> Of the passing many—to bear them
> *Yet* awhile before they are trodden.[24]
>
> [emphasis added]

The sentence structure and syntax of this poem derive from the sonnet, though the spacing of the stanzas and the continuity of the sentence act to obscure it. The poem begins with an "As" clause that runs four lines (and includes two parallel sub-clauses), and then reiterates its subject in a second "as" clause that runs several lines. Had Williams added a third "as" clause, no one would have missed the echo of the English sonnet. To avoid this he split the poem and began the second part with a catalog of colors. At this point he fell into something like the final six lines of an Italian sonnet: the sestet that presents the moral or lesson to be garnered from the preceding section, the wisdom secured from the flux of reality. Lacking confidence in his ability to tie down this knowledge, Williams repeats his intent in the final two lines— reminding the reader of the couplet that closes the English sonnet.

Other modifications Williams tried on the sonnet-form can be seen in "Revelation" and "A Confidence." A more successful and less apparent example, "Pastoral," succeeds by using only the structure of

the sonnet, to which Williams adds a homiletic tone common to Eliza-
bethan verse. The best known and most successful poem in this mode,
however, is "Danse Russe," published by *Others* in December, 1916.

> If when my wife is sleeping
> and the baby and Kathleen
> are sleeping
> and the sun is a flame-white disc
> in silken mists,—
> if I in my north room
> dance naked, grotesquely
> before my mirror
> waving my shirt round my head
> and singing softly to myself:
> "I am lonely, lonely,
> I was born to be lonely,
> I am best so."
> If I admire my arms, my face,
> my shoulders, flanks, buttocks
> against the yellow drawn shades,—
> Who shall say I am not
> the happy genius of my household?[25]

The three phrases beginning "If" and the concluding couplet need no
further comment. It is interesting, though, that the poet, waving his
shirt around his head before the drawn yellow shades becomes himself
the image of the sun—"A flame-white disc / in silken mists"—just like
the painter in Williams' essay "A Matisse." His self-absorption is inno-
cent, but intended, and though it has the result of turning him into a
"happy genius," one sees how Williams could become interested in the
self-conscious narcissism of Marcel Duchamp.

Williams did not pause here to explore or to consolidate his innovations. His struggle was still blind and grasping. As he wrote later,
"The stanzas are short; I was searching for some formal arrangement of
the lines, perhaps a stanzaic form. I have always had something to say
and the sheer sense of what is spoken seemed to me all important, yet I
knew the poem must have shape."

From his friends Demuth and Hartley, and from the concerns of
Arensberg and Duchamp, Williams was becoming aware of Picasso,

Braque, Leger and Gris. From them he discovered point-of-view, although his motivation was different from what one would suppose, and his employment of their techniques more limited than previously thought. An unpublished essay, "What is the Use of Poetry?" throws light on the potential Williams saw. He related multiple points-of-view to the quick-cutting of cinema.

> Some intimation of the character of this force may be discovered, I think, in the much greater interest felt in the snatches of pictures shown at the movies between the regular films to advertise pictures coming the following week—than the regular features themselves. The experience is of something much more vivid and much more sensual than the entire film will be. It is because the banality of the sequence is removed.
>
> The bits exceed the whole in interest—or to be correct let us not say in interest—since interest is too variable a quantity—but in vividness, in sensual reality—an intimation of the very good reason for the brokenness of some modern compositions.[26]

The first poem in which Williams takes any notice of cubism is "Woman Walking," which opens with a description that emphasizes visual flatness, the planes of the objects seen, and the edges and angles of their juxtaposition. After nine lines, however, the poet dismisses this emphasis in favor of the overt sexuality of the woman.

> An oblique cloud of purple smoke
> Across a milky silhouette
> Of house sides and tiny trees
> That ends in a saw edge
> Of mist-covered trees
> On a sheet of grey sky
> To the left, a single tree;
> To the right, jutting in,
> A dark crimson corner of roof.
> God knows I'm tired of it all.
> And God knows what a blessing it is
> To see you in the street again,
> Powerful woman.

This is hardly the immediate, uncritical embrace of cubism by Williams that some scholars propose. That contention is based on three poems:

"To a Solitary Disciple," "Young Housewife," and "Spring Strains."
No more than a fair case can be made for the first poem, published in
Others in 1916.

Rather notice, mon cher,
that the moon is
tilted above
the point of the steeple
than that its color
is shell-pink.

Rather observe
that it is early morning
than that the sky
is smooth
as a turquoise.

Rather grasp
how the dark
converging lines
of the steeple
meet at the pinnacle—;
perceive how
its little ornament
tries to stop them!

See how it fails!
See how the converging lines
of the hexagonal spire
escape upward
receding, dividing!
—sepals
that guard and contain
the flower!

Observe
how motionless
the eaten moon
lies in the protecting lines.

It is true:
in the light colors
of the morning
brown-stone and slate
shine orange and dark blue.

but observe
the oppressive weight
of the squat edifice!
observe
the jasmine lightness
of the moon![27]

Williams' concern here is to defend the qualities that inspire art from assault by dogmatic doctrines, whether in the form of church or that which bruises the flowers. Typifying Williams' modification of the sonnet, this poem employs three parallel clauses: "Rather notice . . ." "Rather observe . . ." and "Rather grasp . . . ." The modifying "rather" ameliorates the explicit command of the verb, but these three sentences are followed by three more naked commands: "See . . ." "See . . ." and "Observe . . . ." A section functioning as the "tag" begins at "It is true:"

The usual interpretation is that the poet is directing a "solitary disciple" of impressionism, who writes poems that are the verbal equivalents of a Renoir or a Monet, to pay attention to line, mass, plane and location—the tools of cubism. One of Charles Demuth's numerous paintings of the Lutheran Church of the Holy Trinity in Lancaster, Pennsylvania, seems to be the model for the steeple described; but one scholar has proposed that the poem concerns the widely anthologized "Ballade a la Lune" by the French poet Alfred de Musset. His poem begins

C'était, dans la nuit brune,
Sur le clocher jauni,
  La lune
Comme un point sur un i.[28]

This striking metaphor, and the deterioration of the rest of de Musset's poem into romantic language, might well have caught Williams' eye. But the purpose of his poem goes beyond visual transcription or simple didacticism.

The steeple is one of Williams' private symbols—and he here attempts to imbue it with communicable meaning. Like the prow of the boat ("The Wanderer," "January Suite") and the canted, receding beams of the attic ("The Attic which is Desire," "Postlude") the steeple-shape represented for Williams an ineffable force. What he wants to demonstrate is that these forces lie beyond the ken of "isms" or schools. ("its little ornament / tries to stop them! / See how it fails!") As Williams writes elsewhere, "Soon we shall have a wakening against all schools and knowledge will begin again. . . . all knowledge vanishing into the apex of a hollow cone—spinning off."[29]

The controversy over whether the steeple represents impressionism or cubism is itself antithetical to the "moon," toward which the steeple reaches and which stands for the forces Williams is trying to revivify. In the "tag" section Williams does not deny the attraction of impressionistic color in describing the steeple, but rather the "oppressive" mass of the lower church, its conservatism and function as a "school." Above both parts and appealing to the sense of smell, is the kinaesthetic "jasmine lightness / of the moon." The poem is more thematically complex than scholars have recognized.

On the other hand, "The Young Housewife," was published in the last *Others* of 1916 and is clearly an experiment in point of view.

At ten A.M. the young housewife
moves about in négligé behind
the wooden walls of her husband's house.
I pass solitary in my car.

Then again she comes to the curb
to call the ice-man, fish-man, and stands
shy, uncorseted, tucking in
stray ends of hair, and I compare her
to a fallen leaf.

The noiseless wheels of my car
rush with a crackling sound over
dried leaves as I bow and pass smiling.[30]

Just as the cubist painters present the subject simultaneously from different points of view, Williams imagines the housewife from three vantages. First she is inside out of his view when he passes in his car. Then she is on the curb, his location is undefined, though he seems to be in his car, and he compares her to a leaf. In the third view her location is undetermined and the poet is in his car, which he drives over the "dried leaves" to unite the final images ("car" and "leaf") of the preceding stanzas. The "noiseless" imaginary nature of the car wheels, and the officious bowing of the poet alert the reader to the playful intent of the poem. In this exercise Williams shows his persistence in adapting artistic techniques, employing point-of-view to achieve unity of metaphor.

Most of the putatively "cubist" poems of this period are so modified that the label is arguable. "Love Song" and "Metric Figure" are usually offered as examples, although the latter (as mentioned previously) Williams considered an exercise in construction of a *new meter*. "Spring Strains" has been repeatedly analyzed for its cubism, but is clearly in the debt of futurism, and in fact participates in the parodying of cubism by futurism.

In a tissue thin monotone of blue-grey buds
crowded erect with desire against
the sky—
            tense blue-grey twigs
slenderly anchoring them down, drawing
them in—
            Two blue-grey birds chasing
a third struggle in circles, angles,
swift convergings to a point that bursts
instantly![31]

This action is not the static state preferred by cubism. True, the emphasis on the monochromatic "blue greys" echoes the drab colors of early cubism, but the inwardly spiraling chase of the birds points to the futurist Giacomo Balla's "Flight of the Swifts." In the longer second stanza Williams shouts encouragement to his composition ("Hold hard, rigid jointed trees!") and employs almost theatrical diction: "Sucking in the sky," "plastering itself against them," "one puckering hold!" and "Sticks through!" His final quatrain,

On a tissue-thin monotone of blue-grey buds
two blue-grey birds, chasing a third,
at full cry! Now they are
flung outward and up—disappearing completely!

shows that dynamic subjects are best captured by the dynamic techniques of futurism.

The passing of Williams' cubist interest was speeded by Arensberg and Duchamp. The Frenchman's intellectualism rubbed off a bit, and Williams began to create obscure titles ("Keller Gegen Dom," "Canthara," and "K. McD.") as well as teasers ("To a Solitary Disciple," "Rendezvous," "Sub Terra," "Rootbuds," and "Portrait of a Woman in Bed"). Duchamp's influence shows itself in another way; in the time of his appearances at Grantwood, Williams attempts frequently either to freeze a moment in time ("Offering") or to render a dynamic moment in a static composition ("Dawn"), which were Duchamp's two principal concerns at the time.

There is little doubt that Williams was also learning something from Duchamp about the erotic in art. In a 1914 poem, "Transitional," Williams had difficulty reconciling his sensuality with his poetic voice.

> First he said:
> It is the woman in us
> That makes us write:
> Let us acknowledge it,
> Men would be silent.
> We are not men.
> Therefore we can speak
> And be conscious
> (O' the two sides)
> Unbent by the sensual,
> As fits accuracy.

Williams' passion is still channeled in this period into Keatsian subterfuges. Such poems as "Sub Terra," "Love Song," and "Naked" dare not imply, much less name, their subjects. The first break in this reticence is "Ogre," published in *Others* in the year that Duchamp arrived.

> Sweet child,
> Little girl with well shaped legs
> You cannot touch the thoughts
> I put over and under and around you.
> This is fortunate for they would
> Burn you to an ash otherwise.[32]

Williams disclaims and censures his speaker with a playfully condemnatory title. But in "Virtue," written a little later, Williams meets his sensuality head on.

> Now? Why—
> whirlpools of
> orange and purple flame
> feather twists of chrome
> on a green ground
> funneling down upon
> the steaming phallus-head
> of the mad sun himself—
> blackened crimson!
>   Now?
> Why—
> it is the smile of her
> the smell of her
> the vulgar inviting mouth of her
> It is—Oh, nothing new
> nothing that lasts
> an eternity, nothing worth
> putting out at interest,
> nothing—
> but the fixing of an eye
> concretely upon emptiness![33]

The phallus is now equated with sun and with color, which were earlier equated with the poet. This is an intuitionalist, sensual nexus of values. "Why now?" Williams asks in response to the sudden rise of sensuality. The cause, however, is nothing seen, for the erotic is "the fixing of an eye / concretely upon emptiness." In a final stanza, to dispel passion Williams fixes his eye on concrete things, cataloging a multitude of men. This is puzzling at first, until one realizes that this visual exercise expends the energy of the forces raised earlier.

This poem and a few others in *Al Que Quiere!* give the reader his first glimpse of the mature Williams. Such a poem as "Winter Sunset" contains all the hallmarks of his style: short lines without capitals, an emphasis on vision and color, a scene constructed for the eye (in this case in layers), the displacement of objects from the usual sense (the cloud becomes a stone), and an "unimpeded grammatical thrust right through the poem."

134

Then I raised my head
and stared out over
the blue February waste
to the blue bank of hill
with stars on it
in strings and festoons—
but above that:
one opaque
stone of a cloud
just on the hill
left and right
as far as I could see;
and above that
a red streak, then
icy blue sky!
It was a fearful thing
to come into a man's heart
at that time; that stone
over the little blinking stars
they'd set there.

This poem is structured, like a sonnet, and yet it makes a picture, like "A Street Market N.Y., 1908" Williams' aim of uniqueness, and the visual way he conceived of it, remind one of that curious figure on the cover of *Al Que Quiere!*

"To me the design looked like a dancer, and the effect of the dancer was very important—a natural, completely individual pattern," said Williams.[34]

8. Kora in Hell *and Duchamp*

For a year I used to come home and no matter how late it was before I went to bed I would write something. And I kept writing, writing, even if it were only a few words, and at the end of the year there were 365 entries. Even if I had nothing in my mind at all I put something down, and, as may be expected, some of the entries were pure nonsense and were rejected when the time for publication came. They were a reflection of the day's happenings more or less, and what I had had to do with them.

Williams

I.

The status of *Kora in Hell* as one of the more garbled, undecipherable poems of the early twentieth century leads one to wonder whether readers have contributed to it all that they might. The "improvisations" have been found by Erich Auerbach to be "fraught with background." Biographer Reed Whittemore writes that *"Kora* had to be murked" in obscurity because that period of Williams' life was rather seamy.[1] The note of uneasiness in both comments epitomizes a more general reader distrust. Despite its classical allusions, its references to Pound, Moore and Stevens, and its hints of deliberate schema, *Kora* seems to lack structure and organizing ideas. It won't come clean in a satisfying literary way.

Much of Williams' genius, however, is keyed to the world of painting, and from the first page *Kora* is a book in which Williams asserts the importance and shows the influence of art. He made a special effort for the second time to get appropriate illustrations. In 1909 he had asked Ed to design a cover. This time he rebelled against classicism; the frontispiece was by a young innovator in art.

I had seen a drawing by Stuart Davis, a young artist I had never met, which

I wanted reproduced in my book because it was as close as possible to my idea of the Improvisations. It was, graphically, exactly what I was trying to do in words, put the Improvisations down as a unit on the page. You must remember I had a strong inclination all my life to be a painter. Under different circumstances I would rather have been a painter than to bother with all these goddamn words. . . . Anyhow, Floss and I went to Gloucester and got permission from Stuart Davis to use his art—an impressionistic view of the simultaneous.[2]

Davis was proud to have been associated with *Kora*. On receiving his copy, he wrote to Williams,

. . . the fact that the expected word doesn't keep dripping on the skull continually is sufficient to recommend it. I see in it fluidity as opposed to stagnation of presentation. It opens a field of possibilities. To me it suggests a development toward word against word without any impediments of story, poetic beauty or anything at all except word clash and sequence. . . . Best of all the book does not suggest any of the modern poets with whom I am familiar. I like the book and am glad to be associated with it.[3]

The cover was another piece of art, showing "the ovum in the act of being impregnated, surrounded by spermatozoa, all trying to get in but only one successfully."

I myself improvised the idea, seeing, symbolically, a design using sperms of various breeds, various races let's say, and directed the artist to vary the shadings from white to gray to black. The cell accepts one sperm—that is the beginning of life. I was feeling fresh and I thought it was a beautiful thing and I wanted the world to see it.[4]

The diction Williams used in discussing the artwork indicates important debts; he was rejecting all the movements in favor of a personal style. "An impressionistic view of the simultaneous" blends impressionism and futurism, the former blurring and bathing in atmosphere the speed and modernity of the latter. "I myself improvised the idea" denoting a theory derived from Kandinsky, by which the flux of emotion is transmuted into "design." It was Williams' genius to equate the "syntax" of poetry with the "composition" in Kandinsky's theory.

Williams took a great stride in *Kora* by attending closely to the lessons painting offered, by approaching the "sheer paint" of words. His method of composition in this book follows his creative theory very closely. He begins in a "fluid state."

In this reverie, Williams experiences two tendencies that he describes in one of the improvisations: "Imagining himself to be two persons he eases his mind by putting his burdens upon one while the other takes what pleasure there is before him." To his "classicist" self Williams assigns his conscience and responsibilities, while the romantic self goes roaming. But the former is not silent, for within Williams there is a constant struggle to *regain* control.

This conflict is evident in some of the sequences, which consist of two and sometimes three improvisations counterpointed. In the clearest example of his classic impulse, Williams complains of a lack of consolidation in romanticism.

> Thinking to have brought all to one level the man finds his foot striking through where he had thought rock to be and stands firm where he had experienced only a bog hitherto. At a loss to free himself from bewilderment at this discovery he puts off the caress of the imagination.[5]

The romantic in Williams, however, enjoys the surreal meld of imagination and reality, and moves aggressively and confidently from one association to the next.

Sometimes, as in the twelfth sequence, Williams arranges these voices in opposition. The first improvisation is the classicist's; the third, the surrealist's. The "interpretation" in the middle describes the "secret delight of the onlooker who is thus regaled by the spectacle of two exquisite and divergent natures playing one against another."

The most distinctive feature of *Kora*'s technique is the division of the one nature (improvisation) from the other (interpretation). Williams explained the genesis of his method in a 1958 interview:

> I was groping around to find a way to include the interpretations when I came upon a book Pound had left in the house, *Varie Poesie* dell' Abate Pietro Metastasio, Venice, 1795. I took the method used by the Abbot of drawing a line to separate my material. First came the Improvisations, those more or less incomprehensible statements, then the dividing line, and in italics, my interpretations of the Improvisations. The book was broken into chapters, headed by Roman numerals; each improvisation numbered in Arabic.[6]

In one sense the use of the line between the parts continues the "tag" function in earlier poems; it is a separation of the wisdom, or "interpretation" that framed the preceding lines, from the body of lines. Williams isolated the romantic impulse and indulged it, then loosed his classical knowledge to interpret it. The separation of the impulses by a *line* has more psychic significance than actual. In separating emotional *mass* from interpretive comment he was identifying his root instincts. The process was probably reinforced by Williams' close friendship with Hartley, whose work employed emphatic line to limit and define the emotion evoked by bold color masses.

Other technical innovations were typographic and derived from the futurism of the *Others* group, most notably the omission of punctuation, and the spacing of words on a line to indicate pauses. *"Most important,"* Williams wrote to Edmund Brown, his printer, "Set up the improvisations exactly as written. Do *not* add to or alter punctuation. Where there is a gap between two words—leave it." The influence of futurism appears repeatedly.

> By the brokenness of his composition the poet makes himself master of a certain weapon. . . . The speed of the emotions is sometimes such that thrashing about in a thin exaltation of despair many matters are touched but not held, more often broken by the contact.[7]

Sequence III reflects Loy's word spacing.

> So far away   August   green as it yet is.   They say the sun still comes up o'mornings and it's harvest moon now. Always one leaf at   the   peak twig swirling, swirling and apples rotting in the ditch.

When he omits punctuation, Williams composes by counterpointing his pauses against the flow of the syntax of his sentence. In another improvisation, which alludes to Pound, Williams blends this technique with punctuation that reasserts itself as the emotions are brought under control.

> Some fifteen years   we'll say   I served this friend, was his valet, nurse, physician, fool and master: nothing too menial, to say the least. Enough of that: so.[8]

The concluding colon refers to a similar conclusion in "Canto 1," where Pound loses control of his translation and reasserts it by resorting to an open-ended colon.

The difficulty of *Kora*'s text *per se* puts off many readers, and leads others to assume that it is "surreal" or lacks organization. In the prologue however, Williams warns us against making the improvisations more obdurate than necessary by reading them as literary documents. He emphasizes that "instability" is characteristic of his mother and himself—the hint is that we ought to think about the way French painters have dealt with the insubstantial world. "The fiber of things is a thin jelly," Williams writes. "The virtue of strength lies not in the grossness of the fiber but in the fiber itself. A poem is tough by no quality it borrows from a *logical* recital of events." [emphasis added.]

Through such comments and his anecdotes about Arensberg and Duchamp, Williams points us toward Marcel Duchamp's ideas. Kandinsky provides the technique of the foreground, but Duchamp provides the informing theory of the background. With a primer on Duchampian novelty and eroticism in hand, one may penetrate the fraughting and murking that have so befogged *Kora in Hell*.

First one must concede that the organization of *Kora* is loose. It begins with a long "prologue" of twenty-four pages. There follow fifty-two pages containing twenty-seven improvisations, some of which have four or five sections when their interpretations are counted. The book is also recapitulative: the points Williams makes were originally scattered in the "data mass" of the improvisations, so he summarized them first in anecdotal form and then in didactic form. The argument can be followed by attending to the prologue, with examples and clarifications drawn from the improvisations themselves.

II.

Finally, when it was all done, I thought of the Prologue which is really an Epilogue. I felt I had to give some indication of myself to the people I knew; sound off, tell the world—especially my intimate friends—how I felt about them.

Williams

It is beyond cavil that an important function of the Prologue is "to sound off." Williams uses it to declare his independence, announce his loyalties, and air his gripes. But he also writes clearly for the first time of the link between his mother, romanticism, imagination and his own poetic abilities; and he includes his "Vortex," the basic elements of a theory of the imagination.

The Prologue opens with a number of anecdotes that appear at first unconnected. Williams writes about his mother, for him the archetype of romanticism, and her "fear of being lost" in Rome, a city to whose spirit he returns later. Then, seemingly without reason, he turns to the fact that "there has always been a disreputable man of picturesque personality associated with" her. Underlying the account of his mother's charity to "William" and to "Tom O'Rourke" is a coyness that hints of the erotic. Elena shares with these free spirits "the most rollicking spirit of comradeship." She is explained as an older, purer form of the same innocence that Williams always maintains is his own animating characteristic; she is "incapable of learning from benefit or disaster." The link is strengthened by Williams' identification of her with Eden, and extended so that she becomes *synonymous* with the imagination: "She might be living in Eden. And indeed she is, an impoverished, ravished Eden but one indestructible as the imagination itself." The Prologue then seems to jump, with quotations from Villon and Carl Sandburg. Actually Williams is about to illustrate, using his mother as an analogue, the chief feature he values in her imagination: that it takes up its home anywhere. The material of the imagination, like the funeral Williams and Elena see from the window, is less important than "the dark turn at the end" by which "she raises her story out of the commonplace." Elena "loses her bearings or associates with some disreputable person or translates a dark mood. She is a creature of great imagination. . . . by this power she still breaks life between her fingers."[9] "Seeing the thing itself" with intensity causes, though Williams does not yet tell *how*, an erotic feeling and an ensuing "translation" via the imagination that is liberating.

Searching the "data base" of the improvisations, one finds several helpful references to Elena. Some of them anticipate her *dichos* in *Yes, Mrs. Williams*. Spanish rolls playfully off her tongue: "Baaaa! Ba-ha-ha-ha-ha-ha Bebe esa purga. It is the goats of Santo Domingo talking. Bebe esa purga! Bebeeesaburga! And the answer is "Yo no lo quiero beber! Yonoloquierobeber!" But the interpretations attached to these appearances are never innocuous; on the above Williams comments:

"The empty form drops from a cloud, like a gourd from a vine; into it the poet packs his phallus-like argument."

Sometimes Williams wants to imitate his mother's "voice," since she is his spiritual progenitor.

> They said I could not put the flower back into the stem nor win roses upon dead briars and I like a fool believed them. But it's all right now. Weave away, dead fingers, the darkies are dancing in Mayaguez—all but one with the sore heel and sugar cane will soon be high enough to romp through.

The interpretation makes this role-playing explicit: "A woman on the verge of growing old kindles in the mind of her son a certain curiosity which spinning upon itself catches the woman herself in its wheel." In other improvisations, using her voice, Williams comments on himself:

> I like the boy. It's years back I began to draw him to me—or he was pushed my way by the others. . . . How the flanks flutter and the heart races. Imagination! That's the worm in the apple. What if it run to paralyses and blind fires, here's sense loose in a world set on foundations. Blame buzzards for the eyes they have.[10]

"Buzzards," Williams notes below the line, "have eyes of a power equal to that of the eagles," although their vision scans the local rather than the lofty. This is the first explicit linkage of Elena, imagination and *vision*.

As if this were a false start on the prologue, Williams attacks from another angle. He tells of "taking lunch with Walter Arensberg," and querying him on the modern painters, "those roughly classed at that time as 'cubists': Gleizes, Man Ray, Demuth, Duchamp. . . . " Arensberg responds "by saying that the only way man differed from every other creature was in his ability to improvise novelty" and in painting anything that is truly a fresh creation is good work. Arensberg illustrates his theory by reference to Duchamp's "Nude Descending a Staircase," and to its retouched photographic copy. Williams wishes to show the reader the similarity between his mother, imagination, and the theory of Duchamp and Arensberg. Using his mother as his representative of the imaginative/romantic, Williams is building outward from his inner concerns to those abstract positions he sees that are compatible, placing himself generally in the futurist camp.

Several paragraphs of praise for Arensberg's activities as a Maecenas follow; then Williams makes a benign but important digression, discussing naive and primitive American art. He wishes that Arensberg "had my opportunity for prying into jaded households where the paintings of Mama's and Papa's flowertime still hang on the walls." This may seem like a note of dissent, but Williams has in mind the sequence that led to cubism in France. He is looking for a domestic equivalent of Picasso's African masks and prehistoric Iberian sculptures. He is acutely aware of the *French* nature of cubism, and wants an American tradition encompassing "prehistoric rock paintings" of "galloping bisons and stags."

The importance of Walter Arensberg is less visible than warranted, though. The techniques Arensberg employed in his poetry appear frequently.

> Where does this downhill turn up again? Driven to the wall you'd put claws to your toes and make a ladder of smooth bricks. But this, this scene shifting that has clipped the cloud's stems and left them to flutter down; heaped them at the feet, so much hay, so much bull's fodder. (*Au moins*, you cannot deny you have the clouds to grasp now, *mon ami!*)[11]

The lapse into French, the reference to "scene shifting," and the allusion to a wall that hides something and needs to be surmounted, (Williams often connects this to memories of Demuth) all allude to the Arensberg circle. In another improvisation, Williams pokes fun at its concerns.

> Security, solidity—we laugh at them in our clique. It is tobacco to us, the side of her leg. We put it in our samovar and make tea of it. You see the stuff has possibilities. You think you are opposing the rich but the truth is you're turning toward authority yourself, to say nothing of religion. No, I do not say it means nothing. Why everything is nicely adjusted to our moods. But I would rather describe to you what I saw in the kitchen last night—overlook the girl a moment:[12]

The intermittently mentioned "girl" is the one whose seduction by a group of men Williams recalls in *The Autobiography* (pp. 140-41), and "the conversation nicely adjusted to our moods" contrasts with Rutherford realities.

The shift in the Prologue to "Fontaine," the urinal that created such a fuss at the 1917 Independents Show, is another apparent leap. The transition lies in the fact that both the prehistoric pictograph artists and Duchamp share with Helena that ability to take "whatever is before her" and to understand it as "sufficient unto itself and so to be valued."

At this point Williams feels he has pointed out enough of a position, and its practitioners—Helena, Duchamp, Arensberg, Man Ray, Gleizes, Demuth, Loy—to stop and make some distinctions. "In contradistinction to this south, Marianne Moore's statement to me . . . sets up a north: 'My work has come to have just one quality of value in it: I will not touch or have to do with those things which I detest.' "

Williams intimates that Moore's fastidiousness contains a nascent classicism. It excludes the local and aligns itself with classicism in placing strictures on technique, subject, emotional range and expression. Williams admires Moore, but in contrasting her work with that of Mina Loy, whose frank erotics captivated him, he establishes an important difference.

Even more distant, Williams wants the reader to know, is Ezra Pound, whose pernicious influence is described in several pages of humorous anecdote. So masterfully does Williams place Pound in his literary past—spinning out quintessential Pound stories as he goes—that one almost misses a deeper, more serious point: the emotional poverty of Pound's classicism. Even Williams' father is permitted to deliver a "triumphant and crushing rejoinder" to Pound's classical imitations. In Pound's letter ("My dear boy you have never felt the woop of the PEEraries. You have never seen the projecting and protuberant Mts. of the Sierra Nevada. WOT can you know of the country?"), Pound tries to include Williams in the camp of "foreigners" by merit of his Spanish blood. But the quote with which Pound concludes embodies the stultifying classicism that Williams warns against. It posits a "cosmopolitisme littéraire" whose enemy is "L'amour excessif d'une patrie," and concludes by slighting the archetype Spanish romantic heroes—El Cid and Don Juan—because professors teach them poorly, an irony Williams intends to be self-evident. Only one improvisation *per se* concerns Pound (VIII-1), and Williams' interpretation dismisses Pound's concerns as "great dudgeon over small profit."[13]

Classicism itself is the next topic of his prologue. "I like to think of the Greeks as setting out for the colonies in Sicily and the Italian peninsula," writes Williams. Ignoring Greece, Williams compares

Rome and America. "The ferment was always richer in Rome, the dispersive explosion was always nearer, the influence carried further and remained hot longer." The point is not to cancel Williams' debt to classicism or to Pound, but to announce the beginning of a new stage in his own development: "Hellenism, especially of the modern sort, is too staid, too chilly, too little fecundative to impregnate my world."[14] The gestative diction deliberately alludes to the cover art of the book—Pound being one of the unfortunate spermatozoa.

The sort of ovum receptive to Pound's advances is Hilda Doolittle, the subject of the following section. Williams includes a letter from Pound's mistress in which she explains why she wants to "delete from your poem all the flippancies." She compares the poem "March" to her favorite in Williams' preceding work, the first, more classic section of "Postlude." She writes, "I feel in the hey-ding-a-ding touch running through your poem a derivative tendency which, to me, is not *you*—not your very self." Manuscripts of the poem in the Yale Beinecke Library show that HD and Pound did, in fact, edit out several lines with the refrain "Hey-ding-a-ding!" along with many other lines that make it apparent Williams wanted to give the poem an ironic, dismissive tone. What eventually appeared as "March"—and concerned Ashur-banipal, the pyramids and Fiesole (which he visited with Ed)—was material at which Williams wanted to poke a little fun, to lighten up.

"The hey-ding-a-ding touch," responded Williams, "*was* derivative, but it filled a gap that I did not know how better to fill at the time. It might be said that that touch is the prototype of these improvisations." A reader acquainted with Duchamp's notion of irony as a tool to avoid "reification" would recognize the derivation of that last line, and of Williams' next comment:

> Oh well, all this might be very disquieting were it not that "sacred" has lately been discovered to apply to a point of arrest where stabilization has gone on past the time. There is nothing sacred about literature, it is damned from one end to the other. There is nothing in literature but change and change is mockery.[15]

The "hey-ding-a-ding touch," Williams continues, marked his discovery of his poetic voice; Pound and HD were impeding him, for "it is to the inventive imagination we look for deliverance from every other mis-

fortune as from the desolation of a flat Hellenic perfection of style."
Lacking an essential place for the individual imagination, Pound's classicism allied itself with the other petrifying forces. The inventive imagination must look "to the field of *art*" to advance. It must proceed "by
compass and follow no path."

The two paragraphs that follow outline Williams' theory of the
poetic imagination, and in a sense presage all that he later attempted. He
announces that he wants "to draw a discrimination between true and
false values." The "true value" of any subject or object "is that peculiarity which gives an object a character by itself." The commonly associated or "sentimental value is the false," and results when the imagination follows the path of least resistance, or delves only into the set of
metaphors and analogues commonly held to be on the same "plane" as
the subject. Instead Williams proposes a "more flexible, jagged resort":

> The imagination goes from one thing to another. Given many things of
> nearly totally divergent natures but possessing one-thousandth part of a
> quality in common, provided that be new, distinguished, these things be-
> long in an imaginative category and not in a gross natural array.

These two sentences announce a new type of poetic imagination, one
demanding a much freer field for metaphor. Williams does not add the
stipulation here, but when we look to his poetry, we find that the field on
which he arranges and associates "things" is predominately a visual
one.

This discussion closes with a look at alternatives. "It is easy to fall
under the spell of a certain mode, especially if it be remote of origin,
leaving thus certain of its members essential to a reconstruction of its
significance permanently lost in an impenetrable mist of time."[16] Cubism is the "mode" under attack; it can never be a crucial part of American art because it was born in the traditions and continuity of French art.
Lacking a Courbet, a Manet, a Cezanne or a Picasso, America can never
assimilate such a revolution successfully. Williams' attention turns to
his locale, just as it did earlier in search of American naive painters. He
finds an enormous difficulty, but one which the French also had to over-
come: " . . . the thing that stands eternally in the way of really good
writing is always one: the virtual impossibility of lifting to the imagination those things which lie under the direct scrutiny of the senses, close
to the nose."

Great cultures use indigenous materials, says Williams; the exotic and faraway, with their great attraction for Americans, cannot produce a "graft" resulting in art. Confront the banality of America, and acknowledge the frustration it creates: "The senses witnessing what is immediately before them in detail see a finality which they cling to in despair, not knowing which way to turn." This frustration usually results in reification, in a victory by forfeit to the scientific order. "Thus the so-called natural or scientific array becomes fixed, the walking devil of modern life," Williams concludes.

There is only one source for these two paragraphs: Marcel Duchamp. It was Duchamp who, by his turn away from cubism when he came to America, showed Williams the foreignness of that creed to American conditions. It was Duchamp who, in his ready-mades, "lifted to the imagination those things which lie under the direct scrutiny of the senses." It was Duchamp whose "Large Glass" showed Williams a "more flexible, jagged resort." Duchamp first proposed to "nick the solidity of this apparition" of scientific materialism. To be sure, Williams cleansed Duchamp's eroticism and futurism of inapplicable elements, but his debt cannot be ignored.

In consolidating his "noumenal" and local emphases Williams moves to distinguish his own world "close to the nose" from Wallace Stevens' "fecundative tropics." He quotes a letter from Stevens that protests the "casual character" of *Al Que Quiere!* He has a "distaste for miscellany."

> Given a fixed point of view, realistic, imagistic or what you will, everything adjusts itself to that point of view; and *the process of adjustment is a world in flux*, as it should be for a poet. But to fidget with points of view leads always to new beginnings and incessant new beginnings lead to sterility.[17]
>
> [emphasis added]

The stressed passage, at first incongruous with the clause preceding it, reveals the broad, but fundamentally classic, framework that Stevens employed: it is a dialectic between process and flux, in which "process" (in Whitehead's sense) subsumes apparent chaos. Stevens rejects cubism (don't "fidget with points of view"), and nominates "process" as a broad but "fixed point of view." Williams goes beyond this, opting for a technique that dissolves "points of view" into hints of the ephemeral. Stevens' classicism is of the rich, fecund type that typified the breakdown of renaissance formalism into impressionism, an irony Williams intends to highlight when he quotes Stevens: "One has to keep looking for poetry as Renoir looked for colors in old walls, woodwork, and so on." He could not have picked a painter more antithetical to Williams' intentions.

"I wish that I might here set down my 'Vortex,' " begins Williams in the second part of the prologue. Echoing Duchamp, he indicates that it matters little to him "whether I live here, there, or elsewhere or succeed in this, that or the other so long as I can keep my mind free from the trammels of literature, beating down every attack of its *retiarii* with my *mirmillones*." Not that he would have a program to offer them: he prefers that they look at his work, from which he has culled some "more or less opaque commentaries" that reiterate in discursive form the argument just made by anecdotes.

The argument begins with an assertion of the literary possibilities of futurism. The "brokenness of his composition" and "speed of the emotions" make the poet "master of a certain weapon" that "does not borrow anything of logic," but rather "from that attenuated power which draws perhaps many broken things into a dance giving them thus a full being." Williams' highly qualified sentence does not locate the power to order the "dance" specifically in either the imagination or in things themselves. It somehow interpenetrates.

The following allusion to basic human drives begins to outline this shared ownership. "It is seldom that anything but the most elementary communications can be exchanged with another. There are in reality only two or three reasons generally accepted as the causes of action."[18] A physician, Williams knows that sexual need, hunger, and shelter are the basic human wants and that desire underlies them: it links the phenomena of the world, providing a unity "vaguely divined by some one person, some half a person whose intimacy has perhaps been cultivated over the whole of a lifetime." In contrast to his earlier advocacy of action ("Action's shining helmet" in *Poems*), Williams now embraces the noumenal realm: "By action itself almost nothing can be imparted. The world of action is a world of stones."

The argument reiterates two points made in the anecdotal section. Language, to convey the verisimilitude of emotion, must be stripped clean of the "sentimental or associational." Words must *move* and their appeal must be to the emotions.

148

Then Williams segues to the lesson to be learned from the French: they know that the world is not made up entirely of virgins, and "they do not deny virtue to the rest because of that." The erotic fabric uniting the "stream of things" is not only erratic and capricious, but also as manifest in the "low" as in the "high."

Williams' sense of the erotic is stimulated by certain clues; these are hints of the sort that he tries to reproduce, or to catch close to their sources, in the body of the improvisations: "Manselle Day, Manselle Day, come back again! Slip your clothes off!—the jingling of those little shell ornaments so deftly fastened-!" These hints surround the body in an aura of the erotic that Williams likens to a dance. "One would say the body lay asleep and the dance escaped from the hair tips, the bleached fuzz that covers back and belly, shoulders, neck and forehead. The dance is diamantine over the sleeper who seems not to breathe! One would say heat over the end of a roadway that turns down hill."

It is deplorable that a great number of people are incapable of sustaining the erotic, says Williams, but it is due to America's sterility.

> Their half sophisticated faces gripe me in the belly. There's no business to be done with them either way. They're neither virtuous nor the other thing, between which there exist no perfections. Oh, but the mothers will explain they are good girls. . . . Dig deeper, *mon ami*, the rock maidens are running naked in the dark cellars.[19]

Always recalling the French, Williams struggles toward a localism that is *also* erotic; he goes *down* into his imagination to produce it.

When the erotic consciousness is present, Williams imparts to desire exactly the right tone of anxiety. As a male he writes:

> I'll not get it no matter how I try. Say it was a girl in black I held open a street door for. Let it go at that. I saw a man an hour earlier I liked better   much better. But it's not so easy to pass over. Perfection's not a thing you'll let slip so easily. What a body. The little flattened buttocks; the quiver of the flesh under the smooth fabric!

And in the female voice:

> . . . our husbands tire of us and we—let us not say we go hungry for their caresses but for caresses—of a kind. Oh I am no prophet. I have no theory to advance, except that it's well nigh impossible to know the wish till after.

Cross the room to him if the whim leads that way. Here's drink of an eye
that calls you. No need to take the thing too seriously. It's something of a
will-o-the-wisp I acknowledge. All in the pressure of an arm—through a
fur coat often. Something of a dancing light with the rain beating on a cab
window. . . . Desire skates like a Hollander. . . . Risk a double enten-
dre. But of a sudden the room's not the same! It's a strange blood sings
under some skin. Who will have the sense for it? *The men sniff suspiciously*; you at least my dear had your head about you. It was a tender
nibble but it really did you credit. But think of what might be! It's all in the
imagination. . . . Your hands please. Ah, if I had your hands.[20]

[emphasis added]

These men are, like Duchamp's Bachelors, eternally frustrated.
While the result of their erotic stimulation is a kind of dance, not all
dancers share common timing, much less syncopation.

The trick of the dance is in following   now the words, *allegro*, now the
contrary beat of the glossy leg: Reaching far over as if—But always she
draws back and comes down upon the word flatfooted. For a moment we—
but the boot's costly and the play's not mine. The pace leads off anew.
Again the words break it and we both come down flatfooted. Then—near
the knee, jumps to the eyes, catching in the hair's shadow. But the lips take
the rhythm again and again we come down flatfooted. By this time bore-
dom takes a hand and the play's ended.

This monologue can be read both as an attempted seduction, in which
the liaison fails, and as a tryst between the poet and his muse: its dual
nature shows how closely Williams linked eroticism and poetry.

One of Williams' major roles in the Improvisations is that of
erotic prospector. He is the satyr, "a bare upstanding fellow whose
thighs bulge with a zest for—say a zest!"

He tries his arm. Flings a stone over the river. Scratches his bare back.
Twirls his beard, laughs softly and stretches up his arms in a yawn—stops
in the midst—looking! A white flash over against the oak stems![21]

The interpretation notes that the satyr "goes in pursuit of a white-
skinned dryad. The gaity of his mood full of lustihood, even so, turns
back with a mocking jibe." Of this terminating self-deprecation, more
in a moment. Meanwhile, the satyr-poet searches the local for the erotic,

determined to find there traces of the fecundity that was Rome. He looks

> to a saloon back of the rail-road switch where they have that girl, you
> know, the one that should have been Venus by the lust that's in her.
> They've got her down there among the railroad men. A crusade couldn't
> rescue her. Up to jail—or call it down to Limbo—the Chief of Police our
> Pluto. . . . They are the same men they always were—but fallen. Do they
> dance now, they that danced beside Helicon? They dance much as they did
> then, only, few have an eye for it, through the dirt and fumes.[22]

The facts upon which this incident is based are given in the interpretation, revealing a more sordid picture: bastardy, retardation, and pneu-
monia. Such unseemly details (the French "know the world is not made
up entirely of virgins") as well as an inevitable post coitium triste, cause
the poet to withdraw when his love/poem is consummated. But he
knows the cycle: "By carefully prepared stages come down through the
vulgarities of a cupiscent girlhood to the barren distinction of this cold
six A.M." He is "an old sinner knows the lit-edge clouds" and "that
beauty stands upon the edge of deflowering." He anticipates his "descent" from desire, and prepares to distance himself from the objects of
his desire. The tool of disengagement is a self-deprecating humor, or
Duchampian irony. This progression is most clearly visible in the sections of sequence XVIII.

> How deftly we keep love from each other. . . . But—it is not that we have
> not felt a certain rumbling, a certain stirring of the earth, but what has it
> amounted to?
> . . . .
> Thus a harsh deed will sometimes win its praise through laughter and
> sometimes through savage mockery, and a deed or simple kindness will
> come to its reward through sarcastic comment. Each thing is secure in its
> own perfections. . . .
>
> What a fool ever to be tricked into seriousness. . . . In his warped brain
> an owl of irony fixes on the immediate object of his care as if it were the
> thing to be destroyed, guffaws at the impossibility of putting any kind of
> value on the object.[23]

Perhaps the summative example of Williams' eroticism is the
interpretation accompanying sequence XVIII, parts 2 and 3. In back to
back interpretive sections Williams discusses lust and the evanescence of

the "music" it produces, which he likens to cheap, indigenous art in which the balance of line and color is "infirm," thus producing "irony."

It is not the lusty bodies of the nearly naked girls in the shows about town, nor the blare of the popular tunes that make money for the manager. The girls can be procured rather more easily in other ways and the music is dirt cheap. It is that this meat is savored with a strangeness which never loses its fresh taste to generation after generation, either of dancers or those who watch. It is beauty escaping, spinning up over the heads, blown out at the overtaxed vents by the electric fans.

In many poor and sentimental households it is a custom to have cheap prints in glass frames upon the walls. These are of all sorts and many sizes and may be found in any room from the kitchen to the toilet. The drawing is always of the worst and the colors, not gaudy but almost always of faint indeterminate tints, are infirm. Yet a delicate accuracy exists between these prints and the environment which breeds them. But as if to intensify this relationship words are added. There will be a "sentiment" as it is called, a rhyme, which the picture illuminates. Many of these pertain to love. This is well enough when the bed is new and the young couple spend the long winter nights there in delightful seclusion. But childbirth follows in its time and a motto still hangs above the bed. It is only then that the full ironical meaning of these prints leaves the paper and the frame and starting through the glass takes undisputed sway over the household.[24]

Once one becomes aware of Duchamp's ideas, his presence in *Kora* is highlighted. "The men sniff suspiciously" reminds the reader of the "gas" decanted for the bachelors in the "Large Glass." The series quoted above, proceeding from "love" to "laughter" to "irony", mimics a Duchampian cycle; its concluding interpretation is distanced, again in the Frenchman's manner. Williams also alludes to Duchamp's idea of non-choice [illustrated in "11 Rue Larrey, Paris," the door that is neither open nor closed].

This pretension of these doors to broach or to conclude our pursuits, our meetings,—of these papered walls to separate our thoughts of impossible tomorrows and these ceilings—that are a jest at shelter. . . . It is laughter gone mad—of a holiday—that has frozen into this—what shall I say? Call it, this house of ours, the crystal itself of laughter, thus peaked and faceted.

Again there is a progression to "laughter" and self-reflexive irony, and finally to the peaked shape of the attic: a complete cycle of desire. A few improvisations later, Williams uses the door image again, this time implying that this cycle makes our decisions for us.

> Doors have a back side also. And grass blades are double-edged. It's no use trying to deceive me, leaves fall more by the buds that push them off than by lack of greenness. Or throw two shoes on the floor and see how they'll lie if you think it's all one way.[25]

This idea dovetails with the fifth point of the prologue, which is similar to Duchamp's idea of non-contradiction. "It is chuckleheaded to desire a way through every difficulty," writes Williams.

> But to weigh a difficulty and to turn it aside without being wrecked upon a destructive solution bespeaks an imagination of force sufficient to transcend action. The difficulty has been solved by ascent to a higher plane.

The recognition of contradiction as an essential part of life is an important part of Duchamp's outlook. Among Williams' unpublished papers at Yale is a note referring to the door paradox: a friend of his, he writes, "is wrong in her assumption [about the door] not so much because we cannot walk through it when it is closed, but precisely because we can, as the imagination proves."[26]

Moving immediately to limit the extent of this noumenal world he has posited, Williams writes that "Nothing is possessed save by dint of that vigorous conception of its perfections which is the imagination's special province but neither is anything possessed which is not extant." Here he parts paths with Duchamp, giving his eroticism a material base and opening the way for a theory of the "local."

The "local" is celebrated in several improvisations, although few tie the American local to classical culture as interestingly as the eighth sequence.

> Hercules is in Hackettstown doing farm labor. Look at his hands if you'll not believe me. And what do I care if yellow and red are Spain's riches and Spain's good blood. Here red and yellow mean simply autumn! The odor of the poor farmer's fried supper is mixing with the smell of the hemlocks, mist is in the valley hugging the ground over Parsipanny—where an old-ish man leans talking to a young woman—the moon is swinging from its star.

The next section of the prologue contains another departure from Duchamp's thinking. When "all manner of things are thrown out of key," as in Duchamp's stained-glass window, "it approaches the impossible to arrive at an understanding of anything." Meaning does not inhere in events, Williams says, clearing up an earlier confusion.

> On the contrary the perfections of the two instruments are emphasized by the joiner; no means is neglected to give to each the *full color* of its perfections. It is only the music of the instruments that is joined and that . . . by virtue of the imagination. On this level of the imagination all things and ages meet in fellowship.[27]
>
> [emphasis added]

This is an important exception to the "all embracing" harmony found in Duchampian and eastern mysticism, and often attributed to Williams. Not everything or everyone is perfect: disparate things are united only by the poet making music of their perfections. Things are "perfect" only insofar as the poet is able to conceive of and to create their "locale." And the prime tool for accomplishing this is *vision*.

> In the mind there is a continual play of obscure images which coming between the eyes and their prey seem pictures on the screen at the movies. Somewhere there appears to me a maladjustment.

Williams wants to "win his way to some hill-top" of clear vision. His "floating visions of unknown purport" need "interpreting as they go." Some days the recognition comes; other times it lacks: "There are days when leaves have knife's edges and one sees only eye-pupils, fixes every catch-penny in a shopwindow and every wire against the sky but—goes puzzled from vista to vista in his own house. . . . "[28] The point at which Williams arrives is *visionary* in the most empirical sense. By *paying attention to our seeing*, we can capture and form into poetry a sense of the unseen, the greater ineffable world.

After this, the prologue becomes digressive. There are several less polished interpretations that are closely related to their improvisations, but most of the vignettes illustrate arguments already made. "A fish swimming in a pond," reflects the poet, is protected above and below by his natural coloration. "A young man, who has been sitting for some time in contemplation at the edge of a lake, rejects with scorn the parochial deductions of history." In other words, the mind is adapted to its element: be of your age. Williams is considering the way in which Kandinsky digested the accomplishments of his predecessors and generalized from them to formulate his triangulated theory. Of his young man Williams adds that "he gives evidence of a bastard sort of knowledge of that diversity of context in things and situations which the great masters of antiquity looked to for the inspiration and distinction of their compositions."

In another place late in the prologue, Williams explains how "eroticism" is lived.

> I have discovered that the thrill of first love passes! It even becomes the backbone of a sordid sort of religion if not assisted in passing. . . . I have been reasonably frank about my erotics with my wife. I have never or seldom said, my dear I love you, when I would rather say: My dear, I wish you were in Tierra del Fuego. I have discovered by scrupulous attention to this detail and by certain experiments that we can continue from time to time to elaborate relationships quite equal in quality if not greatly superior, to that surrounding our wedding. In fact, the best we have enjoyed of love together has come after the most thorough destruction or harvesting of that which has gone before. . . . It is in the continual and violent refreshing of the idea that love and good writing have their security.[29]

The final pages rail against Eliot and Pound, who at one point are associated with "my brother," classicism, and the hated Mr. Jepson. A few debts are acknowledged. Alfred Kreymborg is praised for his "bare irony, gift of rhythm and *Others*." Marcel Duchamp is paraphrased when Williams writes, "Nothing is good save the new. If a thing have novelty it stands intrinsically beside every other work of artistic excellence." Williams bows to Wassily Kandinsky, "who sets down the following":

> Every artist has to express himself
> Every artist has to express his epoch
> Every artist has to express the pure and eternal
>   qualities of the art of all men.

Marsden Hartley's role as a purveyor of Kandinsky and a fellow opponent of Jepson is not mentioned, but a striking number of art-related references do end the prologue. Eliot is compared to "a Whistler at best."

Over him Williams favors the "Adobe Indian hag," whose song "The beetle is blind / The beetle is blind" is repetitive but indigenous. Williams closes with a reference to his favorite image and to Charles Demuth: "There is nothing left in me but the virtue of curiosity, Demuth puts in. The poet should be forever at the ship's prow."[30]

9. *Sour Grapes*

"Eyes have always stood first in the poet's equipment."

Williams

Williams had published no book of poems in four years when *Sour Grapes* appeared on December 9, 1921. It sold for $2.00 in hardback, and contained fifty-two poems and a prose sketch.

Although Williams wrote to Kenneth Burke that "it has been more 'composed' than any [book] so far," there is little discernible relation between the poems beyond a loose chronological arrangement. He apparently meant that the poems themselves were more "composed" visually, and this is true. Williams' later accounting of the title is similarly misleading: "All the poems are poems of disappointment, sorrow . . . But secretly I had my own idea. Sour grapes are just as beautiful as any other grapes."[1] This hardly seems a fair assessment of "Queen Anne's Lace" or "Portrait of a Lady."

A better clue is the book's dedication to Alfred Kreymborg, for *Sour Grapes* includes poems from the *Others* period, recapitulates technical advances made in companionship with Kreymborg, and solidifies Williams' grasp of personal themes that he discovered with the group. On receiving his copy, Kreymborg wrote to Williams, "The dedication bowled me over. I had no idea of this, and I haven't recovered yet."[2]

Some of the poems in *Sour Grapes* first appeared in *Poetry* and *The Dial* between 1917 and 1920, where one can see the increments of Williams' development. The turning points are two groups of poems, one in *The Little Review* in 1920, the other in *The Dial* the same year. *Sour Grapes* reprints these and adds two new interests: the nature poem, a kind of modern "pastoral" in Williams' case; and markedly more visual compositions, moving Williams closer to his painter friends. In fact, his first title for this volume was *Picture Poems*.

The reader is immediately made aware of Williams' life-long interests: in the first poems he highlights his innocence and further modifies the sonnet. In "The Dark Day," for example, (omitted from the *Collected Earlier Poems*) Williams makes small changes in the form he used so successfully in "Danse Russe."

> A three-day-long rain from the east-
> An interminable talking, talking
> 1—Of no consequence—patter, patter, patter.
> Hand in hand little winds
> 2—Blow the thin streams aslant.
> Warm.   Distance cut off.   Seclusion.
> A few passers-by, drawn in upon themselves,
> 3—Hurry from one place to another.
> Winds of the white poppy! there is no escape!—
> An interminable talking, talking,
> 4—Talking . . . it has happened before.
> Backward, backward, backward.
>
> [notation added]

Heavy caesura and ellipsis are added to revive the basic three-sentence-and-a-tag schema. The tag "it has happened before" is advanced a line. This pressing forward appears intended to complement the theme—the poet's ennui in the rain—though the final effect is not enervation, but the strikingly visual way in which the sonnet has been overhauled.

In "Thursday," another sonnet-like poem, Williams arranges the syntax so that the "tag" completes the opening phrase: "I have had my dream—like others / . . . and decide to dream no more." The sonnet underlies a better poem, "The Desolate Field," in which the tag is still evident:

> And amazed my heart leaps
> at the thought of love
> vast and grey
> yearning silently over me.[3]

But Williams had just about exploited the form as much as possible; these small adjustments produced no new "arrangement" capable of bearing the visual burden that Williams more and more wanted his poems to carry.

Some poems in *Sour Grapes* seem to derive from imagism, but only two out of fifty-two can be positively identified as imagist. "Lines" and "Spring" show Williams' persistence in adapting compatible forms.

"Lines"
Leaves are grey green,
the glass broken, bright green
"Spring"
O my grey hairs!
You are truly white as plum blossoms.

Some critics would add to these the poem "Arrival."

And yet one arrives somehow,
finds himself loosening the hooks of
her dress
in a strange bedroom—
feels the autumn
dropping its silk and linen leaves
about her ankles.
The tawdry veined body emerges
twisted upon itself
like a winter wind . . . ![4]

Yet this piece is distinguished as much by its eroticism and its tendrils of syntax as by its central image.

Another cohesive group of poems in *Sour Grapes* reflects Williams' continuing interest in futurism and Duchamp. According to Williams' accounts, "Overture to a Dance of Locomotives" was read at the 1917 Independents Show to Mina Loy's applause. "To Be Closely Written on a Small Piece of Paper Which Folded Into a Tight Lozenge Will Fit Into Any Girl's Locket" has its source in Duchamp's "A Bruit Secret" (1916), which is an unknown "verse" wrapped in a ball of twine and clamped between two steel plates cryptographically encoded by Arensberg. Like Duchamp's verse, Williams' poem—"Lo the leaves / Upon the new autumn grass—/Look at them well!"—is less important than its title and concept. Duchamp's eroticism also animates "The Gentle Man," where the insistence on the *self* before the opposite sex is characteristic of the Frenchman.

159

I feel the caress of my own fingers
on my own neck as I place my collar
and think pityingly
of the kind women I have known.[5]

Lying in the loose ends of this volume there is even a poem ("Man in a Room") that hints Williams was engaged in some translation; and there is a prose piece ("The Delicacies") in which he is again preoccupied by his "townspeople."

More significant than these shards of earlier interests is a group of long-lined, prosy poems that Williams was writing along with the improvisations of *Kora in Hell*. In four pieces between May, 1918, and February, 1919, the reader can see Williams using the prose of *Kora* as a base for experiments in rhythm, caesura and syntax. "A Celebration" in *The Egoist* of May, 1918, is more prosaic than most of the improvisations, but it uses wind metaphorically (like the "tough cords" of *Kora*) and employs strong verbs to "construct" a picture in the reader's mind as Arensberg had advised. The first verse:

A middle-northern March, now as always—
gusts from the south broken against cold winds—
but from under, as if a slow hand lifted a tide,
it moves—not into April—into a second March,
the old skin of wind-clear scales dropping
upon the mould: this is the shadow projects the tree
upward causing the sun to shine in his sphere.[6]

In "Love Song" (June, 1918, *Little Review*) Williams uses this long line again, but he makes it more colloquial, ends lines with prepositions, uses fewer caesuras, and employs irony. Then in "Le Medicin Malgre Lui" (*Poetry*, June, 1918) he shortens the line and imbues his laconic content with crispness by judicious line breaks and continuous enjambment.

Oh I suppose I should
Wash the walls of my office,
Polish the rust from
My instruments and keep them
Definitely in order:

The syntax of this sentence continues for two-thirds of the poem. Williams omits the punctuation that could be used on the enjambed lines, so that we move down quickly to the dash. He then breaks the flow with a question to which he supplies an answer, a tactic still dependent on the "tag," but attempted here with irony.

> If to this I added
> A bill at the tailor's
> And the cleaner's
> And grew a decent beard
> And cultivated a look
> Of importance—
> Who can tell? I might be
> A credit to my Lady Happiness
> And never think anything
> But a white thought![7]

The irony results not just from the blithe spirits of "my Lady Happiness," but also from the placement of the "coloring" words—definitely, gradually, important, new, decent and white—all of which function as rhythmic markers. The initial line position of "definitely" cues the reader to the series.

In the last of the four pieces, "Romance Moderne," Williams opens up his line again and synthesizes the local, the erotic, nature, and futurism.

> Tracks of rain and light linger in
> the spongy greens of a nature whose
> flickering mountain—bulging nearer,
> ebbing back into the sun
> hollowing itself away to hold a lake,—
> or brown stream rising and falling
> at the roadside, turning about,
> churning itself white, drawing
> green over it,- plunging glassy funnels
> fall-[8]

Williams opposed to this natural dynamism "the other world- / the windshield a blunt barrier." In the cleavage the external, natural world becomes Williams' erotic universe, and the interior world remains static, a simulacrum of classicism. Because of "the unseen power of words," the "first desire is / to fling oneself out at the side into / the other dance, to other music." Williams identifies this escape with Peer Gynt (from *Kora*), Rip Van Winkle (a local legend) and Diana (the goddess of the moon). Rip Van Winkle becomes an emblem of the local in the sixth stanza: "I would sit separate weighing a / small red handful: the dirt of these parts." The ephemerality of Diana's presence leads to the inevitable post-erotic irony of the eighth stanza.

> Love you? It's
> a fire in the blood, willy-nilly!
> It's the sun coming up in the morning,
> Ha, but it's the grey noon too, already up
> in the morning. You are slow.
> Men are not friends where it concerns
> a woman? Fighters. Playfellows.
> White round thighs! Youth! Sighs—!
> It's the fillup of novelty. It's—

The erotic, that "fillup of novelty," becomes in the next verse "all stuff of the blind emotions," which in turn awakens his vision. "Stirred, the eye seizes / for the first time—the eye awake!" "All the colors / A good head, backed by the eye—awake!" The yoking of eroticism and vision leads Williams to the edge of a major period. The concerns of this poem combined with the syntax of "Le Medicin Malgre Lui" will produce one of his finest flowerings in the next year.

First, however, two contributory currents in his development merit attention. Williams had long worked within a lyric/epic division: either he wrote in short bursts, such as "Dawn," or he wrote long poems of epic impulse, such as "The Wanderer." He needed to give his poems a foundation in narrative, or at least to hint of a more complex human context, which the reader might flesh out for himself. He apparently recognized this lack of narrative interest and set about remedying it. In a set of eighteen poems published in *Poetry* in March, 1919, and collectively titled "Broken Windows," Williams became a story-teller.

> By constantly tormenting them
> With reminders of the lice in

Their children's hair, the
School physician first
Brought their hatred down on him.
But by this familiarity
They grew used to him, and so,
At last,
Took him for their friend and advisor.[9]

During this period Williams was developing with Marsden Hart-ley (and later with Robert McAlmon) the idea of "contact." In his intro-duction to the journal of like name, Williams explained:

In exploiting his position in America the artist, aware of the universal physical laws of his craft, will however take off only from the sensual accidents of his immediate contacts. This achievement of a *locus*, Contact has maintained, is the one thing which will put his work on a comparable basis with the best work created abroad. Before the approach to anything of a serious character there must be this separate implantation of the sperm in each case.[10]

The half dozen poems he published in *Contact* ("Portrait of the Au-thor," "St. Francis Einstein of the Daffodils," "Complaint," "A Good Night," "Marianne Moore," etc.) pugnaciously subsume all non-local influences to his theory of "contact."

The flowering of this ferment came in late 1919 and early 1920, when Williams published in scattered journals some of his best work: "The Late Singer," "April," "A Coronal," "To Mark Anthony in Heaven," "To a Friend Concerning Several Ladies," "Portrait of a Lady," "To Waken an Old Lady" and others. The "brokenness" of the emotions and the impact of futurism are self-evident in such a poem as "Portrait of a Lady" (which mentions Demuth's favorite eighteenth-cen-tury colorists, Fragonard and Watteau). Less clear may be their role in a poem such as "To Mark Anthony in Heaven."

This quiet morning light
reflected, how many times!
from grass and trees and clouds
enters my north room
touching the walls with
grass and clouds and trees,

Anthony,
Trees and grass and clouds.
Why did you follow
that beloved body
with your ships at Actium?
I hope it was because
you knew her inch by inch
from slanting feet upward
to the roots of her hair
and down again and that
you saw her
above the battle's fury
reflecting—
clouds and trees and grass
for then
you are listening in heaven.[11]

One extraordinary feature of this poem is the way in which it effortlessly subsumes and makes "local" its classical content. Everything in Williams' "system" functions smoothly. He is in his "north room"—the attic of "desire" where he gets a painter's "north light"—and although the light is "quiet" it is also "reflected." It has a "brokenness" that has picked up a hint of everything it has touched: grass, trees, clouds. These items are not only vague in number, but they extend from earth to heaven, connecting the two. They represent the fecundity of the natural world that has become since "Romance Moderne" Williams' most ready analogue for the erotic. By functioning as a refrain, they also emphasize details on the surrounding lines. This "magic nature" penetrates Williams' designated artistic abode, "touching the walls" and making the poet one with it; when the thought of Mark Anthony arises, Williams segues to him by repeating the incantatory "trees and grass and clouds" after his name. In a tactic that will become a hallmark, he sets a number of specific details—"hints" of the erotic, or new vantages on it—against the amorphous "magic" background he has created. Since Williams is puzzled by Anthony's following "that beloved body" to Actium, for he knows that carnage is antithetical to the erotic, he posits in Anthony's mind a few hints, a few of the right details: slanting feet, the roots of her hair. Knowing her "inch by inch," Anthony possesses a grounding in Cleopatra's particulars, a "localism" as it were, which shares in the ambiance of "clouds and trees and grass" that Williams is meditating this morning. That Williams intends to say they are fellow amateurs is clear not only from the final line—"you are listening in heaven"—but also because the new word arrangement (clouds, then trees, finally grass) links heaven to earth.

"To Mark Anthony in Heaven" indicates the approach Williams will take in a number of new poems in *Sour Grapes*, pieces that are among his best. These poems are usually termed Williams' "pastoral" output, a designation that should not be equated with "simple." His poems about nature take form from a complex network of ambitions and experiments. It is by lifting "things under the nose" to his imagination—and what could be more present than trees, grass, flowers, rain and snow?—that Williams puts his poetry on the world stage. Such a poem as "Blizzard" deceives anyone who thinks it a "simple" little nature poem.

Snow:
years of anger following
hours that float idly down—
the blizzard
drifts its weight
deeper and deeper for three days
or sixty years, eh? Then
the sun! a clutter of
yellow and blue flakes—
Hairy looking trees stand out
in long alleys
over a wild solitude.
The man turns and there—
his solitary tracks stretched out
upon the world.

Like "To Mark Anthony in Heaven," this poem moves from the amorphous "years" and "hours" and "drifts" to the particular "solitary tracks" in its conclusion. It begins without "vision," or more accurately with obscured vision, in the abstract diction that represents the flux of the storm. When the sun rises at mid-point, the human eye begins to compose the landscape: the power of the eye is emphasized by the spectrum of color—from yellow to blue, the gamut of the color wheel. Like a camera receding, the poet's eye draws back: from flakes to trees to alleys of trees, from alleys to fields, where footprints stretch outward seemingly over the whole world. At the moment when Williams delivers the last and most specific detail, he has in mind and hopes to communicate to the reader a certain universality "upon the world." Nor is the reader permitted to ignore hints of a self-reflexive nature. The storm is like a man, whose lifespan is "sixty years, eh?" When the poet emerges from the flux that Williams always associated with the gestation of a poem, he "turns and there" almost finished now, are the "solitary tracks"—his poem—that cut his flux into definite shapes. He "wins his way to some hilltop" of clear vision. As much as nature, this poem concerns Williams' way of mediating between the romantic and classic impulses, between flux and form, between mass and line.

The aesthetic of the nature poems is not in every case identical, but the pattern is discernible and consistent. "Spring Storm" begins with "The sky has given over / its bitterness" and progresses to an ending in which the rain "cuts a way for itself / through green ice in the gutters." "Winter Trees" begins with "All the complicated details / of the attiring and / the disattiring" and ends with the discrete, linear shapes of "the wise trees / stand sleeping in the cold." Even in a poem such as "Approach of Winter," which is uniformly permeated with detail, Williams manages to conclude with a hard-edged shape that not only contrasts with the preceding details, but emphasizes the *imaginative* nature of the solution.

> The half-stripped trees
> struck by a wind together,
> bending all,
> the leaves flutter drily
> and refuse to let go
> or driven like hail
> stream bitterly out to one side
> and fall
> where the salvias, hard carmine,—
> *like no leaf that ever was—*
> edge the bare garden.[12]
>   [emphasis added]

If "hard carmine," an intense red oil paint, and the "edge" of the leaves remind one of the precisionists Sheeler and Demuth, it is no doubt because those were the friendships Williams carried away after the demise of the *Others* circle in 1920. But their contributions, like those of the others, Williams has digested; they are of use insofar as they help him decant the vague forces of nature that he identifies with his romantic/formless feelings.

The presence of a distinct detail at the end is not Williams' latent imagism, but a substitute for the "tag" that he used to express awe earlier. Williams hopes this detail, as in "Blizzard," will refer the reader to the thing itself and to the universal. When the technique succeeds, it avoids the kind of static conclusion that forced Duchamp to employ irony.

The best known poems in *Sour Grapes* are the quartet of "Daisy," "Primrose," "Great Mullen," and "Queen-Anne's-Lace." Williams' later comment on them, though notable in its designation of them as "still lifes," is a bit misleading.

> Straight observation is used in four poems about flowers: Daisy, Primrose (this is the American primrose), Queen Anne's Lace, Great Mullen. I thought of them as still-lifes. I looked at the actual flowers as they grew.

Flowers and women and poems were always closely related for Williams. All three represent beauty, secrets and generative mysteries. "Two women, Three women," Williams wrote in *Paterson*, "Innumerable women, each like a flower."

The four flower poems employ the general pattern Williams used in nature poems, and are packed with pansexuality. "Daisy" begins with a quip ("The dayseye hugging the earth"), the orthography of which alludes to Pound and to the generative power Williams associates with the sun. It then moves from its general description of "Spring . . . gone down in purple" to the foreground detail of the "green and pointed scales" of the flower in the poet's hand. The description is profuse, ordered of course by the sun, which Williams gives an androgynous nature: "He lies on his back—/ it is a woman also."[13] The flower of "Primrose" is not only "A man / swinging his pink fists" but also two flowers with feminine names: ladysthumb and birdsbreast. In "Great Mullen" the debate between male and female elements of the flower concerns a trace of incriminating "djer-kis / on your clothes." In fact, "Great Mullen," is the farthest thing imaginable from "straight description."

167

The widely anthologized "Queen-Anne's-Lace" is the most clearly and understandably sexual, for it equates the erotic and the poetic in Duchampian fashion. It is also distinctly local, as the reversed conceit of the first sequence, which calls to mind Shakespeare's sonnet "My mistress' eyes", reminds us.

> Her body is not so white as
> anemone petals nor so smooth—nor
> so remote a thing.[14]

The eroticism is highlighted in a series of personifications. The flower is "taking / the field by force," each flower has a purple "mole," and "Each flower is a hand's span / of her whiteness." The sun again is the creative, male source.

> Wherever
> *his* hand has lain there is
> a tiny purple blemish. Each part
> is a blossom under his touch
> to which the fibres of her being
> stem one by one, each to its end.

Like the poet of "Blizzard," who turns and sees his tracks in the snow, the persona in this poem is a creator; he leaves a trail behind him. Turning on his work, Williams lifts the *entire* field of flowers to an imaginative erotic unity.

> . . . the whole field is a
> white desire, empty, a single stem
> a cluster, flower by flower,
> a pious wish to whiteness gone over—
> or nothing.

The negation of the last line echoes and mystifies the reader when he finishes the poem. The answer begins back with "pious," which Williams means to be taken as "religious" rather than in the modern sense of "hypocritical." The momentum of the "wish to whiteness" exceeds or has "gone over" some lip or precipice, the nature of which is unclear. It is either this success of excess or else "nothing," a word the ambiguity of which presents too many problems to worry about here, except to note that it completes the syntax: "Each part / is a blossom under his touch" "or nothing." Either the poet can fertilize the erotic and poetic potential of the material at hand (under his "nose") or he fails and creates "nothing." Williams intends this as a transcendent statement; if not grasped as such, there is not much the reader can do to unravel it.

Perhaps the best introduction to the final sequence of poems in *Sour Grapes* is a letter to Williams from Edmund Brown of the Four Seas Publishing Company. On February 28, 1921, he wrote: "I received the manuscript of 'Picture Poems' safely. I have not had time to read it entire but there is some great stuff in it." Later statements clarify what Williams intended by "Picture Poems."

> When the mood possessed me, I wrote. Whether it was a tree or a woman or a bird, the mood had to be translated into *form*. To get the *line* on paper. To make it *euphonious*. To fit the words so that they went smoothly and still said exactly what I wanted to say.[15]
>
> [emphasis added]

"Picture" did not mean "image" in the sense of "imagism" to Williams; it meant first a form, second a line, and third a sound. A striking feature of this book is the number of poems constructed out of form and line to present visual compositions.

Such a poem as "The Nightingales" reveals how Williams employed form and layering to create these pictures.

> My shoes as I lean
> unlacing them
> stand out upon
> flat worsted flowers
> under my feet.
> Nimbly the shadows
> of my fingers play
> unlacing
> over shoes and flowers.[16]

This poem shares much with Man Ray's futurist canvas "The Rope Dancer Accompanies Herself with Her Shadows" (1916). In the painting the shadows cast by a girl's jump rope are caught at fixed intervals and expand into graceful, highly stylized signatures of color that fill the canvas and become metaphors for the spirit of the tiny girl in their midst. In like manner the shadows of Williams' fingers become nightingales, metaphors for poetic flight, that follow the "lacing" on one plane but carry import into two others. These three planes are inherent in the phrases "as I lean," "under my feet," and "over shoes and flowers." In a later version Williams cut the fifth line, "under my feet," because it was the only line lacking a sense of movement. His first impulse, though, was to create a poem with visual layers to it. To facilitate the sense of layering he resorts to a shorter line and turns or begins lines on words describing location.

Though Williams is composing visually in many poems at this point, rarely does he give over a whole poem so convincingly as in "Daisy." The strong verbs and futurist elements work almost invisibly beneath his description.

> The sun is upon a
> slender green stem
> ribbed lengthwise.
> . . . .
> round the yellow center,
> split and creviced and done into
> minute flowerheads
> . . . .
>   brownedged,
> green and pointed scales
> armor his yellow.
>
> But turn and turn,
> the crisp petals remain
> brief, translucent, greenfastened,
> barely touching at the edges;
> blades of a limpid seashell.[17]

Williams infuses these "still lifes" with a sense of action. "The Disputants" crackles with the intensity of Van Gogh's sunflowers.

> Upon the table in their bowl!
> in violent disarray
> of yellow sprays, green spikes
> of leaves, red pointed petals

and curled heads of blue
and white among the litter
of the forks and crumbs and plates
the flowers remain composed.
Coolly their colloquy continues
above the coffee and loud talk
grown frail as vaudeville.[18]

Both the conspicuous alliteration of the ninth line and the poet's punning on the 'violent disarray" that he has "composed" interject playful
elements. Williams can not quite admit that he wants only to describe
the flowers, yet "still life" is the impulse here.

"The Tulip Bed" suffers from no such crossed purposes. In this
paradigm of his visual compositions, Williams lays out the elements in
the landscape with the precision of a Canaletto.

The May sun—whom
all things imitate—
that glues small leaves to
the wooden trees
shone from the sky
through bluegauze   clouds
upon the ground.
Under the leafy trees
where the suburban streets
lay crossed
with houses on each corner,
tangled shadows had begun
to join
the roadway and the lawns.
With excellent precision
the tulip bed
inside the iron fence
upreared its gaudy
yellow, white and red,
rimmed round with grass,
reposedly.[19]

In painterly fashion Williams decides on the source of light, then paints
from the background to the foreground, from the top to the bottom. In

passing he cannot resist implying that the poet is an analogue of the sun, but in the same brushstroke he leafs out his trees and paints in the sky-scape: "shone from the sky / through bluegauze clouds." Having laid in the foliage, he drops "under the leafy trees" and fills in details closer to the reader/viewer. There are crossed streets, houses on each corner, and shadows that blur the edges of lawn and roadway. In the foreground and at the bottom of the canvas is "the tulip bed / inside the iron fence" where the tulips thrust up their "gaudy/yellow, white and red." As befits a poet who in his first published essay called Whitman a "colorist," Williams inclines to the fauve in his description of the flowers, but he has learned not to let his color run off the canvas. The tulips must be "rimmed round with grass/reposedly." The whole effect of the poem lies in the exuberance of its painting, the way the poet can imitate with words on paper the effect of the light of the sun.

The last poem in *Sour Grapes* is "The Great Figure," an especially visual poem and one that seems to defy exegesis. A comparison of two early versions of the poem with the final draft lays bare some of the elements crucial to its success. Below are the three versions in chronological order.

Among the rain
and lights
I saw the figure 5
gold on red
moving
with weight and urgency
tense
unheeded
to gong clangs
siren howls
and wheels rumbling
through the dark city.

Among the rain
and lights
I saw the figure 5
in gold
on a red
firetruck
moving

with weight and urgency
tense
unheeded
to gong clangs
siren howls
and wheels rumbling
through the dark city.

Among the rain
and lights
I saw the figure 5
in gold
on a red
firetruck
moving
tense
unheeded
to gong clangs
siren howls
and wheels rumbling
through the dark city.[20]

In the first two versions Williams did not use to his advantage the potential of the colors. In "gold on red" he attempts by elision to impart the
sense of speed: gold red stands for the firetruck. Yet to complete his
impression of the event, he needs to give some indication of the size and
purpose of the hurtling object, so he decides that it moves "with weight
and urgency." Williams solved the first problem first: he isolated the
colors on lines of their own, and added "firetruck." This did not slow the
syntax of the sentence, and it emphasized the colors while creating a
definite *sequence* among the details: rain and lights / figure 5 in gold /
red background of the firetruck. This is a dynamic version of his "layering" technique, in which Williams' eye approaches or retreats from the
subject in a series of steps. When he zooms in, it is generally quite fast.
When he retreats, it is more slowly. In this poem the nature of the event
demanded both techniques, one after the other. With this sequence
worked out, "weight and urgency" could be omitted, since it only speci-
fies qualities inherent in "firetruck," is redundant, and freights the
speed of the lines.

These changes present the reader with a series of clear and distinct visual impressions that approximate the action of a camera that first focuses and then dissolves: figure 5 / gold / red / firetruck and—zip—it's gone into the "dark city." The poem both opens ("Among the rain / and lights") and closes ("dark city") with the kind of vague, hazy descriptions that Williams favored in his nature poems. Between the vague moments he created an instant out of time by recording accurately the way in which the eye perceives things. It is no accident that when Charles Demuth was commissioned by Stieglitz to do a poster series of his friends, he decided to illustrate this poem as his tribute to Williams. Perhaps the fact that Williams was on his way to visit Hartley's studio when he saw the fire engine put him in this visual frame of mind.

It may also be that Hartley introduced Williams to the poem "Klange" (or "Sounds") by Kandinsky, which begins with the line "There was a big figure 3 - white on dark brown." On the way to Hartley's he could have had the sonorous title and opening line in mind at the propitious moment, as one scholar maintains.[21]

"The Great Figure" marks a stage of technical mastery for Williams; there was no need, as there had been in *Kora*, to be coy about his alliance with the painters. He was writing poems for the eye, and he would insist on that fact. Others would write the poems of the ear, and the poems of the intellect. Williams was composing *pictures*, reawakening the eye that slept, and he had announced that his poetry was intended to register meaning in the same way that a painting did.

10. *Dada Spring*

> *"How easy to slip*
> *into the old mode, how hard to*
> *cling firmly to the advance—"*

> Williams

Spring and All (1923) is informatively paired with *Kora in Hell*: both explore the contrasts and commonality of prose and poetry; both intersperse passages of one with the other. But while *Kora*'s confusion is partially cleared by its "prologue," the dada "unsequencing" of *Spring and All* makes it more frustrating. As an elaboration of Williams' technique and ideas, however, it makes important advances upon *Kora*. To discover these one must first work through the other motifs in the volume.

There is a parodic element that must be understood. *"Spring and All* was a fooling around book that became a crucial book," according to a Williams' editor, and Williams himself said:

> It was written when all the world was going crazy about typographical form and is really a travesty on the idea. Chapter headings are printed upside down on purpose, the chapters are numbered all out of order, sometimes with a Roman numeral, sometimes with an Arabic, anything that came in handy. The prose is a mixture of philosophy and nonsense. It made sense to me, at least to my disturbed mind—because it *was* disturbed at that time—but I doubt if it made sense to anyone else.[1]

The "typographic form" that Williams pokes fun at had become prevalent in Stieglitz' publications, especially the Picabia-edited *391*. A close friend of Duchamp's, Picabia was given free rein at *391*. His taste ran to Breton and Apollinaire, and by reprinting the Frenchmen he added to the ferment that produced New York dada. A close friend of Williams and Sheeler, Marius De Zayas, was among the leading "typographical poets." By 1918 not only Picabia but also Duchamp and Arensberg were serious about dada. Hartley soon caught the fever.

A minority of the circle, which included Williams, was less enthusiastic about the new *ism*. At the same time that he wrote *Spring and All*, Williams was writing *The Great American Novel*, a dada novella that is as much parody as profession. For Williams the new *ism* was an ally in the battle against classicism, as he showed by dismissing contemporary classicists in the *Novel*.

> What good to talk to me of Santayana and your later critics. I brush them aside. They do not apply. They do not reach me any more than a baby's hand reaches the moon. I am far under them. I am less, far less if you will, I am a beginner. I am an American. A United Stateser.[2]

Out of the crisp, mature style of *Sour Grapes*, Williams was writing with his other hand the poems in *Spring and All*. The interaction of the *Sour Grapes* style with dada creates the parodic elements and also the difficulty of *Spring and All*. Williams recognized that dada applied to poetry would lead to the *reducto ad absurdum* of the "brokenness"—and consequent lack of clarity—that characterized *Kora*. Therefore, he tried to insulate his poems from the dada prose. "The poems were kept pure—no typographical tricks when they appear—set off from the prose. They are numbered consistently; none had titles though they were to have titles when they were reprinted."[3] This could be a slip of the memory, for some of the poems appear to be parodies, too. This excerpt of "To Have Done Nothing," (No. 6) is far removed from Williams' style, but does recall the experimental poetry of Walter Arensberg.

> nothing
> I have done
> is made up of
> nothing
> and the dipthong
> ae
> together with
> the first person
> singular
> indicative
> of the auxiliary
> verb
> to have. . . . [4]

This piece is paired with a better poem, presumably to indicate the contrast. Williams uses this tactic again with the poem "The Rose" ("The rose is obsolete") and the Dada exercise "At the Faucet of June" (poem VIII). The references in the latter to J. P. Morgan, Renaissance painters, and classical allusions are an anthology of Williams' dislikes.

> pulling at the
> anemones in
> Persephone's cow pasture—
> When from among
> the steel rocks leaps
> J.P.M.
> who enjoyed
> extraordinary privileges
> among virginity
> to solve the core
> of whirling flywheels
> by cutting
> the Gordian knot
> with a Veronese or
> perhaps a Rubens—[5]

Once the dada has been dispersed, *Spring and All* is more legible. In the manner of *Kora* it begins with a contentious forward, but one more analytic than anecdotal. This dais is intended to raise the serious material above the parody. Williams announces the problem: "There is a constant barrier between the reader and his consciousness of immediate contact with the world." Most writers and critics have a vested interest in this separation, Williams says, because their work "has been especially designed to keep up the barrier between sense and the vaporous fringe which distracts attention from its agonized approaches to the moment. It has always been a search for 'the beautiful illusion.' Very well, I am not in search of the 'beautiful illusion.' " Williams sees himself as an iconoclast, stripping cherished fictions from addicted critics.

> "You have robbed me, God, I am naked. What shall I do?"—By it they mean that when I have suffered (provided I have not done so as yet) I too shall run for cover; that I too shall seek refuge in fantasy. And mind you, I do not say that I will not. To decorate my age.[6]

Even while owning that his intention to unify imagination and reality might be "pompous," Williams asserts that "to refine, to clarify, to intensify, that eternal moment in which we alone live there is but a single force—the imagination." Williams is its apostle, a fact to keep in mind in the ensuing sections.

Williams intends the typographic subversion of chapter headings to indicate the parodic intent of the first few chapters. In the first section, he proposes to "kill every man woman and child in the area west of the Carpathian Mountains," in other words the whole of western Europe. In particular he singles out the highly cultured nations, those that have made Americans conscious of a certain literary hegemony from which they are excluded: "The English, the Irish, the French. . . . " The shadow of T. S. Eliot and the immediate success of "The Wasteland" hang over Williams as he writes, "If I could say what is in my mind in Sanscrit or even Latin, I would do so. But I cannot." His first poem ("By the road to the contagious hospital") concerns spring and echoes Eliot's line "April is the cruellest month," though Williams' "Rhine maidens" ("Weialala leia / Wallala leialala" wrote Eliot) only chant "ula lu la lu . . . and and and . . . O la la."

The next section "Chapter XIII" provides the reader with a close-up of the hours before destruction. "How funny it seems. All thought of misery has left us. Why should we care? Children laughingly fling themselves under the wheels of the street cars, airplanes crash gaily to the earth." So much for compassion, and as for religion, "The new cathedral overlooking the park, looked down from its towers today, with great eyes, and saw by the decorative lake a group of people staring curiously at the corpse of a suicide."[7] So much, Williams adds, for Parson Eliot's religion.

In the third section, "Chapter VI," "all human flesh has been dead upon the earth for ten million, billion years." But through some miracle, "EVOLUTION HAS REPEATED ITSELF FROM THE BEGINNING." Williams begins to loosen the parodic framework, intending the reader to grasp by this paradox his own "first time" manner of seeing: "A perfect plagiarism results. Everything is and is new. Only the imagination is undeceived." He delivers a knock to Pound and Eliot when he asks, "Why are we here?" and answers "Dora Marsden's philosophic algebra." Then he has a vision—a sort of American *Odyssey*—about the re-culturing of Europe.

It is HOPE long asleep, aroused once more. Wilson has taken an army of advisors and sailed for England. The ship has sunk. But the men are all good swimmers. They take the women on their shoulders and bouyed on by the inspiration of the moment, they churn the free seas with their sinewy arms, like Ulysses, landing all along the European seaboard.[8]

The introduction of the American imagination as a serious force requires a further fading of parodic background. But since Williams still has much to say to the critics with whom he parried in his "forward," the prose sections become didactic. On one side are Williams, evolution and the imagination; on the other, Eliot, Pound, the critics, the classics, the dead, Europe, and the forces of emotional repression. The latter are branded "the Traditionalists of Plagiarism" and are represented by Samuel Butler, who is envisioned "trying to get hold of the crowd," and fooling men with "crude symbolism" and religion. Aligned against him are stout fellows Demuth, Hartley, Moore and Kreymborg. This fray could be a repeat of the battle in the Prologue to *Kora*, except that rather than propose a theory of imagination, Williams advances an elementary metaphysics, one too crude to be called a philosophy, but workable enough as a poetic paradigm.

The essential natures of things, he writes, can be known only through their "contact" realities, which are illustrated by the next several pages of prose and the first two poems ("Spring and All—I," "A Pot of Flowers"). Beyond and in some senses opposed to this is the other great force—the imagination, which receives examination in its functions as designer ("The Farmer" III), unmasker ("Flight to the City" IV), and unifier ("The Black Winds" V). Imagination is a kind of noumenal atmosphere that floats through and dominates the world; it is even capable of destroying the world, as the dada sections are intended to show. But it is difficult to grasp; man exists in a lacuna of planning and designing. Williams' poems begin to illustrate this theme:

The farmer in deep thought
is pacing through the rain
among his blank fields, with
hands in pockets
in his head
the harvest already planted.
A cold wind ruffles the water

among the browned weeds.
On all sides
the world rolls coldly away:
black orchards
darkened by the March clouds—
leaving room for thought.
Down past the brushwood
bristling by
the rainsluiced wagonroad
looms the artist figure of
the farmer—composing
—antagonist.[9]

The farmer who walks on the ground but is stroked by a "cool wind" (the "tough cords" in *Kora*) "in his head / the harvest already planted" is like the artist plotting to break through to revelation. He is the "composing-antagonist" in these periods because contact with "the world rolls coldly away." He is getting ready to create, to merge the real and the imaginary by the "author's classic caress." This division and recombination is what Williams has come to understand as the core of the poetic event.

He begins to explain this conception in a long prose section at the end of the fourth poem ("The Flight to the City," IV). A few pages later he summarizes it succinctly. He begins by alluding to the sky in the poem he has just finished:

So long as the sky is recognized as an association
     is recognized in its function of accessory to vague words
whose meaning it is impossible to rediscover
     its value can be nothing but mathematical certain limits
of gravity and density of air
     The farmer and the fisherman who read their own lives
there have a practical corrective for—

Williams wants to strip language of "the patina of use" as he did in *Kora*. Sentimental, romantic associations with the sky will not do: the sky must be a simple physical entity until, like the fisherman or the farmer, the poet makes his own essential contact with it. Those people who go about their business among the elements of nature

rediscover or replace demoded meanings to the
religious terms
    Among them, without expansion of imagination,
there is the residual contact between life and
the imagination which is essential to freedom.[10]

But the rest of mankind "contends with the sky through layers of demoded words and shapes."
    Williams summons up possible alternatives to this scheme but
doesn't find them credible. There is symbolism, but he calls it "crude." It
associates "emotions with natural phenomena such as anger with
lightning, flowers with love." "Such work is empty . . . It is not only
typical of most writers," he adds, but also of most of his own work.
    Use of simile typifies another kind of poetry, against which he
railed in *Kora*. Now Williams says that imagism, too, is only simile written large. "It is typified by use of the word 'like' or that 'evocation' of the
'image' which served us for a time. Its abuse is apparent. The insignifi-
cant 'image' may be 'evoked' never [sic] so ably and still mean
nothing."[11]
    Working first by exclusion and then by comparison with his fel-
low poets, as he did in the prologue to *Kora*, Williams turns to Kreymborg, Sandburg and Moore. For all his faults, Kreymborg never forfeited
to symbolism, simile or imagism—and that makes him valuable. Sandburg, however, succumbs to "an empty symbolism" when "uninspired
by intimacies of the eye and ear." But "Marianne Moore escapes."
Though formerly she represented the "north" to Williams' "south," she
has more "new composition" than her peers. Williams has come to share
her perspective. He allies himself with her when he writes:

> What I put down of value will have this value: an escape from crude sym-
> bolism, the annihilation of strained associations, complicated ritualistic
> forms designed to separate the work from "reality"—such as rhyme, meter
> as meter and not as the essential of the work. . . .
>   The word must be put down for itself, not as a symbol of nature but
> a part, cognizant of the whole—aware—civilized.[12]

After two intervening poems, Williams summarizes the *modus
operandi* of this "new creation," which, like Moore's, "will have

nothing to do with that which I detest." The basis throughout his work now is vision—the world *seen*. The following passage recapitulates a theme present in every book since *The Tempers*, where Williams posited vision "winning its way to some hill-top."

> The inevitable flux of the seeing eye toward measuring itself by the world it inhabits can only result in himself crushing humiliation [sic] unless the individual raise to some approximate co-extension with the universe. This is possible by aid of the imagination. Only through the agency of this force can a man feel himself moved largely with sympathetic pulses at work—

Every work of art must aim "to release the sense in accordance with this major requisite" of "co-extension with the universe." And the working ground of this "release" is composition.

> In the composition, the artist does exactly what every eye must do with life, fix the particular with the universality of his own personality.—Taught by the largeness of his imagination to feel *every form which he sees moving within himself*.[13] [emphasis added]

Through an "embodiment," the poem becomes the "contraction" of the "form" that is seen "moving within himself." All of this is "anterior to technique, that can have only a sequent value."

Williams expressed these same feelings less clearly in other poems ("A Street Market in N. Y., 1908," "Con Brio," "To a Solitary Disciple," "Pastoral"). The painters have taught him that the human eye never sees a whole scene, but composes in a series of independent flashes. The poet, too, must "fix the particular" on each line of a poem with the "approximate co-extension with the universe." The poet's line serves him as the painter's does: it makes visually co-extensive objects discrete by indicating their relations. It is the ground of composition, where the classic and romantic elements of a personality such as Williams' meet in a moment of tension to produce art. No better example of this fusion exists than the first poem in the book.

"Spring and All" was originally titled "It Quickens." Few if any of the appreciations of it note the futurist tone of the first title or emphasize the visual nature of the "composition" that occurs. As he did in the painterly poems of *Sour Grapes*, Williams works from top to bottom,

background to foreground, in the traditional painter's fashion. What he
does new and exceptionally well is break his lines to imbue words with
added significance.

By the road to the contagious hospital
under the surge of the blue
mottled clouds driven from the
northeast—a cold wind. Beyond the
waste of broad, muddy fields
brown with dried weeds, standing and fallen

patches of standing water
the scattering of tall trees

All along the road the reddish
purplish, forked, upstanding, twiggy

stuff of bushes and small trees
with dead, brown leaves under them
leafless vines—[14]

The first section is almost devoid of any verb forms except participles,
but is nonetheless extremely active. A series of locating words—"By,"
"under," "Beyond" and "All along"—guide the eye in recreating the
scene. The first one ("By") gestures to an unpainted foreground to
which the poet will return, and indicates the topic while creating an
expectation to fulfill. Then the background is filled in: "*under* the surge
of the blue / mottled clouds." This line break not only intensifies "blue"
and "mottled" by giving them the first and last line positions, but seems
to redouble the force of "surge." This impetus continues through the
subsequent line and its break, "driven from the / northeast," where the
final article sends the reader skipping ahead to find its noun—an ab-
straction isolated in a new stanza.

As the eye drops down just "beyond" the road, it catches the vista
of fields "brown with dried weeds, standing and fallen." Colors are emphasized by prominent line location, and the positions of the weeds are
replicated in words by the caesura before "standing" and the final position of "fallen." Even closer to the eye are isolated, unmoving "patches
of standing water / the scattering of tall trees," items that are isolated
fragments of lines, devoid of connectives and end-stopped. In the close
foreground, at eye level "all along the road," are the famous bushes. The
length along which they border the road is indicated by the absence of

end-stopping. The bright colors in the bushes hold down prominent line positions ("Reddish/purplish") while more nondescript colors are located in the interior of the line ("with dead, brown leaves under them"). As a visualization of the stuff of bushes, the line "purplish, forked, upstanding, twiggy" speaks for itself far more eloquently than any explicator.

From the bushes Williams' gaze travels down to the "dead, brown leaves under them" and the "leafless vines." The eye is at the bottom of the canvas, immediate foreground.

Then Williams backs off, generalizing outward from the scene he has painted to the abstract. "Lifeless in appearance, sluggish / dazed spring approaches." This draws on the technique he mastered in the nature poems of *Sour Grapes*. The non-specificity of the "they" and "them" in the coming section will create a feeling of universal sympathy, of "approximate co-extension with the universe." The reader is able to watch the opposed sides of the poet rise toward a moment of tension in which line and discrete shape will fuse.

> One by one objects are defined—
> It quickens: clarify, outline of leaf.

Williams resolves the conflict and asserts his control of the poem by being the one who draws the line, by deciding what will take shape, what will be defined. Yet he must be careful not to over-define; he wants to engage the vague forces of "profound change" and "stark dignity" in his lines. Suddenly he gets the concluding line: "rooted they / grip down and begin to awaken." The speed of the insight is transferred to the reader by uniting in the same line the opposing senses of "grip down" and "to awaken," which beckons upwards.

This speed is one of the differences between poetry and prose, a distinction Williams raised and neglected in *Kora in Hell* and raises again in *Spring and All*. The discussion begins immediately after "To Elsie" (XVIII), the last few lines of which must be quoted to give the bridge to the argument that follows.

> It is only in isolate flecks that
> something
> is given off

No one
to witness
and adjust, no one to drive the car.

Or better: prose has to do with the fact of an emotion;
poetry has to do with the dynamization of emotion into a
separate form. This is the force of imagination.
prose: statement of facts concerning emotions, intellectual
states, data of all sorts—technical expositions, jargon,
of all sorts—fictional and other—
poetry: new form dealt with as a reality in itself.

The form of prose is the accuracy of its subject matter—
how best to expose the multiform phases of its material
        the form of poetry is related to the movements of the
imagination revealed in words—or whatever it may be—
the cleavage is complete.[15]

With this gloss the poem that on first reading seemed a narrative takes on
new significance. Besides the predicament of the American imagination,
Elsie represents the American mania for creating and disseminating
"facts" and "data" that is itself antithetical to the noumenous quality of
poetry.

as if the earth under our feet
were
an excrement of some sky
and we degraded prisoners
destined
to hunger until we eat filth

But the urge that animates poetry does not settle for this. While the prosaic forces denigrate existence,

        the imagination strains
after deer
going by fields of goldenrod in
the stifling heat of September.

Inarticulate and uncultured as she is, Elsie has the potential for "expressing with broken / brain the truth about us," if only there were someone to *give form* to it—"to drive the car."

In the prose that follows the bridging section, Williams buttresses this argument by analogy to painting.

> I mean that there will always be prose painting, representative work, clever as may be in revealing new phases of emotional research presented on the surface.
>
> But the jump from that to Cezanne or back to certain of the primitives is the impossible.
>
> The primitives are not back in some remote age—they are not BEHIND experience. Work which bridges the gap between the rigidities of vulgar experience and the imagination is rare. It is new, immediate.[16]

Elsie is, of course, a primitive (an intervening poem, in fact, has mentioned the primitive paintings of "prehistoric caves / in the Pyrenees") and when Williams resumes the debate in the next prose section, he focuses on the essence of prose. He comes to two tentative conclusions: "There is no form to prose but that which depends on clarity" and "form in prose ends with the end of that which is being communicated."

The two poems that follow are counterpointed to demonstrate the "separate origins" of prose and poetry. "Rapid Transit," (XXV) consists of prose arranged in lines, some of them culled from subway posters and the whole seemingly inspired by Stuart Davis' collages.

> Somebody dies every four minutes
> in New York State
> ....
> Careful Crossing Campaign
> Cross Crossings Cautiously
> ....
> Ho for the open country
> Don't stay shut up in hot rooms
> Go to one of the Great Parks
> Pelham Bay for example
> It's on Long Island Sound
> with bathing, boating
> tennis, baseball, golf, etc.

Amid these slogans are vernacular interruptions, possibly the comments of the typesetters.

186

What the hell do you know about it?
. . . .
What's the use of sweating over
this sort of thing, Carl; here
it is all set up—

Paired with this is "At the Ball Game," a poem that demonstrates the "separate origin" of poetry. At the ball park, they are "moved uniformly / by a spirit of uselessness / which delights them." Rather than prose operating to "clarify" something (the need to cross safely), the crowd admires "all the exciting detail / of the chase / and the escape / the error / the flash of genius- / all to no end save beauty / the eternal."[17] The relation of this collective spirit, unnamed but analogous to "imagination," to the specific individuals in the crowd comes about when the eye defines the concrete.

So in detail they, the crowd,
are beautiful
for this
to be warned against
saluted and defied—
It is alive, venemous
It smiles grimly
its words cut.

Williams picks out two people to "get it," to act as the locus of the spirit. They are the only individuals he needs to define against the amorphous background, for the point is, as he concludes, that "the crowd is laughing / in detail."

The concern for painting in *Spring and All* is announced by its dedication to Charles Demuth. Williams' comment on it reveals the importance of his male friendships and indicates a steeping in personal sources as he grew older.

I met him almost at once when I went down to Penn in my Freshman year and we became at once lifelong friends. The men I met in those years I have clung to forever; that's the way I felt about it from the first, that it would be forever, and that's the way it has turned out. With *Spring and All*, it was his turn for a dedication and tribute.[18]

There are an unusual number of references in *Spring and All* to various painters, and several of the poems have been explained in terms of work by specific artists. These citations also function within Williams' lifelong system of artistic analogues.

The first reference is to Greek culture, which Williams thought less fecund than Roman, but which he tied to futurism.

> In that majestic progress of life, that gives the exact impression of Phidias' frieze, the men and beasts of which, though they seem of the rigidity of marble are not so but move, with blinding rapidity, though we do not notice it. . . . [19]

This passage occurs in "The Traditionalists of Plagiarism" and ends with the phrase "at last SPRING is approaching." Apparently spring will break the static force of Phidias' frieze, which shows the pan-Athenic procession. Parts of it comprise the Elgin marbles that Williams saw in the British Museum when he visited Pound in 1910.

Another classicist of Williams' youth who comes up for judgment early is Holbein, to whom the poet referred often as the embodiment of mimetic art:

> The great furor about perspective in Holbein's day had as a consequence much fine drawing, it made coins defy gravity, standing on the table as if in the act of falling. To say this was lifelike must have been satisfying to the master, it gave depth, pungency.
>
> But all the while the picture escaped notice—partly because of the perspective. Or if noticed it was for the most part because one could see "the birds pecking at the grapes" in it.[20]

He evidently knew of Barrhasios' fabled grapes, so realistic that they reportedly fooled the birds. Williams implies his disapproval of Rubens and Veronese by including them in the piece parodying dada poetry. He would like to admire Goya and Velazquez ("I don't know what the Spanish see in their Velazquez and Goya but—") yet lacking at this point a background in the tradition of Spanish painting, he brushes them aside.

For Williams the world of art breaks cleanly in two with the advent of Cezanne. The mere mention of Cezanne is felt to be self explanatory:

Cezanne -
The only realism in art is of the imagination. It is only thus that the world
escapes plagiarism after nature and becomes a creation.

Even his favorite, Juan Gris, is designated to a place "coming after the
impressionists, the expressionists, Cezanne—." Williams cites the certain obsolescence of the "prose painters" because they cannot "jump
from [their work] to Cezanne" without the lengthy and complete overhaul that the master undertook.[21]

    Duchamp is not mentioned in *Spring and All*, but Williams con-
tinues to build on what he learned from him. Ideas that he attributed to
Duchamp or Arensberg in *Kora*, Williams articulates now in his own
way. The image of the shattered stained-glass window appears several
times, though not as a metaphor for the creative act. Williams pictures
that as a gunshot through glass, the broken fragments futuristically frozen as they spiral out.

Burst it asunder
break through to the fifty words
necessary
. . . .
stars of tinsel
from the great end of a cornucopia
of glass.
. . . .
Clean is he alone
after whom stream
the broken pieces of the city-
flying apart at his approaches[22]

    Duchamp's mark appears when Williams writes of "leaving off
the g / of sunlight and grass—impossible," for he is referring not only
to such work as Arensberg's "Ing," but also to Duchamp's experiments
with a "new language." The unity that Duchamp discerned in eroticism
and that Williams developed in *Kora* is still present. "It is one." "It is the
same," he repeats in "Black Winds." Williams even begins to think that
art should be put at the service of the intelligence: "A work of the imagination which fails to release the senses in accordance with this major
requisite—the sympathies, the intelligence in its selective world, fails at
the elucidation." He endorses more explicitly than before the parting

irony that mitigates the artist's connection to his work: " . . . at the end of the feast nothing would be left but suicide. That or the imagination which in this case takes the form of humor, is known in that form—the release from physical necessity."[23]

Williams demonstrates an understanding of the way that art can use "the precise and exact aspect" of science in its craftsmanship to produce a result that undermines the claims of science.

> . . . we are beginning to discover the truth that in great works of the imagination A CREATIVE FORCE IS SHOWN AT WORK MAKING OBJECTS WHICH ALONE COMPLETE SCIENCE AND ALLOW INTELLIGENCE TO SURVIVE—his picture lives anew. It lives as only pictures can: by their power to ESCAPE ILLUSION and stand between man and nature as saints once stood between man and the sky.

Most importantly Williams has learned to avoid reification. After the puzzling lines that end "The Right of Way"—"I saw a girl with one leg / over the rail of a balcony"—Williams comments: "When in the condition of imaginative suspense only will the writing have reality as explained partially in what precedes."[24] "Imaginative suspense" is not only a narrative tactic—here the girl is caught in a vaguely erotic pose reminiscent of some of Edward Hopper's women—but also a syntactic technique. Suspense can be created by elaborating a sentence structure that breaks lines into tantalizing but incomplete parts, impelling the reader onward by virtue of a need for grammatical completion.

Marsden Hartley is also a strong presence and one to whom Williams indicates his debt more clearly. He makes several references to Hartley's *Adventures in the Arts* (1921). "Nothing is put down in the present book . . . which is not intended as of a piece with the 'nature' which Shakespeare mentions and which Hartley speaks of so completely in his *Adventures*."

> That is why boxing matches and
> Chinese poems are the same—That is why
> Hartley praises Miss Wirt [sic]

May Wirth is the subject of "A Charming Equestrienne," a chapter in *Adventures in the Arts*. Hartley considers her an artist, and Williams seconds the motion that "consummate mastery" in any field creates art.

As befits a book developed out of common interests, Williams ends *Spring and All* with a reference to the last chapter of Hartley's work:

> Sometimes I speak of imagination as a force, an electricity or a medium, a place. It is immaterial which: for whether it is the condition or a place or a dynamization its effect is the same: to free the world of fact from the impositions of "art" (see Hartley's last chapter) and to liberate the man to act in whatever direction his disposition leads.[25]

It is possible that the famous bushes of "Spring and All" owe something to Hartley's paintings "Desertion" (1912) and "New Mexico Reflections" (1923). The dramatically forked trees in the foreground of these paintings impressed Williams and he mentioned them repeatedly.

Charles Demuth, to whom the book is dedicated, receives early mention in the text and is drafted as an ally in Williams' central battle: "Demuth and a few others do their best to point out the error, telling us that design is a function of the imagination, describing its movements, its colors—but it is a hard battle." The poem "The Pot of Flowers" that precedes this passage is, by common consent, a treatment in poetry of Demuth's watercolor "Tuberoses," (1922) which later became part of Williams' collection.

Pink confused with white
flowers and flowers reversed
take and spill the shaded flame
darting it back
into the lamp's horn

petals aslant darkened with mauve

red where in whorls
petal lays its glow upon petal
round flame green throats
petal radiant with transpiercing light
contending
        above
the leaves
reaching up their modest green
from the pot's rim
and there, wholly dark, the pot
gay with rough moss.[26]

Working with his customary ways, Williams begins at the top of the scene and works down. The pink and white flowers are a confusion of "flowers and flowers reversed." Their essence is unbounded color, so he is careful not to ascribe discrete shapes or forms to them. They "take and spill the shaded flame" of the light source, an element foremost in the mind of the painter, and reflect "it back / into the lamp's horn" that is later located "above." The actual colors are placed in prominent line positions, but the uninterrupted sentence flow indicates an oceanic form-lessness to their mingling. Only as the poem grows is there a need for form. Williams sees "petals aslant," which are described in painterly diction as "darkened with mauve." Colors become gradually associated with defined shape: "red where in whorls / petal lays its glow upon petal / round flame-green throats." Then Williams' eye falls on the "leaves / reaching up their modest green," and on "the pot's rim" and finally on the "rough moss" adhering to it. In part the poem takes its cues from the painting, for in the water color Demuth makes dramatic use of the white space between the flowers and leaves. The objects are mingled, yet they are defined precisely, too, seeming to float above the paper, free of the background.

The genius of this apparently "factual" poem lies in a similar ordering of the "confused" flowers by the poet through his line. In earlier days Williams' fauve instincts would have led him to give over the poem to the brilliant light and color: it would have been a lyric. Now his practiced hand sets down what his eye sees in its instantaneous "vision" and he frames a poetic line that either continues or stops according to the next action of the eye. The triumph in "The Pot of Flowers" is the mastery of the formless and its attachment to a place "wholly dark the pot / gay with rough moss."

Other painters are mentioned, of course. Williams refers to Juan Gris twice in the most complimentary terms: once as a representative of his contact theory and again as the progeny of Cezanne. Williams tops this tribute with the poem "The Rose," which is preceded by this passage.

> But such a picture as that of Juan Gris, though I have not seen it in color, is important as marking more clearly than any I have seen what the modern trend is: the attempt is being made to separate things of the imagination from life, and obviously, by using the forms common to experience so a not to frighten the onlooker away but to invite him.[27]

Dada Spring

Gris' collage "Roses" (1912) consists of flowers that are photographed, cut out of a magazine or catalog, and pasted into the composition. The black and white reproduction that Williams saw would have obscured the color and rendered more sharply the edge and definition.

The rose is obsolete
but each petal ends in
an edge, the double facet
cementing the grooved
columns of air—The edge
cuts without cutting
meets—nothing—renews
itself in metal or porcelain—

whither? It ends—

But if it ends
the start is begun
so that to engage roses
becomes a geometry—

Sharper, neater, more cutting
figured in majolica—
the broken plate
glazed with a rose

Somewhere the sense
makes copper roses
steel roses—

The rose carried a weight of love
but love is at an end—of roses

It is at the edge of the
petal that love waits

Crisp, worked to defeat
laboredness—fragile
plucked, moist, half-raised
cold, precise, touching

What

The place between the petal's
edge and the

From the petal's edge a line starts
that being of steel
infinitely fine, infinitely
rigid penetrates
the Milky Way
without contact—lifting

from it—neither hanging
nor pushing

The fragility of the flower
unbruised
penetrates space.[28]

There has been considerable debate about this poem. Dijkstra, Townley and recently Fure have asserted that it is a transcription, in some form, of the painting, even though it seems a meditative rather than literal rendering. But Sayre argues that when the text resumes with this description,

> Here is a shutter, a bunch of grapes, a sheet of music, a picture of sea and mountains (particularly fine) which the onlooker is not for a moment permitted to witness as an "illusion." One thing laps over on the other, the cloud laps over on the shutter, the bunch of grapes is part of the handle of the guitar, the mountain and sea are obviously not "the mountain and sea," but a picture of the mountain and sea.

it is clearly describing Gris' "The Open Window," which had appeared in black-and-white in the January, 1922, issue of *Broom*. He votes to discard the correspondence, arguing that "this close a connection between text and poetry rarely, if ever, appears in *Spring and All*," which is clearly not true.[29]

Other scholars have praised this poem because it "describes and delineates rather than imposing a . . . specific interpretation of meaning."[30] All of this fails to explain the obsessive attention given to those futuristic edges and their meaning. Actually the poem describes Williams' vision into Gris' "composition," an area in which they share a

194

common technique. This is announced in the first line: "The rose is obsolete." It is obsolete because, like the sky in Williams' earlier exposition on technique, it has been "demoded." It is no longer sufficient to convey "love," which Williams makes explicit:

> The rose carried the weight of love
> but love is at an end—of roses

Williams directs the reader to the location of a meaningful verbal approximation of love:

> It is at the edge of the
> petal that love waits
> . . . .
> The place between the petal's
> edge and the

Love begins here because "definition" begins here; composition acts here to mediate between the amorphous force of the "Milky Way" and the "Crisp / worked to defeat / laboredness - fragile / plucked, moist, half-raised / cold, precise, touching" specifics that can be attributed to the flower. How much to define? Williams defines only enough to give an effective intimation of the tangible yet vulnerable: "The fragility of the flower / unbruised / penetrates space."

In such an act of composition Williams creates, as he writes at another point in *Spring and All,* "A world detached from the necessity of recording it, sufficient to itself . . . with which he has bitter and delicious relations and from which he is independent—moving at will from one thing to another—as he pleases, unbound—complete." He successfully balances his romantic and classic impulses.

Spring and All represents an advance over *Kora* for that reason: the process that a careful reader could discern developing in Williams' unconscious is made conscious and grasped in *Spring and All.* Williams acknowledges this in two prose sections of the volume. "I think of my earlier work," he writes, "and what it has cost me not to be clear. . . . Now I have come to a different condition. I find that the values there discovered can be extended."[31]

11. *One Gesture*

"If I did not achieve a language, I at least stated what I would not say. I would not melt myself into a great universal sea of love with all its shapes and colors."

Williams

The Arensbergs' move to Hollywood in 1920 marked the end of the salon, but did not end the close friendships within the circle. Few of his friends knew that Arensberg had faced financial ruin after World War I. He was a private man. When they came to Hollywood, he was still the genial host, still the patron who minimized his own role and cultivated the success of his artists. When a biographer attempted to assemble a few pages on Arensberg in the fifties, he found that everyone remembered the paintings, the food, and the celebrities, but few remembered Arensberg.

It was different for Williams and a few others, notably Sheeler, for whom the circle was a great formative experience. It was an initiation, a revelation, and an accomplishment, so that other parties and cliques seemed at best copies of a thing they had seen in the original.

As is often the case when strong bonds are forged among young men, the principals of the circle kept in touch. Though Williams turned his attention to an American program for poetry, in the forties he wrote to Arensberg that

> it has been a number of years since our first encounters centering about your studio and its life in—when was that? Just as alive today as then. Curious how little meaning the years really have. I mean to say that the important contributive moments are just as dissociated from the element of time today as they have always been. . . . The French are swarming in New York as they did in 1917-18 and some of the old ones still among them.[1]

196

When he travelled to California for a reading at U.C.L.A. in the fifties, Williams wrote ahead to invite Arensberg: "I thought you might like to know of it and for sure I'd like to see you there or afterward."[2] He closed with information about their friend Charles Sheeler. Arensberg probably smiled when he read the letter: Williams had become a famous poet, but the patron was in reduced circumstances.

Duchamp was a frequent visitor in Hollywood. At first he came to help Arensberg obtain the best prices for his Brancusis, but when finances improved, he returned to help Arensberg buy them back from the new owners. Arensberg set up several shows for Duchamp on the West Coast in the thirties, and there is a voluminous correspondence about these affairs that continues until 1945.

Duchamp encouraged Arensberg to buy more of Charles Sheeler's work; he admired the exacting technique and preternatural clarity of the American's work, even though his French friends were cool to Sheeler. The three men kept in close touch through the twenties and thirties, as one of Sheeler's notes to Arensberg in 1927 shows:

I only saw Marcel a couple of times before he left for Chicago with the show. He had hopes that it would go to Los Angeles, but they backed down.[3]

Charles Demuth, though an ailing diabetic, kept in touch with Arensberg and Duchamp by mail. He wrote to Arensberg of seeing "dear Marcel" on a rare trip to New York and "how much good it did my heart." Williams, of course, went to see and treat Demuth with the newly discovered insulin in the twenties.

In the thirties Sheeler thought about becoming a cinematographer and moving to Hollywood, which was drawing writers and painters from New York to its sun-drenched hillsides. He learned to use the motion picture camera, and wrote happily to Arensberg that he would be living in Hollywood soon. But his apprenticeship was not easy, and Sheeler finally concluded that it was "a considerable grind and incidentally much tension."

For Williams, at least, the circle continued to provide sustenance. He looked at the work of Sheeler, of Demuth, of Hartley and Duchamp and he saw the analogues and implications of his own work. They were more valuable to him than other painters because he had followed them through the revolutions. He seems to have heeded Duchamp particularly, putting himself on guard against coming to the end in his own art. That he dropped such promising forms as that of "The Red Wheelbarrow," which he repeated only in "Between Walls" in the thirties, may owe to his perception of it as a kind of verbal "readymade," and his memory of where that form led the Frenchman.

He proceeded to have one of the most productive, technically innovative careers of all American poets. Each book, or at least every other one, opened up a new avenue of invention. But it would be wrong to claim that the analogue he discovered in painting, and the use he made of it, are developments that can be traced cleanly through his work after the twenties. Between 1909 and 1923 the component parts of Williams' poetry are visible to an unusual degree; in *Spring and All* (1923) one already senses that his work is entirely his own, that any trace of apprenticeship has vanished. More and more the value of painting to Williams became the metaphor it provided. He was constantly struggling to eliminate the inessential, to reveal as Brancusi had revealed in stone the essential forms of his art. What he finally discovered was a simple, fluid mode that is related to painting only in that realm in which all art is united.

This is not to say that he abandoned his word painting. As late as 1929, in *The Descent of Winter*, Williams wrote poems that were strikingly visual in the manner of his earlier work. Passages such as the following are self-sufficient picture poems:

> that brilliant field
> of rainwet orange
> blanketed
> by the red grass
> and oilgreen bayberry
>
> the last yarrow
> on the gutter
> white by the sand
> rainwater
>
> and a white birch
> with yellow leaves
> and few
> and loosely hung.

But he consolidated these themes and techniques in the *Collected Poems 1921-1931*, and drawing the implications of his work therein, he moved to revamp even more basically his technique. In "The Wind Increases," a poem that harks back to the "tough cords" in *Kora in Hell*, he wrote:

```
Good Christ what is
a poet—if any
                    exists?
a man
whose words will
        bite
            their way
home—being actual
having the form
            of motion.
                    [emphasis added]
```

"The form of motion," that durable legacy of futurism, constitutes one of three lasting influences of the 1909-1923 period on Williams' later work. The others were Kandinsky, upon whose charged physical forms and special social role for the artist Williams built, and Duchamp. It was not until "The Descent" that Williams found a poetic equivalent of Duchamp's "Three Standard Stoppages" - the variable foot. In it he saw a measure elastic enough to encompass change and chance, even to admit that all might be flux or "process," and yet firm enough to establish the rhythms required by his sense of structure.

In *Paterson* Williams took up the thematic concerns of the "Large Glass" again: divorce, the separation of man from his physical world, and of man from woman. As Sayre notes, "It is divorce which 'blocks' the poem's fulfillment in 'spring time.' "

That Williams diminished his alliance with avant-garde painting is perhaps fortunate. Harold Rosenberg has noted that Picabia and Man Ray and others of the Stieglitz group became "self appointed leaders inspired with the belief that they and their contemporaries could equal and surpass the greatest feats in history."

Williams' subsequent poetry was less visual, less visually structured, and more dependent on the dynamism of the lines themselves. His use of painters and painting, most notably in *Pictures from Brueghel*, was consciously metaphoric. For Williams, Pieter Brueghel was a "localist,' whose meticulous attention to things-in-themselves and to life as it was lived in his epoch gave his painting that preternatural quality which Kandinsky thought the result of fidelity to age and locale. Williams gave himself over to admiration of the earlier localist:

> The living quality of
> the man's mind
> stands out
>
> and its covert assertions
> for art, art, art!
> painting
>
> that the Renaissance
> tried to absorb
> but
>
> it remained a wheat field
> over which the
> wind played

In this volume, only "The Fall of Icarus" and "The Hunters in the Snow" attempt in the telling to replicate the sequence of sensation that the painter achieved on canvas.

When his fame spread, Williams repeated for eager audiences some of his early lessons. In his speech of acceptance before the Academy of Arts and Letters in 1951, he told the "Hartpence story," and made its lesson elastic enough to stretch from Cezanne to the present.

> From that through cubism, Matisse to Motherwell, the ultimate step is one gesture. And it is important because it says that you don't paint a picture or write a poem *about* anything, you *make* a picture or a poem of *anything*.

Williams' friend and nemesis Ezra Pound wrote that "the arts bear witness and define for us the inner nature and conditions of man." More than most of his fellows, Williams dedicated his artistic life to the exploration and reportage of the inner nature in conflict with the twentieth century. He knew something about the magic of shape, of vision, that we still struggle to name. The painter Jean Bazaine said that "a form that can reconcile man with his world is an 'art of communion' by which a man at any moment, can recognize his own unformed countenance in the world." Somehow Williams apprehended this "communion" early, and dedicated himself to its transfer to poetry. It gives us some intimation of why, despite the comparative clumsiness of writing about such things, Williams has always enjoyed tremendous respect among people alive to color and form and nuance of speech. What he invented has expanded our means and added to our perceptive lexicon. What he apprehended at that deep level of consciousness where the primordial relations of things gain a foothold in the human consciousness, we now recognize in our own lives.

Notes

Notes—Chapter 1

1. William Carlos Williams, in *Speaking Straight Ahead: Interviews with William Carlos Williams*, ed. Linda Welshimer Wagoner (Middletown, Conn.: Wesleyan University Press, 1972), p. 154. I am indebted to Ms. Wagoner's earlier studies, *The Poems of William Carlos Williams* (Wesleyan, 1963) and *The Prose of William Carlos Williams* (Wesleyan, 1970), which identify in different terms many traits of Williams' work that I discuss in this study.

2. Paul Mariani's biography was published after this volume had been set in type; I am happy to note, however, that most of the new information he provides complements this study. The other recent studies I have found helpful or thought-provoking are these: James E. Breslin, "William Carlos Williams and Charles Demuth: Cross-Fertilization in the Arts," *Journal of Modern Literature*, 1977, vol. 6, p. 248; Suzy Michel, "The Identity of William Carlos Williams' 'Solitary Disciple,' " *Modern Language Review*, 1978, vol. 73, p. 741; Gail Levin, "Wassily Kandinsky and the American Avant-Garde," *Criticism*, 1979, vol. 21, p. 347; Jacqueline Saunier-Ollier, "Dans le sillage de l'Armory Show," *Revue Francais des Etudes Americaines*, 1979, vol. 7, p. 51; Rob Fure, "The Design of Experience: William Carlos Williams and Juan Gris," *William Carlos Williams Newsletter*, 1978, vol. 4, no. ii, p. 10; Henry Sayre, "Distancing 'The Rose' from 'Roses,' " *William Carlos Williams Newsletter*, 1979, vol. 4, no. 1, p. 18; Henry Sayre, "The Poetics of Marcel Duchamp and William Carlos Williams," *Journal of Modern Literature*, Winter 1981, p. 3; Peter Schmidt, "Some Versions of Modernist Pastoral: Williams and the Precisionists," *Contemporary Literature*, Summer 1980, p. 383.

3. Bram Dijkstra, *The Hieroglyphics of a New Speech*: Cubism, Stieglitz and the Early Poetry of William Carlos Williams (Princeton, N.J.: Princeton University Press, 1969), p. 86.

4. Alfred Stieglitz, Stieglitz Archive (Yale Za Stieglitz), Beinecke Manuscript Library, Yale University.

5. Ibid.

6. Ibid.

7. Ibid.

8. Ibid.

9. Williams, unpublished draft of "What of Alfred Stieglitz?" (Yale Za Wms. 262-a-b) Beinecke Manuscript Library, Yale University.

10. Ibid.

11. Alfred Kazin, *New York Jew* (New York: Knopf, 1978), pp. 90–91.

12. Williams, "The Delicacies," *Sour Grapes* (Boston: Four Seas Co., 1921), p. 40.

13. Beatrice Wood, interview with the author.

14. Patrick L. Stewart, "The European Invasion of American Art and the Arensberg Circle, 1914–1918" *Arts*, May, 1977, p. 108.

15. Alfred Kreymborg, *Troubadour* (New York: Boni & Liveright, 1925), p. 219.

16. Anne d'Harnoncourt, "A. E. Gallatin and the Arensbergs" *Apollo*, July, 1974, pp. 52–53.

17. Beatrice Wood, interview with the author.

18. d'Harnoncourt, p. 53.

19. Stewart, p. 108.

20. Williams, *The Autobiography* (New York: Random House, 1951), p. 138.

21. Williams, draft of *Voyage to Pagany*, Beinecke Manuscript Library, Yale University, unpaginated.

22. See especially the unpublished essay "The Baroness Elsa von Freitag Loringhoven" at the Beinecke Manuscript Library for a more explicit explanation of pre-writing. This phrase is taken from that essay.

23. The phrase is that of J. Hillis Miller in his introduction to *William Carlos Williams: a Collection of Critical Essays* (Englewood Cliffs: Prentice Hall, 1966), p. 6.

24. Wagoner, *Interviews*, p. 53.

Notes—Chapter 2

1. Marsden Hartley, letter to Alfred Stieglitz, Oct. 9, 1923, Stieglitz Archive, Beinecke Library, Yale University.

2. Williams, quoted by Dickran Tashjian, *William Carlos Williams and the American Scene* (New York: Whitney Museum, 1979), p. 10.

3. Williams, unpublished manuscript of *The Autobiography*, (Yale Za Williams Autobiography), Beinecke Library, Yale University.

4. Williams, *Yes, Mrs. Williams* (New York: McDowell, 1959), p. 3.

5. Reed Whittemore, *William Carlos Williams, Poet from Jersey* (Boston: Houghton Mifflin, 1975), pp. 14–15.

6. Williams, *The Autobiography*, p. 36.

7. Stanley Koehler, "William Carlos Williams" *Paris Review*, VIII, no. 32, Summer-Fall, 1962, p. 120.

8. Williams, *The Great American Novel* in *Imaginations* (New York: New Directions, 1971), p. 188.

9. Williams, *Yes*, p. 5; Wagoner, *Interviews*, p. 19.

10. Whittemore, *Williams*, p. 14; Williams, *Yes*, p. 5.

11. Williams, *Autobiography*, p. 10; *Yes*, p. 17; and an unpublished version of *I Wanted to Write a Poem* (B4c), S.U.N.Y.—Buffalo.

12. Williams, *I Wanted to Write a Poem* (Boston: Beacon Press, 1958), p. 3.

13. Williams, "The Painting," *Agenda* (London), April, 1960, p. 1.

14. Williams, *Selected Essays* (New York: New Directions, 1969), p. 3.
15. Williams, *Yes*, p. 75, p. 100.
16. William Carlos Williams, *The Selected Letters of William Carlos Williams* (New York: McDowell, Obolensky, 1957), p. 275.
17. Williams, *Yes*, p. 94, p. 13.
18. Williams, *Autobiography*, p. 15.
19. Wagoner, *Interviews*, p. 9; Williams, *Autobiography*, p. 52; *Imaginations*, p. 207; *Autobiography*, p. 52.
20. Williams, *Letters*, p. 5; *Autobiography*, p. 53, p. 151.
21. Williams, unpublished letter, (Buff F1107) S.U.N.Y.—Buffalo Library.
22. Emily Farnham, *Charles Demuth: Behind the Laughing Mask*, (Norman: U. of Oklahoma Press, 1971), p. 45.
23. Williams, "Introduction," *Selected Essays* (unpaginated); *Autobiography*, pp. 61–62.
24. Williams, *Letters*, p. 14.
25. Williams quoted in Bram Dijkstra's *A Recognizable Image: William Carlos Williams on Art and Artists* (New York: New Directions, 1978), p. 11, p. 12. F-1118, S.U.N.Y.—Buffalo.
26. Williams, unpublished letter, April 6, 1909, to Ed. (Yale Za Williams), Beinecke Library, Yale University.
27. Williams, *Letters*, p. 15; p. 18.
28. Williams, *Autobiography*, p. 120; *Letters*, p. 312; *The Embodiment of Knowledge* (New York: New Directions, 1977), p. 114.
29. Williams, *Autobiography*, p. 117; *Voyage to Pagany* (New York: New Directions, 1970), p. 24, p. 33.
30. Williams, *Autobiography*, p. 120.
31. Williams, *Pagany*, p. 117, p. 116.
32. Wagoner, *Interviews*, p. 72; *Autobiography*, p. 121.
33. Williams, *Pagany*, pp. 100–103; p. 102.
34. Williams, *Autobiography*, p. 124.
35. Koehler, *Paris Review*, p. 133.
36. Williams, unpublished ms. of *Autobiography*, Beinecke Library, Yale University; and *Letters*, p. 55, p. 28.
37. Williams, unpublished letter, June 23, 1951, Beinecke Library, Yale University; *Autobiography*, p. 237.
38. Williams, *To Write a Poem*, p. 3.

Notes—Chapter 3

1. Williams, unpublished note (Yale Za 174 misc.) Beinecke Library, Yale University.
2. Williams, note (Yale Za 22) Beinecke Library, Yale University.
3. Williams, *Autobiography*, p. 106.
4. Ibid., p. 47, pp. 130–131.
5. Florence Williams, quoted by Edith Heal, "Interview with Flossie," *The William Carlos Williams Newsletter*, vol. 2, no. 1, Fall 1976, p. 11.

6. Quoted in Milton W. Brown, *The Story of the Armory Show* (Princeton: Princeton University Press, 1955), p. 156.

7. Williams, *Letters*, p. 23.

8. Farnham, *Demuth*, p. 20; p. 12.

9. Williams, *Autobiography*, p. 177.

10. Quoted in Farnham, *Demuth*, p. 110.

11. Ibid., pp. 130–136.

12. Williams, *To Write a Poem*, p. 19.

13. Tashjian, *American Scene*, p. 18.

14. Williams, *To Write a Poem*, p. 20; *Autobiography*, p. 148.

15. Williams, *Letters*, p. 27; A *Recognizable Image*, pp. 57–58.

16. Williams, "Spring Letter" to *The Egoist* (London), vol. 3, no. 9, 1916, p. 137.

17. Williams, *To Write a Poem*, p. 34; *Autobiography*, p. 134.

18. Farnham, *Demuth*, p. 104.

19. Williams, quoted by Dijkstra in *A Recognizable Image*, p. 17 S.U.N.Y.—Buffalo (C57).

20. Williams, *Autobiography*, pp. 380–381.

21. Wagoner, *Interviews*, p. 64.

22. Tashjian, *American Scene*, p. 50; Williams, *Autobiography*, p. 168.

23. Williams, *Pagany*, pp. 46–47. Dating the Williams-Sheeler meeting is difficult. Both were at Arensbergs' (Sheeler photographed the art). Josephson dates the meeting at his return, but in *The Autobiography* Williams put it in 1923. Florence Williams cited a 1924 date, but I opt with Josephson, at least for the meeting of the men individually.

24. Williams, *Autobiography*, p. 195, p. 213.

25. Ibid., p. 217; *Pagany*, p. 239.

26. Williams, *Letters*, p. 62; *Pagany*, p. 128.

27. Williams, *Letters*, pp. 60–61; p. 64.

28. Williams, *Pagany*, p. 218; p. 242; *Selected Essays*, p. 157.

29. Williams, *Letters*, p. 69; *The Little Review* (May, 1929) p. 87; *Autobiography*, pp. 299–300; *Letters*, p. 124.

30. Williams, quoted in Dijkstra, *A Recognizable Image*, p. 4; *Letters*, p. 181; Florence Williams, "Interview," p. 4.

31. Williams, *Letters*, p. 218.

32. Florence Williams in Koehler, *Paris Review*, p. 135; pp. 111–112.

33. James Laughlin, "Dev Evans," *William Carlos Williams Newsletter*, vol. 4, no. 1, Spring 1978, p. 1.

34. Florence Williams, "Interview," p. 13; Koehler, *Paris Review*, p. 120.

Notes—Chapter 4

1. Alfred Kreymborg, *Troubadour* (New York: Boni and Liveright, 1925), pp. 200–201.

2. Ibid., p. 221.

3. Ibid., p. 222.

4. Man Ray, "An Interview with Man Ray," *Arts*, May, 1977, p. 117.

5. William Carlos Williams, *To Write a Poem*, p. 20. Despite his declaration of exclusiveness, Williams submitted work to many magazines in this period.

6. Kreymborg, p. 236.

7. Quoted in Caroline Burke, "Becoming Mina Loy," *Women's Studies*, London, 1980, vol. 7, p. 141, a study to which I am in debt.

8. Quoted by Wagoner, *Poetry*, p. 77.

9. Kreymborg, p. 233; Williams, "Spring Letter," p. 137.

10. Kreymborg, p. 238.

11. Ibid., p. 240.

12. Williams, in Koehler, *Paris Review*, p. 116.

13. Kreymborg, pp. 242–243.

14. Williams, *Autobiography*, pp. 135–136.

15. Jacqueline Saunier-Ollier, "Dans le sillage de l'Armory Show," *Revue Francais des Etudes Americaines*, vol. 7, pp. 54–55; Duchamp remark in Stewart, "The European Invasion of American Art," *Arts*, p. 109.

16. Williams, unpublished manuscript, "Marianne Moore," S.U.N.Y.— Buffalo (C-90); and "Marianne Moore," *Imaginations*, ed. Webster Schott, (New York: New Directions, 1970), p. 311.

17. Williams, unpublished manuscript, "Mina Loy," (Yale Za Williams-65-66), Beinecke Library, Yale University.

18. Williams, "Spring Letter," p. 137.

19. Ibid.; *Autobiography*, p. 153.

20. The most nearly complete work on Arensberg has been done by Francis Nauman, in "New York Dada," *Arts*, February, 1980, p. 144.

21. Williams, unpublished fragment, *The Autobiography*, (Yale Za Williams Autobiography, p. 10), Beinecke Library, Yale University.

22. Florence Williams, "Interview," p. 136. Williams, *Autobiography*, p. 136.

23. Beatrice Wood, interview with the author.

24. Gabrielle Picabia-Buffet, *Aires Abstraites* (Geneva: Pierre Cailler, 1957), p. 164.

25. William Innes Homer, *Alfred Stieglitz* (Boston: New York Graphic Society, 1977), p. 172, p. 179.

26. Williams, *Autobiography*, p. 138.

27. Homer, *Stieglitz*, p. 290.

28. Ibid., p. 184.

29. Williams, Prologue to *Kora in Hell*, in *Imaginations*, p. 8. tions, p. 8.

30. Walter Arensberg, "Arithmetical Progression of the Verb 'To Be' " *The Revolution of the Word*, ed. Jerome Rothenberg (New York: Seabury Press, 1974), p. 6, p. 8.

31. Ibid., "Ing," p. 4.

32. Ibid., "Vacuum Tires," p. 5.

33. Williams, in Stewart "The European Invasion of American Art," p. 111.

34. Homer, p. 290.

35. Stewart, "The European Invasion of American Art," p. 112.

Notes—Chapter 5

1. Williams, *Autobiography*, pp. 136–137.

2. Beatrice Wood, interview with the author. Duchamp's letters to Arensberg are held by the Beinecke Library, Yale University, the Francis Bacon Foundation, Pomona, Ca., and the Philadelphia Museum of Art.

3. Williams, *Imaginations*, pp. 8–9.

4. Williams, *Autobiography*, p. 137; Duchamp, *Dialogues with Marcel Duchamp* (New York: Viking, 1971), p. 53, p. 24.

5. Duchamp, *Dialogues*, p. 16, pp. 35–36, p. 40.

6. Williams, *Letters*, p. 24.

7. Robert Lebel, *Marcel Duchamp* (New York: Grove Press, 1959), p. 29; Arturo Schwarz, *Duchamp* (New York: Abrams, 1975), p. 70. Translations are those of Schwarz.

8. Williams, *Essays*, p. 63.

9. Rothenberg, *Revolution*, p. 34.

10. Williams, *Selected Poems*, p. 16.

11. Duchamp, *Dialogues*, p. 70.

12. Williams, unpublished notebook, (Yale Za Williams-misc. n.p.), Beinecke Library, Yale University.

13. Williams, *Essays*, p. 196; "Interview," *Paris Review*, p. 73.

14. Duchamp, *Dialogues*, p. 16.

15. Williams, *Imaginations*, p. 14; Schwarz, *Duchamp*, p. 20.

16. Lebel, *Duchamp*, p. 1; Williams, *Imaginations*, p. 38.

17. Williams, *Imaginations*, p. 19, pp. 16–17, p. 33.

18. Williams, *Imaginations*, p. 65; unpublished fragment, (Yale Za Williams-B123), Beinecke Library, Yale University.

19. Duchamp, *Dialogues*, p. 88.

20. Williams, "Beginnings: Marsden Hartley," *A Recognizable Image*, p. 153.

21. Excellent research on Hartley and the Blaue Reiter group has been done by Homer, *Stieglitz*, pp. 157–164; Levin, "Wassily Kandinsky and the American Avant-Garde," *Criticism*, vol. 21, p. 347; and Barbara Haskell, *Marsden Hartley* (New York: N.Y.U. Press, 1980).

22. Unsigned letter in *The Little Review*, November 1916, p. 25; Gertrude Stein, quoted in Donald Gallup, "The Weaving of a Pattern: Gertrude Stein and Marsden Hartley," *Magazine of the Arts*, November, 1948, p. 259.

23. Mabel Dodge quoted in Gallup; locales and Williams' comment in *A Recognizable Image*; Arensberg information in "Cryptography and the Arensberg Circle," Francis Naumann, *Arts*, May, 1977, p. 80; Hartley's activity

in Elizabeth McCausland, *Marsden Hartley* (Minneapolis: U. of Minnesota Press, 1952).

24. Williams, *Imaginations*, p. 24; Hartley, "Breakfast Resumé," *The Little Review*, November, 1918, p. 47, p. 48.

25. Margaret Anderson, "A Discussion," *The Little Review*, July 1919, p. 55; and Jane Heap, *The Little Review*, October, 1919, p. 29.

26. Williams, *Essays*, p. 34; *Imaginations*, p. 26; note in Levin, p. 359.

27. Hartley, *The Little Review*, October, 1919, p. 25.

28. Hartley, "Indian Point" in *Selected Poems of Marsden Hartley* (New York: Viking, 1945), p. 4.

29. Ibid., "Solar Sanctity," p. 87; "Squirrel," p. 36.

30. Williams, *A Recognizable Image*, p. 152.

31. Hartley, *Poems*, p. 129, p. 110.

32. Williams, *Autobiography*, pp. 172–173; unpublished draft of *The Autobiography*, (Yale-Za-Williams-Autobiography), Beinecke Library, Yale University, p. 55, p. 12.

33. Hartley, letter to Williams, F216, Lockwood Memorial Library, S.U.N.Y.—Buffalo.

34. Williams, unpublished essay, "The Baroness Elsa Freytag von Loringhoven," (Yale-Za-Williams-22), Beinecke Library, Yale University.

35. Hartley quoted in Tashjian, *Primitives*, p. 61; and Williams, *Autobiography*, p. 177.

36. Hartley, "Tribal Esthetics," *The Dial*, November 16, 1918, p. 6; Williams, *Letters*, p. 121.

37. Hartley, "Dissertation on Modern Painting," *The Nation*, February 9, 1921, p. 235; *Adventures in the Arts* (New York: Hacker Art Books, 1972), p. 9, p. 13, p. 31.

38. Williams, *Imaginations*, pp. 176, 200.

39. Williams, *Recognizable Image*, p. 152; *Letters*, p. 121.

40. Williams, *Recognizable Image*, p. 153; *Letters*, pp. 167–168.

41. Williams, *Letters*, p. 183; recounted by Tashjian, *Scene*, p. 51.

42. Williams, *Letters*, pp. 216–217.

43. Quoted in Tashjian, *Scene*, p. 74.

44. Constance Rourke, *Charles Sheeler, Artist in the American Tradition* (New York: McGraw Hill and Co., 1954), p. 34; Martin Friedman, *Charles Sheeler* (Washington, D.C.: Smithsonian Press, 1968), p. 14.

45. Friedman, p. 33; Sheeler, quoted in *Sheeler: Retrospective Exhibition* (Los Angeles: U.C.L.A. Art Galleries, 1954), p. 17.

46. Rourke, pp. 49–50.

47. Williams, *Letters*, pp. 180–181.

48. Williams, "Introduction," *Charles Sheeler: Paintings, Drawings, Photographs* (New York: Museum of Modern Art, 1939), p. 6.

49. Williams, introduction, *Sheeler Retrospective*, n.p.

50. Sheeler, letter, Arensberg Archives, Philadelphia Museum of Art, August 7, 1939.

51. Williams, *Autobiography*, pp. 332–334.

Notes—Chapter 6

1. Hartley, *Adventures in the Arts* (New York: Boni and Liveright Inc., 1921), p. 32, pp. 35–36.

2. H. H. Arnason, *History of Modern Art* (New York: Abrams, 1977), p. 49.

3. Rudolph Arnheim, "The Intelligence of Perception" in *Visual Thinking* (Berkeley: U. of California Press, 1969) and *Art and Visual Perception* (Berkeley: U. of California Press, 1964.)

4. Brown, *Armory Show*, pp. 229–230.

5. Williams, *The Embodiment of Knowledge*, p. 10; *The Autobiography*, pp. 380–381; *Interviews*, p. 53.

6. Roger Fry, in Alfred Barr, *Cezanne* (New York: Museum of Modern Art, 1954), p. 149; Williams' library described in WCWN, vol. 4, no. i, p. 20.

7. Tashjian, *Scene*, p. 30; Williams, *Essays*, p. 11.

8. Alfred Barr, *Matisse: His Art and His Public* (New York: Museum of Modern Art, 1960), p. 115; Tashjian, *Scene*, p. 30, postulates that Williams' concurrent editorship of *Contact* provided the occasion for "A Matisse." "Williams felt challenged to write an appreciation of Henri Matisse for the second issue of *Contact* in January, 1921. What better way to confound the charges of provincialism than to address the French in a magazine that declared itself for an American art? The object of the piece was "The Blue Nude," painted in 1907 and on loan from Leo Stein at the 1913 Armory Show. Subsequently the painting was shown at the De Zayas Gallery in December, 1920, and purchased by John Quinn . . ."

9. Williams, *Essays*, pp. 30–31.

10. Williams, *Letters*, p. 107; "The Fault: Matisse," unpublished manuscript, Lockwood Memorial Library, S.U.N.Y.—Buffalo, (D6(c)1).

11. Barr, *Matisse*, p. 563.

12. Barr, *Matisse*, p. 86; Jacques Lassaigne, *Kandinsky* (Paris: Skira, 1964), p. 17.

13. Williams, *Letters*, p. 333.

14. Wassily Kandinsky, *The Art of Spiritual Harmony* (London: Constable and Co., Ltd., 1914), p. 5; Williams, *Essays*, p. 23.

15. Williams, *Imaginations*, p. 173, p. 174.

16. Levin, "Kandinsky," p. 358.

17. Arnason, *History*, p. 130.

18. Guy Habasque, *Cubism* (Paris: Skira, 1959), p. 17; Williams, *Recognizable Image*, p. 223.

19. Williams, *Pagany*, p. 239.

20. Ibid., p. 11, pp. 10–11.

21. Williams, *Embodiment*, p. 21, p. 84.

22. Williams, *Recognizable Image*, p. 8; *Letters*, p. 133.

23. Williams, *Recognizable Image*, pp. 223–224.

24. Williams, *The Hudson Review*, XVI, no. 4, Winter, 1963, p. 515.

25. Edwin Mullins, *The Art of Georges Braque* (New York: Abrams, 1968), p. 72.

26. Ibid., p. 34.

27. Williams, *Pagany*, p. 39.

28. Williams, *Essays*, p. 304; *Interviews*, p. 69.

29. Daniel Henry Kahnweiler, *Juan Gris* (New York: Abrams, 1946), p. 87, p. 198.

30. Williams, *Imaginations*, p. 283, p. 284, p. 287.

31. Max Kozloff, *Cubism/Futurism* (New York: Charterhouse, 1973), p. 147.

32. Williams, *Autobiography*, p. 232.

33. Schwarz, *Marcel Duchamp*, unpaginated.

34. Ibid.

35. Williams, *Embodiment*, p. 23, p. 117.

36. Williams, *Essays*, p. 157.

37. Williams, *Embodiment*, p. 21.

38. Williams, *Essays*, p. 202, p. 204.

39. Williams, *Embodiment*, p. 95; *Essays*, p. 305.

40. Williams, *Letters*, p. 104; *Essays*, p. 34.

41. Williams, *Essays*, p. 330, p. 334; *Embodiment*, p. 176.

42. Williams, *Essays*, p. 198; p. 212.

43. Ibid., pp. 198, p. 203.

44. Ibid. p. 123.

45. Ibid.

46. Ibid. p. 126, p. 130, p. 124, p. 126.

47. Ibid. p. 307, p. 213, pp. 107–108.

48. Ibid. p. 130.

Notes—Chapter 7

1. Quoted by Ron Loewinsohn in his "Tracking William Carlos Williams' Early Development," *Sumac*, May, 1977, p. 129.

2. Williams, *I Wanted to Write a Poem*, p. 14, p. 10, p. 10.

3. Williams, *Poems* (Rutherford: Reid Howell, 1909), p. 20, p. 1.

4. Williams, *I Wanted*, p. 10.

5. Wagoner, *Poetry*, p. 76.

6. Williams, *Poems*, p. 8, p. 20.

7. Ibid., p. 13, p. 20.

8. Pound, quoted in *I Wanted*, p. 12.

9. Williams, *The Tempers* (London: Elkin Mathews, 1913), p. 7, p. 14.

10. Ibid., p. 21.

11. Williams, *I Wanted*, p. 18.

12. Williams, *The Tempers*, p. 17, p. 22.

13. Williams, *The Tempers*, p. 8; *I Wanted*, p. 17.

14. Williams, *Letters*, p. 147.

15. Williams, *I Wanted*, p. 15, p. 23; pp. 21–22.

16. Williams, "Invocations," *The Egoist*, December 1, 1914, p. 444.

17. Williams, *I Wanted*, p. 65.

18. Pound, "London Letter," *The Egoist*, March 16, 1914, p. 109.

19. Williams, *I Wanted*, pp. 21–22; "Gulls," *The Egoist*, August 15, 1914, p. 307.

20. Williams, "Tract," *Others*, Fall, 1916, p. 140; "Chicory and Daisies," *The Collected Earlier Poems of William Carlos Williams* (New York: New Directions, 1951), p. 122.

21. Williams, *Collected Earlier Poems*, p. 138.

22. Williams, *Letters*, p. 50; *Others*, Fall, 1916, p. 145.

23. Wagoner, *Poetry*, p. 80.

24. Williams, "Offering," *The Egoist*, August 15, 1914, p. 308.

25. Williams, "Danse Russe," *Others*, December 1916, p. 23.

26. Williams, *I Wanted*, p. 22; "What is the Use of Poetry?" Lockwood Memorial Library, S.U.N.Y.—Buffalo, C150.

27. Williams, "Woman Walking," *The Egoist*, December 1, 1914, p. 444; "To a Solitary Disciple," *Others*, December 1916, pp. 145–147.

28. Suzy Michel, "Solitary Disciple," *Modern Language Review*, 1978, vol. 73, p. 741.

29. Williams, *Pagany*, pp. 92–93.

30. Williams, "The Young Housewife," *Others*, December, 1916, pp. 18–19.

31. Williams, *Collected Earlier Poems*, p. 159.

32. Williams, "Transitional," *The Egoist*, December 1, 1914, p. 444; "Ogre," *Others*, August, 1915, p. 24.

33. Williams, *Collected Earlier Poems*, p. 152.

34. *Collected Earlier Poems*, p. 127; *I Wanted*, p. 18.

Notes—Chapter 8

1. Erich Auerbach, "Odysseus' Scar," *Mimesis: The Representation of Reality in Western Literature* (Princeton: Princeton University Press, 1969), p. 2; Reed Whittemore, *William Carlos Williams: Poet from Jersey* (Boston: Houghton Mifflin Co., 1975), pp. 157–158.

2. Williams, *I Wanted*, p. 29.

3. Stuart Davis, Letter to Williams, S.U.N.Y.—Buffalo, (F-140).

4. Williams, *I Wanted*, p. 29.

5. Williams, *Imaginations*, p. 53, p. 52.

6. Williams, *Imaginations*, pp. 79–80; *I Wanted*, p. 27.

7. Williams, quoted in Townley, *The Early Poetry*, p. 109; *Imaginations*, p. 16.

8. Williams, *Imaginations*, p. 34, p. 35.

9. Ibid., p. 7, p. 88.

10. Ibid., p. 89, p. 62, p. 77.

11. Ibid., p. 8, p. 69.

12. Ibid., p. 73.

13. Ibid., p. 10, p. 45.

14. Ibid., p. 12.
15. Ibid., p. 13.
16. Ibid., p. 14.
17. Ibid., p. 15.
18. Ibid., pp. 16–17.
19. Ibid., p. 16, p. 35, p. 47, p. 54.
20. Ibid., p. 55, pp. 49–50.
21. Ibid., p. 55, p. 60.
22. Ibid., p. 61.
23. Ibid., pp. 65–66.
24. Ibid., pp. 75–76.
25. Ibid., p. 72, p. 80.
26. Williams, *Imaginations*, p. 18; manuscripts at Lockwood Memorial Library, S.U.N.Y.—Buffalo, (C-124).
27. Williams, *Imaginations*, p. 46, p. 19.
28. Ibid., p. 67.
29. Ibid., p. 48, p. 22.
30. Ibid., p. 26, p. 28.

Notes—Chapter 9

1. Williams, *Letters*, p. 53; *I Wanted*, p. 33.
2. Alfred Kreymborg, letter, Lockwood Memorial Library, S.U.N.Y.—Buffalo, (F-283).
3. Williams, "The Dark Day," *Poetry*, March, 1919, p. 304; *Collected Earlier Poems*, p. 196.
4. Williams, *Collected Earlier Poems*, pp. 205–206, p. 215.
5. Ibid., p. 205.
6. Ibid., p. 188.
7. Ibid., p. 36.
8. Ibid., p. 181.
9. Williams, "Broken Windows," *Poetry*, March, 1919, p. 301.
10. Williams, *Contact*, 1921, p. 18.
11. Williams, "To Mark Anthony in Heaven," *The Little Review*, January, 1920, p. 51.
12. Williams, *Collected Earlier Poems*, p. 198, p. 197.
13. Williams, *I Wanted*, p. 35; *Paterson* (New York: New Directions, 1963), p. 15; *Collected Earlier Poems*, p. 208.
14. Williams, *Collected Earlier Poems*, p. 210.
15. Edmund Brown, quoted in Townley, *The Early Poetry*, p. 115; Williams, *I Wanted*, pp. 34–35.
16. Williams, *Collected Earlier Poems*, p. 224.
17. Ibid., p. 208.
18. Ibid., p. 218.
19. Ibid., p. 221.
20. Williams, cited in Townley, *The Early Poetry*, pp. 124–125.
21. Gail Levin, "Solitary Disciple," p. 360.

Notes—Chapter 10

1. Webster Schott, *Imaginations*, p. 85; Williams, Ibid., p. 85.
2. Williams, *Imaginations*, p. 175.
3. Williams, *I Wanted*, p. 37.
4. Williams, *Collected Earlier Poems*, p. 247.
5. Ibid., p. 251.
6. Williams, *Imaginations*, p. 89.
7. Ibid., p. 92.
8. Ibid., p. 93, p. 97.
9. Ibid., p. 98.
10. Ibid., p. 100.
11. Ibid., p. 101.
12. Ibid., p. 102.
13. Ibid., p. 105.
14. Ibid., p. 95.
15. Ibid., p. 133.
16. Ibid., p. 134.
17. Ibid., pp. 146–147.
18. Williams, *I Wanted*, p. 36.
19. Williams, *Imaginations*, p. 94.
20. Ibid., p. 112.
21. Ibid., p. 111, p. 117, p. 134.
22. Ibid., p. 115.
23. Ibid., p. 105, p. 106.
24. Ibid., p. 112, p. 120.
25. Ibid., p. 101, p. 103, p. 150.
26. Ibid., p. 98, p. 96.
27. Ibid., p. 117, p. 107.
28. Ibid., pp. 107–109.
29. See note 1 of Chapter One for the location of the various articles. The debate has gone so far afield that most participants are in error on the date (1912) and original title ("Flowers.")
30. Dijkstra, *Cubism, Stieglitz and the Early Poetry*, p. 175.
31. Williams, *Imaginations*, p. 121, pp. 115–117.

Notes—Chapter 11

1. William Carlos Williams, letter 4/4/44, Arensberg Collection, Francis Bacon Library, Pomona, California.
2. Williams, letter 6/1/51, Francis Bacon Library.
3. Sheeler, letter 1/10/27, Arensberg Archive, Philadelphia Museum of Art.

Selected Bibliography

Anderson, Margaret. *My Thirty Years' War*, New York: Hermitage House. 1953.
Angoff, Charles, editor *William Carlos Williams*, Rutherford, N.J.: Fairleigh Dickinson University, 1974.
Apollinaire, Guillaume. *Les Peintres Cubistes* (1913), ed. L. C. Breunig and J. Cl. Chevalier: Paris, 1965.
Arnason, H. H. *History of Modern Art*, New York: Prentice-Hall, Abrams, 1977.
Arnheim, Rudolph. *Visual Thinking*, Berkeley: U. of California Press, 1969.
_____. *Art and Visual Perception*, Berkeley: U. of California Press, 1964.
Barr, Alfred. *Masters of Modern Art*, New York: Simon & Schuster, 1954.
_____. *Matisse: His Art and His Public*, New York: Museum of Modern Art, 1951.
Breslin, James E. *William Carlos Williams, An American Artist*, New York: Oxford University Press, 1970.
Brown, Milton W. *The Story of the Armory Show*, Princeton: Princeton University Press, 1955.
Buffet-Picabia, Gabrielle. *Aires Abstraites*, Geneva: Pierre Cailler, 1957.
Coles, Robert. *William Carlos Williams: The Knack of Survival in America*, New Brunswick, N.J.: Rutgers University Press, 1975.
Cowley, Malcolm. *Exile's Return*, New York: Viking Press, 1951.
Delevoy, Robert L. *Leger*, Paris: Skira, 1962.
_____. Bruegel, Paris: Skira, 1959.
Dijkstra, Bram. *The Hieroglyphics of a New Speech: Cubism, Stieglitz, and the Early Poetry of William Carlos Williams*, Princeton, N.J.: Princeton University Press, 1969.
_____. ed. *A Recognizable Image: William Carlos Williams on Art and Artists*, New York: New Directions, 1978.
Duchamp, Marcel. *Dialogues with Marcel Duchamp* (ed. Pierre Cabanne), New York: Viking, 1971.
Farnham, Emily. *Charles Demuth: Behind a Laughing Mask*, Norman: University of Oklahoma Press, 1971.
Frank, Waldo, Lewis Mumford, Dorothy Norman, Paul Rosenfeld, and Harold Rugg, eds. *America and Alfred Stieglitz*. New York: Literary Guild, 1934.
Friedman, Martin L. *Charles Sheeler*, New York: Watson-Guptill Publications, 1975.
_____. *The Precisionist View in American Art*, Minneapolis, Minn.: Walker Art Center, 1960.
Grohman, Will. *Wassily Kandinsky*, New York: Abrams, 1958.

Guimond, James. *The Art of William Carlos Williams*, Urbana: University of Illinois Press, 1968.

Habasque, Guy. *Cubism*, Paris: Skira, 1959.

Hartley, Marsden. *Adventures in the Arts*, New York: Boni and Liveright, 1921.

———. *Selected Poems*, New York: Viking, 1945.

Josephson, Matthew, *Infidel in the Temple: A Memoir of the Nineteen-Thirties*, New York: Alfred A. Knopf, 1967.

Kahnweiler, Daniel Henry. *Juan Gris*, New York: Abrams, 1946.

Kandinsky, Wassily. *The Art of Spiritual Harmony*, London: Constable and Co., 1914.

———. *Concerning the Spiritual in Art*, New York: Prentice-Hall, 1964.

Kenner, Hugh. *A Homemade World*, New York: Knopf, 1975.

———. *The Pound Era*, Berkeley: University of California Press, 1971.

Koehler, Stanley. "William Carlos Williams," *The Paris Review*, VIII, No. 32, Summer-Fall, 1962.

Kozloff, Max. *Cubism/Futurism*, New York: Charterhouse, 1973.

Kreymborg, Alfred. *Troubadour*, New York: Boni and Liveright, 1925.

Laforgue, Jules. *Oeuvres Completes de Jules Laforgue*, Paris: Mercure de France, 1922.

Lassaigne, Jacques. *Kandinsky*, Paris: Skira, 1964.

Lebel, Robert. *Marcel Duchamp*, New York: Grove Press, Inc., 1959.

Leymarie, Jean. *Braque*, Paris: Skira, 1961.

Mariani, Paul. *William Carlos Williams: The Poet and His Critics*, Chicago: American Library Association, 1975.

———. *William Carlos Williams: A New World Naked.* New York: McGraw-Hill, 1981.

Mazzaro, Jerome. *Profile of William Carlos Williams.* Columbus, Ohio: Charles Merrill Publishers, 1971.

McAlmon, Robert. *Being Geniuses Together: 1920–1930.* Revised and with supplementary chapters by Kay Boyle, Garden City, N.Y.: Doubleday, 1968.

McCausland, Elizabeth, *Marsden Hartley*, Minneapolis: University of Minnesota Press, 1952.

Millard, Charles W., III. *Charles Sheeler: American Photographer*, in *Contemporary Photographer* VI, no. 1 (1967).

Miller J. Hillis. *Poets of Reality: Six Twentieth-Century Writers*, Cambridge, Mass.: Harvard University Press, 1966.

——— (ed). *William Carlos Williams: A Collection of Critical Essays*, Englewood Cliffs, N.J.: Prentice-Hall, 1966.

Mullins, Edward. *The Art of Georges Braque*, New York: Abrams, 1968.

Murphy, Richard W., *The World of Cezanne*, New York: Time-Life Books, 1968.

Pound, Ezra. *Literary Essays*, New York: New Directions, 1968.

———. *Selected Essays.* New York: Random House, 1954.

Raynal, Maurice. *Cezanne*, Paris: Skira, 1954.

Rose, Barbara. *American Art Since 1900: A Critical History*, New York: Frederick A. Praeger, 1967.

Rothenberg, Jerome. *Revolution of the World*, New York: Seabury Press, 1974.

Rourke, Constance. *Charles Sheeler, Artist in the American Tradition*, New York: McGraw-Hill & Co., 1954.

Schwarz, Arturo. *Marcel Duchamp*, New York: Abrams, 1975.

Sheeler, Charles. *Sheeler: Retrospective Exhibition*, Los Angeles: U.C.L.A. Art Galleries, 1954.

Tashjian, Dickran. *Skyscraper Primitives*, Middletown: Wesleyan University Press, 1975.

––––––. *William Carlos Williams and the American Scene, 1920–1940*. Berkeley: University of California Press, 1979.

Tomlinson, Charles. (ed.) *William Carlos Williams: a Critical Anthology*, Baltimore: Penguin, 1972.

Townley, Rod. *The Early Poetry of William Carlos Williams*, Ithaca: Cornell University Press, 1975.

Wagoner, Linda Welshimer. *The Poems of William Carlos Williams*, Middletown, Conn.: Wesleyan University Press, 1963.

––––––. *The Prose of William Carlos Williams*. Middletown, Conn.: Wesleyan University Press, 1970.

Wallace, Emily. *A Bibliography of William Carlos Williams*, Middletown: Wesleyan University Press, 1968.

Weaver, Mike. *William Carlos Williams: The American Background*, Cambridge: Cambridge University Press, 1971.

Whittaker, Thomas R. *William Carlos Williams*, New York: Twayne Publishers, 1968.

Whittemore, Reed. *William Carlos Williams: Poet from Jersey*, Boston: Houghton Mifflin, 1974.

Williams, William Carlos. "Appreciation," *John Marin Memorial Exhibition*, Los Angeles: Art Galleries, University of California, 1955.

––––––. *The Autobiography*, New York: Random House, 1951.

––––––. *The Collected Earlier Poems*, Norfolk, Conn.: New Directions, 1951.

––––––. *The Embodiment of Knowledge*, ed. Ron Loewinsohn, New York: New Directions, 1974.

––––––. *The Farmers' Daughters*, Norfolk, Conn.: New Directions, 1961.

––––––. *I Wanted to Write a Poem*, reported and edited by Edith Heal, Boston: Beacon Press, 1958.

––––––. *Imaginations*, ed., Webster Schott, New York: New Directions, 1970.

––––––. *In the American Grain*, New York: New Directions, 1956.

––––––. "Introduction," *Charles Sheeler: Paintings, Drawings, Photographs*, New York: Museum of Modern Art, 1959.

––––––. *Paterson*, Norfolk, Conn.: New Directions, 1963.

––––––. *Pictures from Brueghel*, Norfolk, Conn.: New Directions, 1962.

––––––. *Selected Essays*, New York: New Directions, 1969.

––––––. *Selected Letters*, ed., John C. Thirlwall, New York: McDowell, Obolensky, 1957.

––––––. *Speaking Straight Ahead: Interviews with William Carlos Williams*, ed.

Linda Welshimer Wagoner, Middletown, Conn.: Wesleyan University Press, 1975.

———. *Voyage to Pagany*, New York, New Directions, 1970.

———. *Yes, Mrs. Williams: A Personal Record of My Mother*, New York: McDowell, Obolensky, 1959.

Index

218

"Folly of Preoccupation, The," 112
"Fontaine," 29, 50, 63, 143
"Fool's Song, The," 116
Ford, Ford Maddox, 33
Forum Exhibit, 49
Fragonard, 16, 163
Frank, Waldo, 77
"French Painting," 103
"Fresh Widow," 59
Fry, Roger, 88, 91
Futurism, 7, 38–39, 42–43, 47, 53, 72, 99, 101–102, 124, 132–133, 148, 170, 188–189, 194, 199

Gaudier, Brzeska, 27, 32
Gide, Andre, 25
Glebe, The, 36–37
Gleizes, Albert, 6–7, 28, 31, 45, 49
Gould, Wallace, 3, 71–72
Grantwood, 5, 26–27, 36–37, 40–44, 46, 103, 108, 120–121
Great American Novel, The, 53, 62, 94, 176
"Great Figure, The", 32; versions, 172
"Great Mullen," 168
Gris, Juan, 49, 98–100, 189, 192–193; theory, 99
Guggenheim, Peggy, 34
"Gulls," 122

Halpert, Samuel, 36, 40, 47
Hartley, Marsden, 2–4, 6, 9, 25, 31, 34, 43, 47, 67, 70–72, 77–78, 154, 163, 174–175, 179, 190–191; as colorist, 70, 74; dadaism, 76; death, 80; personal life, 74; poems, 78; writing, 74; technique, 73
Hartpence, Alanson, 30, 45, 86, 110, 200
"Hat Rack," 63
Haviland, Paul, 69
Heap, Jane, 71
Hemingway, Ernest, 100
Herman, Charlotte, 113
Holbein, 19, 188

"Hunters in the Snow, The," 200
"Hymn to Perfection," 111
"Hymn to the Spirit of Fraternal Love," 111

I Wanted to Write a Poem, 125
Idols, 47
"Il Penseroso," 14
Imagism, 36–37, 50, 73, 115, 121, 257, 179
Impressionism, 27, 30, 32, 44, 131, 137, 148
Impressions d'Afrique, 59
"In Advance of a Broken Arm," 58, 63
In the American Grain, 22, 29, 77, 79
Independents Show, 143, 157
"Innocence," 111
Intimate Gallery, 29
"Invitation," 122

Jacob, Max, 57, 95
Jepson, Edgar, 70, 155
"Jeune Homme Triste Dans un Train," 57
"Joie de Vivre," 88
Josephson, Matthew, 31, 80
Joyce, James, 30–31

Kahweiler, Daniel Henry, 99
Kandinsky, Wassily, 68–70, 72, 91, 94, 102, 154, 174, 199–200; theory, 92–93, 137
Kazin, Alfred, 5
Keats, John, 8, 125
"King and Queen Surrounded by Swift Nudes," 58, 102
"Klange," 174
Knoedler's Gallery, 28, 87
Kora in Hell, 30, 50, 53, 56, 61, 64–65, 70, 72, 93–94, 103, 136, 145, 151–153, 154, 160, 175, 180, 189; Arensberg's role, 143; composition, 138; cover, 136; eroticism, 150; organization, 140; prologue, 140–141, 153; theory, 139; typography, 139

220

Picabia, Francis, 6–7, 30–31, 49, 53, 60, 175, 199
Picabia-Buffet, Gabrielle, 48
Picasso, Pablo, 5, 25, 29, 32, 43, 47, 49, 95, 96; theory, 95
"Picasso Breaks Faces," 95
Pictures from Brueghel, 199
"Pig Cupid," 38
"Pink Lady Slippers," 34
Poems (1909), 18, 111–115
Poems (Arensberg), 46
Poetry, 24–25, 37, 39, 120, 157, 162
"Portent," 117
"Portrait of a Niece in Mayaguez," 13
"Portrait of Mlle. Yvonne Landsberg," 47
"Postlude," 118, 145; manuscripts, 145
"Pot of Flowers, The," 191
Pound, Ezra, 2, 5, 10, 15, 19, 24, 26–27, 33, 36–37, 40, 44, 50, 65, 68, 70–71, 73, 106, 115, 117, 120–121, 138–139, 144, 146, 154, 188, 200
Precisionism, 82, 167
"Preoccupation," 112
"Primrose," 167

"Queene Anne's Lace," 168
Quinn, John, 82, 89

"Rapid Transit," 184
Ray, Man, 6, 31, 36–37, 42, 45, 47, 62, 169, 199
Recognizable, Image, A, 35
Red Wheelbarrow, The," 83
Rembrandt, 19, 22
Renoir, Jean, 148
"Revelation, The," 120, 126
Rhyer, Ferdinand, 46
Ridge, Lola, 47–48
"Right of Way, The," 190
Riordan, John, 9–10
Roche, Henri, 7, 48
Rogue, 6, 26, 36–37, 46
"Romance Moderne," 161, 164
Ronnebeck, Arnold, 69

"Rope Dancer Accompanies Herself," 169
"Rose, The," 177, 192–194
Rosenberg, Harold, 62, 199
"Roses" (collage), 100, 193
Roussel, Raymond, 59
Rutherford, Williams' relations with, 2, 5, 7, 11, 13, 23, 33, 36, 45, 123, 160

Sandburg, Carl, 141
Santayana, George, 176
Schamberg, Morton, 6, 25, 49, 81
"Sea Elephant," 59
Sheeler, Charles, 6, 25, 31, 34–35, 49, 54, 80, 85, 95, 167, 175, 196; cinematography, 197; friendship with Arensberg, 197, in Arensberg circle, 81; on Williams, 84; photography, 82, 84; themes, 83; theory, 81–82
Slinkard, Rex, 71–72
"Smell," 64
Societe Anonyme, 70
Society of Independent Artists, 49
Sour Grapes, 157–174, 176; title, 157
"Speculation," 60
Spingarn, Joel, 24
"Spring," 159
Spring and All, 61, 100, 175–195, 198
"Spring and All," 182, 184
"Spring Storm," 166
"Spring Strains," 129, 132
Steichen, Edward, 29, 87–88
Stein, Gertrude, 25, 30, 36, 46, 50, 68–69, 88, 101
Stein, Michael, 81, 88–89
Stella, Joseph, 6
Stevens, Wallace, 5–7, 36, 40, 46–47, 147
Stieglitz, Alfred, 2, 3–6, 26, 29, 30, 34, 48–49, 68, 69–70, 78–79, 174, 199
"Still Life: The Table," 49
"Street Market, N.Y. 1908," 114, 135
"SurCENsure," 60
Surrealism, 27